EVOLUTIONARY PATTERNS OF LOCAL INDUSTRIAL SYSTEMS

Evolutionary Patterns of Local Industrial Systems

Towards a cognitive approach to the industrial district

Edited by

FIORENZA BELUSSI and GIORGIO GOTTARDI
University of Padua, Italy

Ashgate

Aldershot • Brookfield USA • Singapore • Sydney

Published by
Ashgate Publishing Ltd
Gower House
Croft Road
Aldershot
Hants GU11 3HR
England

Ashgate Publishing Company
Old Post Road
Brookfield
Vermont 05036
USA

Ashgate website: http://www.ashgate.com

British Library Cataloguing in Publication Data
Evolutionary patterns of local industrial systems
    1. Industrial organization (Economic theory) 2. Small
    business - Italy 3. Regional economics
    I. Belussi, Fiorenza II. Gottardi, Giorgio
    330.9'45'0929

Library of Congress Catalog Card Number: 99-75550

ISBN 1 84014 520 X

Printed in Great Britain by
Antony Rowe Ltd, Chippenham, Wiltshire

Contents

Part III: The dynamics of local industrial systems: empirical evidence

List of Contributors

Jonathan Michie: Birkbeck College in London.

Fiorenza Belussi: Department of Economics "Marco Fanno" at the University of Padua.

Giorgio Gottardi: Department of Engineering of Vicenza at the University of Padua.

Mauro Lombardi: Department of Economics at the University of Firenze.

Silvano Bertini: Institute for Labour in Bologna.

Fabio Arcangeli: Department of Engineering of Vicenza at the University of Padua.

Christian Genthon: Department of Engineering of Vicenza at the University of Padua and in the University of Paris.

Luciano Pilotti: Department of Economics "Marco Fanno" at the University of Padua.

Paolo Calza Bini: Department of Sociology at the University of Rome.

M. Carmela Bosco: Department of Sociology at the University of Rome.

Monica Tamisari: Department of Economics at the University of Bocconi in Milan.

Foreword

JONATHAN MICHIE

The need to continually innovate and invest in upgrading quality, particularly in global markets, is illustrated by the story of a British company in the 1950s using a Japanese supplier for the first time. The firm instructed the Japanese supplier regarding their required quality levels, which was to receive no more than 5 faulty components per 10,000. When the first 10,000 components were delivered from Japan they came with a cover letter saying 'We were unsure as to what you wanted us to do with the 5 faulty components, so we have wrapped these separately'.

So quality standards in global markets is a continually moving target. The economies that have been most successful in matching and setting these targets since the Second World War have done so through active public policies, including interventionist industrial and innovation policies. Some argue, though, that such policies are no longer on the agenda - that globalisation rules out active industrial and technology policies by government, and that instead we are limited to just promoting education and training, plus perhaps labour market deregulation.

Against this, I would make the following three points. Firstly, on these sorts of claims regarding globalisation — there is often rather less to them than meets the eye. Secondly, the key to promoting prosperity remains in boosting investment through active public policy; indeed without this, the potential benefits from education will be largely lost. And thirdly, that pursuing labour market deregulation is likely to be a dead end — or even a low road to nowhere.

Globalisation

Firstly, then, 'Globalisation' is sometimes depicted as being driven by technological developments — the fax, satellite communications, the internet, the World Wide Web. It is important, though, to counter four myths.

Firstly, the global operation of companies has *not* in most cases led to them abandoning their home bases or becoming in some sense 'non-national'. Professor Daniele Archibugi of the Italian National Science Council and I analysed patenting data and found that the huge increase which had indeed occurred in international patenting was basically by firms that remained rooted in their home base but who wanted to exploit their innovations in foreign markets.

Secondly, the work reported in that same article — in the *Cambridge Journal of Economics* in 1995 - found that the globalisation of technology had *not* broken down differences between national markets — if anything differentiation and specialisation has increased. Thirdly, the globalisation of technology has *not* replaced distinctive *National* Systems of Innovation, nor undermined the importance of national government action that underpins and promotes these distinctive systems.

And to these three I would add a fourth, that although technology has made currency speculation easier, that same technology can be — and is — used to monitor and regulate such activities.

It is quite wrong to adopt some sort of technologically determinist view of the globalisation of economic activities. On the other hand, it has to be recognised that powerful global forces are indeed at work, as described in the following passage:

All old-established national industries have been destroyed or are daily being destroyed. They are dislodged by new industries, whose introduction becomes a life and death question for all nations, by industries that no longer work up indigenous raw materials, but raw material drawn from the remotest zones; industries whose products are consumed, not only at home, but in every quarter of the globe. In place of the old wants, satisfied by the productions of the country, we find new wants... We have universal inter-dependence of nations. And as in material, so also in intellectual production.

This depiction — of powerful globalising forces — may be accurate. But it should not be accepted as being a completely new, *unprecedented* phenomenon. On the contrary, this characterisation of globalisation was actually published more than 150 years ago, in *The Communist Manifesto*.

The basic idea that globalisation has been around for a while is illustrated by the joke about the Native American attending a conference in New York, who, because he was wearing traditional tribal dress was asked whether he had been to New York before. 'No', he replied. 'Well, how do you like our City?', he was asked. 'Fine', he replied, 'how do *you* like *our* country?'.

Because of course the global migration of labour was greater pre-WW1 than it is today. And other measures of globalisation such as openness to trade had also reached high levels pre-WW1, before the big de-globalisation shift during the inter-war period. What *is* new is the *scale* of *speculative* activities following the abandonment of exchange controls during the 1980s. The McKinsey Global Institute estimated the stock of financial assets traded in global markets to have risen from $5,000 billion in 1980 to $35,000 billion in 1992, and set to reach $83,000 billion by the year 2000. This would be about three times the total national income of the world's richest economies.

Financial markets are peculiarly subject to herd-like behaviour, leading to speculative bubbles and irrational crashes. Keynes described the problem by analogy with a beauty competition run in one of the newspapers of his day. Presented with photographs of various 'beauties', the reader in those politically incorrect days had to guess which one would be chosen as the beauty queen by the panel of no-doubt expert judges. To win the competition, Keynes pointed out, it was no good saying who *you* thought was the most beautiful. What you had to do, was guess what the *panel* would think.

And so it is in financial markets. It matters not what you think the fundamentals might be. All that matters is what the other speculators think. Will they buy or will they sell? The pressure is always to go with the crowd — follow the herd. Even though from time to time it turns out to be a herd of lemmings heading for a cliff.

Their expectations become self-fulfilling. If they all think that a currency will be devalued, and so they all sell, then unless the government responds by open market operations, or through imposing exchange controls — or using existing exchange controls — then the currency will most likely be devalued. In this case, even if they are lemmings, it is still probably best to follow the herd. It is still in the interest of the *individual* speculator to sell, and contribute to the collective jump off the cliff, than be left alone at the top, holding the currency that gets devalued.

It may not be in the interest of the country or the economy for all to follow each other in an irrational jump off the cliff, but that is a different matter entirely. Hence the need for Government intervention to rein in such behaviour. That has to be a matter for *public* policy.

Labour market deregulation

It is sometimes argued that to have an innovative economy, we need a flexibly labour market. In theory, labour market flexibility allows labour to be reallocated more easily to more productive tasks and firms. One of the downsides is that increased labour turnover reduces the incentive for firms to invest in training, or in new technology, since much of the payback will come over future years, from the *tacit* knowledge that gets created within the workforce — the ideas and know-how acquired through work.

Simple-minded models and policy prescriptions often miss the importance of knowledge and ideas. Indeed, one of the greatest ever economists Keynes, when writing in *The Economic Journal* about the other great economist — and one of Keynes's teachers — Alfred Marshall, quoted him approvingly as saying that 'If I had to live my life over again I should have devoted it to psychology. Economics has too little to do with ideas.'

Two research projects within the School of Management and Organisational Psychology at Birkbeck College — involving Professor David Guest, Dr Maura Sheehan, Dr Sharon Milner, Dr Melvina Methochi, Dr Neil Conway and myself — are investigating the role that training, flexibility and other Human Resource Management practices play in corporate performance. This work - funded by the Leverhulme Trust, the ESRC's Future of Work Programme, and the Institute for Personnel and Development - is still at an early stage and we will be reporting on the results over the next 3 years and beyond.

However, initial work using the existing Workplace Industrial Relations Survey data does suggest that one can indeed characterise firms according to whether they are attempting to take advantage of the sort of flexibility created by labour market deregulation, or not. There are then differences between the behaviour of the two categories of firms as regards innovation.

In a paper published in the journal *Industrial & Corporate Change* (June 1999), Maura Sheehan and I found that policies aimed at increasing more marginal forms of employment — such as short-term and casual contracts, and reducing trade union recognition — are negatively correlated with the probability of firms engaging in R&D and introducing new technology. Firms adopting what we would characterise as more progressive Human Resource Management practices, were more likely to engage in R&D and to introduce technical change.

In a separate paper — to be published later this year in the journal *Economic Analysis* — we looked specifically at employee participation and representation at work — things which labour market deregulation generally tries to do away with. Again, we found these to be *positively* correlated with the likelihood of firms innovating.

Thus, promoting what might be termed a 'low road' approach to labour market flexibility — in particular the use of marginal types of employment contracts — appears unlikely to be associated with creating an innovative and dynamic economy.

Conclusion

Economic reality is rather more complex than many simple-minded theories and their associated policy agendas would suggest. One of the complexities that gets missed by many is the importance of the human agent in these economic processes, and the fact that a firm cannot be treated as just some sort of production function.

What a manager gets out in terms of production will depend crucially on what is essentially a co-operative process amongst the workforce as well as between firms. How productive the workforce is will depend in part on the degree of tacit knowledge built up over time. Tacit knowledge and collaborative work relations requires investment not only in education and training but — crucially — also in new technology and the design of new products. It is not a simple process to transfer these things between firms or across borders.

These are, for example, conclusions that my colleagues Daniele Archibugi, Jeremy Howells and I have drawn regarding technology transfer to developing countries:

Policies directed towards competence (such as those favouring training, education, the acquisition of managerial skills, and encouraging technological change) become crucial instruments to allow national communities to take advantage of — or at least protect themselves in the face of — the processes of globalisation.

(Archibugi, Howells & Michie, *Technology Analysis & Strategic Management*, 2000)

These are also conclusions that came out of the UK Economic and Social Research Council's 1992-97 Contracts & Competition programme (of which I was the Director). Problems with imposed contracting in the health service and local government were found to be due in part to a rather simple minded view of how contracting actually works between successful firms in the private sector (as discussed in Buckley and Michie, *Firms, Organisations and Contracts*, Oxford University Press, 1996). Long term relations are often built up with suppliers, in contrast to the compulsory contracting forced on the public sector in the 1980s and 1990s.

One of the researchers within the Contracts & Competition Programme admitted that his starting assumption had been that the reason for contracts existing must be because the world is full of people trying to maximise their own profits at the expense of everyone and anyone else. So without contracts everyone would be trying to take advantage of each other the whole time. In other words, that no one trusts anyone else, so they have to agree contracts. (And yes, the person with this worldview was an economist).

He was therefore rather taken aback on his first Site Visit when a top Executive reported telling all his managers — 'never sign a contract with someone you don't trust'. The economic reality — and the role of trust within and between firms - is thus rather more complex than might at first be assumed. This is all written up admirably in Seumas Milne's pamphlet, *Making Markets Work: Contracts, Co-operation and Competition*, available free of charge from myself (J.Michie@bbk.ac.uk).

In conclusion I would suggest that policies that attempt to leave things to the 'free' market are often based on rather simplistic and unrealistic notions of how markets actually operate.

Birkbeck College, July 1999

Acknowledgements

This book has its origins in the conference *Industrial districts and the global economy: the Italian case* held under the auspices of the Departments of Economics of the University of Udine and the University of Padua, 15 and 16 December 1995 in Udine. Chapters 2 and 9, by Giorgio Gottardi and Monica Tamisari respectively, have appeared in an earlier form in *Journal of Industry Studies*. We also would like to acknowledge that part of the funds used to realise this book from the C. N. R. (the Italian National Research Council) and M. U. R. S. T. (the Ministry of Universities and Scientific and Technological Research). We would also like to thank Ralph D. Church, Lecturer of English, in the Faculty of Political Science, at the University of Padua, for his collaboration and assistance both for the English in the articles and the preparation of the camera-ready copy of the text.

Fiorenza Belussi
Giorgio Gottardi

Introduction

FIORENZA BELUSSI AND GIORGIO GOTTARDI

... É nel nucleo dei valori, conoscenze e aspirazioni, nella forma mentis dominante, nel grumo culturale e istituzionale di un luogo, che è racchiuso il ventaglio dei sentieri di sviluppo aperti, in ogni dato momento, ad una comunità. Sarà l'incontro di esso con le circostanze "esterne" in senso lato a determinare quale, fra le diverse storie possibili, diverrà quella effettiva. (Becattini, 1999)

... It is in the core of values, ideas, and aspirations, in the dominant mind sets, in the cultural and institutional agglomeration of a place, that the array of possible developmental paths of a community at any time is enclosed. It will be the meeting of these factors with "external" circumstances in the broadest sense of the term that will determine which of the possible futures will become real. (Becattini, 1999)

To the roots of a widely used concept

The variety of research contributed to the international debate in the last two decades by Italian economists (e.g. Becattini, Brusco, Garofoli, Fuà, and Rullani among others) has brought the concept of industrial district to general attention.

In the beginning, the analysis of this particular mode of industrial organisation has been applied in order to explain the development of peripheral areas in the less developed regions of Italy. This field of study has interpreted the emergence of industrial districts (locally interconnected systems of small firms) as a "poor" model of industrialisation in areas lacking of capital, technology, and modern forms of industrial organisations (Bagnasco and Messori, 1975).

Then, the "egalitarian" social structure which exists in many industrial districts located in the North of Italy administered by the Left (Emilia-Romagna and Tuscany) has attracted the interest of many political economists, even in the US. The focus has shifted towards the analysis of social and economic conditions that have generated a new historical regime (or industrial divide) in the pattern of industrialisation of some late arriving regions which are more favourable to labour. Here the roots of the "community" district can be found: the development of small firms and the political culture of solidarity, trust and co-operation, interpreted as the basis of a more progressive social model (Piore and

1

Sabel, 1984; Becattini, 1987; Dei Ottati, 1994), and an example of formation of a collective social capital.

Now, in Italy, a third, more atheoretical and exploratory phase of research on the industrial district model is occurring (Belussi, 1996; Cossentino, Pyke, and Sengenberger, 1996; Bramanti and Maggioni, 1997). The aim, once the genotype has been identified and discussed, is not just to evaluate their importance and consistency within the Italian economy, but also to study the process of "districtualisation" of local economies, and the laws of its growth and transformation (Belussi, 1999) of these local structures (for instance: the extent of inter-firm division of labour; the process of local accumulation of tacit and codified knowledge; the prevailing mode of firm governance, between the alternatives of extreme decentralisation or high hierarchisation).

In an evolutionary perspective, recent research has tried to classify and identify the numerous, differentiated, and even "hybrid" forms, of local "industrial districts" (Moussanet and Paolozzi, 1992), because it is ever more evident that in the future they could become active nodes and levels of industrial policy. In order to include a variety of models of local development, a loose definition of local production system (LPS) has been used here. In this regard, attention has been shifted from the static conditions that gave rise to a geographical concentration of a specific type of industry (static Marshallian districts), to the evolutionary dynamics of these industrial structures (evolutionary local systems), in which differentiated patterns of growth have be found and analysed. Indeed this book is devoted to in depth discussion of the reasons behind this type of development and to the illustration of several significant examples of accelerated growth (as well as decline) of LPSs located mainly in Northeast Italy.

The macrodynamics of LPSs: a model of industrialisation resilient to the pressures of globalisation

The presence of differentiated LPSs characterises the remarkable competitiveness of the whole Italian economy, but particularly of some of the fast-growing (and wealthy) regions of the Northeast (Emilia Romagna, Veneto, Friuli Venezia Giulia, and Trentino). This area of the country, in the last decades, has exhibited an extraordinary performance in terms of growth, and even a counter-cyclical intensification of its industrialisation pattern. To validate our analysis some data reflecting the general circumstances of the evolutionary pattern of Northeast Italy is presented. As pointed out in Tables 1.1, 1.2, and 1.3, the regions of the Northeast Triangle, particularly at the end of 1980s, have activated a striking catching-up pattern in relation to the traditionally more industrialised areas of the Italian Industrial Triangle (the Northwest regions of Lombardy, Piedmont and Liguria). As shown in Table 1.1, during the 1970s and 1980s, a striking redistribution of industrial activities has taken place between the more industrialised North and the Northeast regions of Italy. While at the beginning of the period analysed (1971) the weight of the industrial structure for the whole Northeast was only 33.3% of the total for the North, after 20 years, it has reached 40.7% (on the contrary, the Northwest has gone from 66.7% to 59.3%). In these years, the level of productivity of firms localised in the more peripheral areas of the Northeast has been significant, following the growth of productivity (measured in Table 1.2 by the indicator of gross product per employee) of the more advanced areas. The same trend can be observed in other indicators, such as expenditures on personnel or the amount of fixed investment per employee. So, at the beginning of 1990s, the density of the productive and industrial structure, in the two sets of regions (measured by the number of productive units and by the number of employees per 100 inhabitants) was already converging towards a model of high industrialisation and tertiarisation. As appears in the data presented, the performance of the Northeast regions was quite different from the rest of the country.

Table 1.1   Distribution of Employment and productive units in the North regions of Italy

Macro Regions	Sectors	Productive units 1971	1981	1991	Employment 1971	1981	1991
Northeast	Industry	42.9	44.8	44.8	33.3	38.1	40.7
	Services	41.0	44.0	44.0	39.4	41.8	42.0
	Total	42.0	44.5	44.3	35.5	40.0	41.4
Northwest	Industry	57.1	55.2	55.2	66.7	61.9	59.3
	Services	58.4	55.6	56.0	60.6	58.2	58.0
	Total	58.0	55.5	55.7	64.5	60.0	58.6
North Italy	Industry	100.0	100.0	100.0	100.0	100.0	100.0
	Services	100.0	100.0	100.0	100.0	100.0	100.0
	Total	100.0	100.0	100.0	100.0	100.0	100.0
North/ Italy	Industry	55.4	59.5	57.8	67.8	64.2	63.0
	Services	50.5	50.2	49.6	53.5	50.2	49.7
	Total	51.9	52.9	51.8	61.7	56.3	54.8

Source: Our elaboration of National Census (1971, 1981, 1991) and Marcato (1997)

The microdynamics of local technological change

Despite the common view which predicts the end of diversity and the elimination of geographic differences with the coming of globalisation, regional diversities persist. Regions are indeed reinforcing their specialisation, and the process of economic and technological re-organisation has not changed the rank of the best performing regions significantly (Archibugi and Michie, 1997). Today it is widely accepted that high growth rates mainly depend on the presence, on the regional and local level, of a dynamic mixture of knowledge and learning capabilities. Innovation is a peculiar and localised process which is difficult to imitate or reproduce in other contexts. This specific combination of intangible resources is the foundation of the development of competitive industrial clusters, and it is at the root of the competitive success of LPS. Consequently, local systems and districts are starting to be considered as hubs in the generation of knowledge and learning in the new age of global capitalism.

Table 1.2   Productivity indicators: survey on Gross product, personnel expenditures and investment in manufacturing firms with more than 20 employees (millions of Italian lire)

Macro Regions	Gross product Per employee		Personnel Expenditures Per employee		Fix investment Per employee		Δ 83-92 Employment
	1983	1992	1983	1992	1983	1992	1983-1992
Northeast	33.2	74.6	21.7	48.4	4.9	12.9	+ 5.3
Northwest	34.9	80.0	23.0	52.9	4.7	13.9	- 12.9
Northeast/ Northwest	95.3	93.3	94.4	91.4	104.2	92.8	- - -
North Italy	34.3	78.0	22.6	51.2	4.7	13.5	- 6.9
Italy	33.5	75.6	22.0	49.7	5.7	15.3	- 5.8

Source: Our elaboration on ISTAT and Marcato (1997)

The first chapters of the book (Part I) are devoted to the study of the models of innovation and learning that characterise the dynamics of LPSs. An endogenous model of technological change is described by Fiorenza Belussi and Giorgio Gottardi in chapter 1, where the dynamics of the Italian LPS is explained through a model of knowledge creation, based on incremental innovations. According to our view, the following factors need to be stressed:
-   the influence of agent proximity in knowledge transmission,
-   the development and transfer of tacit (non-codified) knowledge,
-   the importance of (non-R&D based) incremental innovations,

- the crucial role of accumulation of practical knowledge and its localised nature,
- the systemic nature of the LPS model, where productivity appears to be also the regulative outcome of agents interactions,
- the extent of the division of labour among the various productive units induced by a "spontaneous order" in which agents are organised in co-evolving networks,
- the role of institutions (collective actors), that may function as meta-organisers in the diffusion and creation of knowledge.

Table 1.3 Density of the productive and industrial structure

Macro-regions	Sectors	Productive Units/100 inhabitants			Employees/100 inhabitants		
		1971	1981	1991	1971	1981	1991
Northeast	Industry	1.7	2.6	2.6	14.3	17.3	17.0
	Services	3.6	5.4	6.0	9.9	19.2	22.3
	Total	5.3	7.9	8.6	24.2	36.5	39.3
Northwest	Industry	1.5	2.1	2.2	19.5	19.2	17.2
	Services	3.5	4.6	5.3	10.4	18.2	21.4
	Total	5.0	6.7	7.5	29.9	37.3	38.6
North	Industry	1.6	2.3	2.3	17.4	18.4	17.1
Italy	Service	3.5	4.9	5.6	10.2	18.6	21.7
	Total	5.1	7.2	7.9	27.6	37.0	38.9
Italy	Industry	1.3	1.8	1.8	11.7	13.0	12.1
	Services	3.2	4.4	5.0	8.7	16.8	19.5
	Total	4.5	6.2	6.8	20.5	29.9	31.7

Source: Our elaboration on ISTAT

Economic theory has recently devoted large intellectual resources in order to explain the development of regions and the increasingly evident concentration of activities in industrial clusters, without coming up with solid explanatory models. In particular, these processes of agglomeration of industrial activities, have been set at the centre of the New international economics by Krugman (1991), who has tried to explain and generalise the process of concentration of similar activities as the result of imperfect competition. Another stream of research has in contrast focused its attention on the creation of localised knowledge, the diffusion of spill overs, and the emergence of externalities (Antonelli, 1992; 1994), which determine an increasing return to invested capital. More in tune with this approach, Giorgio Gottardi in chapter 2 uses a conceptual framework in which the model of the industrial district/LPS is inserted in a systemic analysis of the co-evolution of knowledge, competitiveness, learning procedures, and specialisation of agents. A cognitive approach to the study of the LPS is developed by Mauro Lombardi in chapter 3. Lombardi describes the model of the LPS as a stable network of relationships, characterised by systemic properties: self-containment, operational flexibility and strategic rationality.

The dynamics of local systems and the links with local institutions

Nowadays, many countries provide direct incentives to support the introduction of technological change on the local level. Indeed, centralised policies do not work very well in transferring basic research to production activities. Central policy is effective in overcoming market failures in basic research, but the other stages in the development of new technology (with their applications to products and processes) require highly specific skills and entrepreneurial and professional capabilities which exist only in production systems and enterprises.

Innovation is generated when there are enterprises capable of transforming technical and applied knowledge into economic value, e.g. to rapidly transform such knowledge into sales, products, and services.

In contrast to price competitiveness (that can be externally influenced by price regulating policies), innovation competitiveness cannot be created artificially, that is, independently of entrepreneurial efforts. The essential issues are corporate strategy and entrepreneurial risk taking. For these reasons many countries no longer limit public intervention to pre-competitive research, but provide incentives for industrialisation and propagation directly by supporting firms (e.g. by financing projects up to the development of prototypes) or indirectly by public purchases.

The propensity to delegate at least part of national or "extra-national" policies on innovation to local policy levels is becoming widespread: science and technology parks, innovation centres, co-operative R&D projects managed at the local level. For instance, large American technology parks, the French network of *Centres Règionaux d'Innovation et de Transfert de Technologie*, or Japanese *kohsetsushi*, are all structures to catalyse innovation processes on the local level. These centres involve various operators: firms, universities, local levels of government, with the aim of setting up infrastructure capable of producing specialised services to support the entire innovation cycle. To add a new perspective to the international debate, the Italian case has been presented here, as an original model in which local policies have been directed largely to reinforce the mechanisms of collective learning and social interaction, in which (collective or individual) local actors may also play a strategic role as meta-organisers in the local innovative process.

The second part of the book discusses the LPS model in relation to its implications for policy. Silvano Bertini, in chapter 4, outlines a broad variety of organisational forms of LPS, deriving from a process of SME evolution into more coherent local systems, where expansion and consolidation phases are clearly identified. From the Italian experience some lessons for development policies are drawn, in terms of liberalisation of markets, support of national demand, and economic democracy. Given the complex and comprehensive character of the mobilisation and creation of knowledge at the local level, Fiorenza Belussi, in chapter 5, associates the role of local policies to the collective mechanism of learning, by developing an operational approach to establishing a normative (knowledge-intensive) model of intervention, based on the Italian experience. Belussi develops a tool box of concepts, processes, levels of intervention, and specific options that can be adapted to other contexts. The development of multimedia technologies, which represents a potential area of (direct or indirect) policy intervention, is explored by Christian Genthon and Fabio Arcangeli, in chapter 6, as a new organisational challenge for the development of LPSs, in which they contrast post-Fordist organisations with the small organisations of LPSs.

The evolutionary dynamics of the LPS

It is clear from the perspective adopted here that there is no single LPS model. In any case there may be some regularities in their evolutionary character, such as path dependency, accelerated dynamics of growth, and a high rate of new firm formation. The hinge in LPS dynamics is found in their innovative capability. How are they able to reproduce and generate new knowledge? And which subjects possess the relevant tacit knowledge that accumulates over time within LPSs?

In the third part of the book some case-studies are presented which illustrate the variety of LPS evolutionary patterns. LPSs cannot by any means be considered homogeneous systems in terms of the structure of firm governance and mechanisms of learning and knowledge creation, such as some international literature based on secondary sources has sometimes assumed. A quite static evolutionary path is described by Paolo Calza Bini and M. Carmela Bosco in chapter 8, for the case of Civita Castellana, where the local system is characterised, above all, by the processes of diffusion and socialisation of existing tacit skills, competencies are continuously re-created. A different model of LPS is described by Monica Tamisari in chapter 9, which discusses the chair-manufacturing district of the Manzano area near Udine. This LPS constitutes a good example of a moderately evolutionary path. The LPS contains many improver firms, and, over time, a process of accumulation of tacit knowledge has occurred. Small improvements introduced in the firm production cycles have rendered this local system extremely competitive, however, the Manzano area, is still based on small firms (new leading firms have emerged only recently), limited local networks of subcontracting, and little new knowledge creation. Luciano Pilotti in chapter 7 contrasts two very different LPSs: one exhibits a strong evolutionary pattern (the case of Montebelluna), the other is quite stationary (the case of Maniago). The Montebelluna district of ski boots is characterised by firms capable of generating original innovations. The district is populated by large Schumpeterian firms and by a dense network of subcontractors which amplify their global influence through long-distance relational links. Many actors have generated a social process of knowledge generation and transmission. The complexity of relationships, incorporated in the Montebelluna district, has pushed Pilotti to interpret the function of this LPS as a "neural network". In contrast, the case of Maniago represents a static district, where local firms are scarcely innovative. As emerges from the empirical analysis, no significant learning processes have taken place in recent decades, and within this LPS, there are no strategic actors capable of activating processes of new knowledge generation.

References

Antonelli C. (1992), *The Economics of Information Networks*, Amsterdam, North-Holland.

Antonelli C. (1994), Technological districts, localised spillovers, and productivity growth. The Italian evidence on technological externalities in the core regions, *International Review of Applied Economics*, n.8.

Archibugi D. and Michie J. (1997), (eds.), *Technology Globalisation and Economic Performance*, Cambridge, Cambridge University Press.

Bagnasco A. and Messori M. (1975), *Tendenze dell'economia periferica*, Turin, Valentino Editori.

Bagnasco A. (1977), *Le tre Italie: la problematica territoriale dello sviluppo*, Bologna, Il Mulino.

Becattini G. (1987), (ed.), *Mercato e forze locali: il distretto industriale*, Bologna, Il Mulino.

Becattini G. (1999), Quella forza porta successo, Il Sole 24 Ore, 6 June.

Belussi F. (1996), Local systems, industrial districts and institutional networks: towards a new evolutionary paradigm of industrial economics?, *European Planning Studies*, vol.4, n.1.

Belussi F. (1999), Policies for the development of knowledge-intensive local production systems, *Cambridge Journal of Economics*, vol. 26, n. 6.

Bramanti A. and Maggioni M. (1997), (eds.), La dinamica dei sistemi produttivi territoriali, Angeli, Milan.

Cossentino F., Pyke F., and Sengenberger W. (1996), (eds.), *Local and regional response to global pressure: the case of Italy and its industrial districts*, Geneva, Ilo.

Dei Ottati G. (1994), Trust, interlinking transaction and credit in the industrial district, *Cambridge Journal of Economics*, vol.18.

Krugman P. (1991), *Geography and Trade*, New York, The Mit Press.

Marcato G. (1997), L'evoluzione della struttura industriale del nord-Italia, aspetti territoriali e settoriali, paper presented at the conference "La molteplicità dei modelli di sviluppo dell'Italia del Noprd, Parma, 6-7 November.

Moussanet M. and Paolazzi L. (1992), (eds.), *Gioielli, bambole, coltelli. Viaggio nei distretti produttivi italiani*, Milan, Il Sole 24- Ore.

Piore M. and Sabel C. (1984), *The Second Industrial Divide: Possibilities for Prosperity*, New York, Basic Books.

Part I

Innovation and learning

1 Models of localised technological change

FIORENZA BELUSSI AND GIORGIO GOTTARDI

The role of knowledge as a latent explanation of growth in local economies

Economic theory has devoted recently a large amount of intellectual energy to explain the uneven development of regions and the increasingly evident concentration of activities in industrial clusters, without producing any solid explanatory models. In particular, these processes of agglomeration of industrial activities, have been placed in the centre of the New international economics of Krugman (1991), who has tried to explain and generalise the process of concentration of similar activities as the result of imperfect competition induced by the creation of externalities (Antonelli, 1992; 1994), which determine an increasing return to the invested capital.

Other theories of endogenous growth, have focused their analysis on the dynamic role of human capital (Romer, 1987, and 1994; Lucas, 1988). So, within a determined production function, the use of more qualified labour (in terms of years of education), could explain, over the long term, an increase in final output, which opens up the way to the growth of the economy. Such theories seem to offer only partial explanations.

In fact, empirical research in Italy has confirmed that, historically, the growth of industrial districts has emerged in very competitive markets (with low entry barriers and the absence of oligopolistic actors). In addition, investment in education does not seem to have been influential, given the fact that, workers employed by firms located in the Northeast have comparatively low levels of formal education, well below the Italian average.

Thus, these questions still remain open. When does geographical concentration start? The concentration of similar activities in a specific area goes back to unbalanced growth[1] in which firms located in the area become more efficient and competitive. But, why do resources located in local firms become more productive over time? And, relatedly:

-When are stationary conditions within local economies broken?
-What are the fundamental forces behind the development of specific areas?

Clearly, the process envisaged in this book does not depend on an

13

increase in the quantity of locally available factors (in particular, stocks of capital and labour, according to processes *à la* Harrod-Domar).

In our view, it is the sequence of changes (the so called *empirical regularities*) linked to knowledge absorption, creation, and diffusion among the actors participating in the process of the enlargement of the local industrial structure that need to be considered. The industrial district *story* tells us how, the diffusion of practical knowledge among potential entrepreneurs, together with some favourable market conditions, can start a recurring process of knowledge accumulation and expansion. Thus, growth appears to be founded principally on the expansion and deepening of knowledge, and consequently on broad application of innovation and incremental modification of products and processes. The accumulation of knowledge is related to the processes of task and product specialisation that characterises all local industrial districts studied in this volume.

This gradually leads to a process of cognitive division of labour among firms. The notion of cognitive division of labour has evolved from the thought of Adam Smith. However, while a Smithian division of labour focuses on the productivity of partitioning tasks (an intra-firm division of labour), the cognitive division of labour operates on a system level within each industrial structure (an inter-firm division of labour). The process envisaged here is a process of slow differentiation and specialisation of firms, which can be further qualified.

Within each industrial district some firms use their resources to perform routine activities (which usually are subcontracted by the final assembler). Other firms, more strategically placed, specialise their activities in the production of intermediate components and often develop a crucial competence for the final assemblers; a dense productive network of relationships is established which leads to externalities and the spillover of knowledge; over time, the accumulation of localised knowledge influences the intrinsic quality of the components and semi-finished goods and their average cost; the lowering of costs increases the global competitiveness of the final firms which compete in international markets. Clearly, specialisation also accelerates learning within firms. The growth of their market shares increases the scope of the process of specialisation and the division of labour among firms. Thus, the system may become even more competitive, and the scale and scope of the economies can be more widely exploited. Finally, in this schematic description of the systemic specialisation of the industrial structure, there is the category of firms identified as final assemblers. They devote much of their resources to the more creative tasks of product design, engineering, marketing, innovation, and new product development. In each local industrial district final assemblers are at the centre of the cognitive division of labour and typically specialise in the less routine activities. These most strategic agents are the dominant actors of the productive filière. In fact, the average level of innovation in each industrial district depends greatly on them. On one hand, they are responsible for the absorption of external knowledge which always needs to be adapted quickly to local conditions and socialised by the firms belonging to the networks of subcontractors and specialised producers. On the other hand, they are able, given their position in the chain of interactions between producers and final users (with their antennas in markets that put them in direct contact with the consumer needs), to make original innovations, particularly in product. In this interpretation, the cognitive division of labour structurally imposes firm diversity. This also explains why local industrial districts are populated by differentiated agents: routine producers, innovative agents, and sometimes collective meta-organisers and problem-solvers (the district's regulative institutions).

As discussed elsewhere (Belussi, 1996), evolutionary economic theories provide a suitable approach to describe the processes operating within industrial districts.

In an evolutionary perspective, physical and cognitive resources are asymmetrically distributed in the economic space. A territorial milieu is characterised by competencies and skills that do not exist in other contexts. The economic space represents the locus where factors and inputs are consciously organised and enriched in cognitive content. The firms are linked to their environment in a twofold way. First, they use local resources (various competencies, manual abilities, professional skills are historically ingrained in some districts, while they are lacking in others). Second, they contribute, by solving productive problems, to framing and giving significance and value to these resources. Therefore, they contribute to *qualify* the local context: within this space, new technological opportunities are tried, and new capabilities and organisational routines are produced.

In a simple neo-classical world the firm is considered to be a black box, a pure mechanism of adjustment between prices and quantities as well as certain proportions of input factors, principally labour and capital. Technology is assumed as a given, provided externally by the economic system. Moreover, all firms are presumed to have equal access to similar resources and similar technological capabilities, and all depend on the fact that there is only one optimal solution for organising production.

In this book on the other hand, an approach to the theory of the firm which considers firms as partially responsible for the creation (or acquisition) of their technology will be examined (Nelson and Winter, 1982; Nelson, 1978; 1987; 1990; Foray, 1990; Kline and Rosenberg, 1986; Rosenberg, 1992; Winter, 1987; Cohendet et al., 1991; Demsetz, 1988; Langlois and Robertson, 1995; Metcalfe, 1997). Firms are viewed as evolving, creative and differentiated agents, and thus as loci of productive knowledge. It is the evolving nature of firms which explains the dynamics of each economic system.[2]

In this analytical context, the adjustment of firms to market conditions are not externally given but are related to the firms' active mechanism for selecting among various technological choices (Amendola and Gaffard, 1988) and among several modes of factor co-ordination (for instance, the boundaries of the firm, determined by the buy or make choice, or again, the extent to which firms may follow different strategies of product differentiation, etc.). In line with recent industrial economics, economic agents modify their environment instead of being subjected to predetermined conditions (Jacquemin, 1987), and the industrial structure and organisation of firms is the outcome of deliberate strategies as well as the initial conditions of the market structure (Saviotti and Metcalfe, 1992; Antonelli, 1995). All this renders firms' choices indeterminate, because technologies and demand only define opportunities.

In this perspective, firms are differentiated agents, able to formulate diversified strategies. So, local industrial districts may follow different paths of growth because they are formed by a differentiated population of economic agents. If firms are a mixture of resources and skills that evolve in an original and not in a predetermined way, within the boundaries imposed by market demand and by technological opportunities (Malerba, Orsenigo, and Peretto, 1997), the rate of development of each district is related by the kind of learning processes that take place and by the frequency with which innovations are introduced in firms. The presence of network externalities is a factor in determining the innovative capabilities of firms. In this volume the thesis, found in a wide range of the literature, that the origin of most Italian districts is based on favourable conditions of market demand and factor prices (related, above all, to labour costs), will be discussed. However, the most dynamic districts are those in which these initial conditions were paired with specific technological competencies.

On the local dimension of technical progress

The competitiveness of these models of industrial organisation has led to the abandonment of some common descriptions, such as those which regarded small enterprise districts as technologically poor units, incapable of generating innovation and endogenous growth factors. In addition, the study of districts has led to the discovery of the importance of the proximity factor and the local dimension of technical progress. Most analyses of the impact of new telecommunication technologies support the notion that geographical barriers and physical distance are being overcome. Many scholars think that, in a world of instantaneous and free communication, as well as transportation that can connect all parts of the globe, suppliers and sub-suppliers will be able to deliver just in time to their clients, independently of the physical distance. However, the role of proximity remains decisive in the organisation of economic activities. Even though transportation and telecommunication technologies are becoming more sophisticated, "we are very far from freeing all forms of interactions from the necessity of propinquity" (Storper and Scott, 1995).

Distances are important for many kinds of transactions, and transactions sustain all economic and social processes. The formation of an industrial district consists of the formation of a community of economic subjects that share technical know-how, common practices and rules of behaviour. The survival and growth of a district depend on regular and frequent exchange of information, goods and experience and involve a large number and variety of transactions. Transactions impose important constraints on the geographical distance at which they may be carried out.

This does not mean that every exchange must necessarily take place over a short distance. Transactions occur on different geographical scales, ranging from the highly localised to the international. But in general production activities, businesses and competition are not socially de-contextualised: they are modelled by local culture and institutions (law, norms, markets, inter-organisational relations, trust, and so on). In this regard local environments differ profoundly from one another, even if their industrial structure and sectorial composition is similar.

The rediscovery of proximity has led to reflection on innovation models and questions about the origins and consequences of technical progress; in particular the acknowledgement of its local dimension.

In orthodox theories, technical progress has been considered the mechanical consequence of the R&D activity, and its dynamic has been associated to a given probability distribution function, or alternatively to totally exogenous factors. Innovation has been studied by industrial economists and by policy makers as an output of highly formalised and planned efforts. But, in our view, this is a partial and incomplete description of the path required to generate and develop new technologies. In the real world, technical progress is difficult to predict and plan, and there is a high risk factor for the subjects involved. The sources of innovation are found in complex and intricate networks of ideas, relationships, techniques and routines, and in a myriad of small improvements that determine continuous growth and evolution. The interactions of agents are specialised and involve localised supplier chains and industrial systems, with their territorial and economic-production specificity. These networks are the depositories of specialised production capacities and skills. From this point of view, technology is not something universally available, but it is rather incorporated in clusters of firms (and networks of personal relationships) and it is developed within the transactions rooted in these particular contexts (Spender, 1996). Technical change can hardly be planned through large R&D investments, when it is manifest in a long chain of small scale events.

This approach, in contrast to the traditional one, comes from a great number of case studies and some theoretical work within the so-called Schumpeterian tradition. The most significant contributions to the theory of the firm that embody this interpretation of technical progress are those of Richard Nelson and Sidney Winter (Winter, 1964; Nelson, 1959a; 1959b; 1962; 1963; Nelson, Peck and Kalachek, 1967). Their work gave rise to the evolutionary theory, a theory that seems extremely fertile both from a theoretical and applied perspective and has stimulated most of the work in this volume. The empirical evidence provided by the research work presented here on the sources and modalities of technology innovation in local industrial systems and industrial districts supports the complex nature of these processes. In particular, the importance of incremental innovations, that are not based on formal R&D activities, but on minor discoveries and on a type of non-codified, tacit and localised knowledge (Stiglitz, 1987; Antonelli, 1995). Today it is recognised that there is a close relationship between technology, growth in individual industries and regional or local development. For some ten years now there has been an important research trend dedicated to the study of innovation processes at the regional level (Amin and Robins, 1990; Romer, 1990; Camagni, 1991; Harrison, 1992; Vet, 1993; Teitz, 1994; Cooke, 1995; Audretsch and Feldman, 1996). The reason for this new direction is justified by the effects of de-centralised dynamics on growth, in which the importance of local-endogenous factors of growth are emphasised. According to recent research, the development of knowledge is a social and economic process. Knowledge is rather scarce and it is asymmetrically distributed among subjects in an economic space. This uneven distribution and diversity of knowledge also depends on the different 'genetic' routines that are embodied in the firms. Of course, these features are profoundly influenced by the specific localisation of each economic entity.

There is a clear spatial and sectorial dimension to the process of growth even though its implications are not fully understood. This is because the generation of new knowledge through R&D, the transfer of new technologies from one sector or region to another, the adaptation of new parameters to particular applicative conditions have been more difficult than expected.

There is also a close relationship between the creation and absorption of technology and the development of the local environment (David and Rosenbloom, 1990; David, Foray, and Dalle, 1997). When industries having similar or complementary technologies are localised in close proximity, economic growth, technological development and the rate of innovation are stimulated by the aggregation and transferability of technological and production competencies (Edquist, 1997). In industries and supplier firms that benefit from high tech-productive proximity, the transferability of technology and the benefits that are generated from this, produce continual innovative flows. Most of the firms located within these supplier-client chains benefit from these results and may base their expansion on these new developments.

If there is physical and technological proximity, synergetic effects from two-way flows of applicative knowledge are combined with the traditional economies of agglomeration (Richardson, 1995; Harrison, 1992; Feldman, 1994) to form one of the main causes of long term stability and growth of networks, local industrial systems, or local clusters of districts. The mechanisms that lead to these results have recently been examined (Antonelli and Gottardi, 1991; Antonelli, 1995; Gottardi, 1996). These effects influence and support each other, and activate various learning processes that transfer the benefits of innovations to the entire local system. The co-ordinated evolution of these structures (networks or clusters) is a specifically local process, that is difficult to imitate or reproduce in other contexts and profoundly characterises each local industrial system. Today, it is widely recognised that high growth rates strictly depend on the presence, on the local level, of dynamic and competitive industrial networks or clusters. As a result, regions and local systems are becoming the focal point for the creation of knowledge and learning in a new era of capitalism that is global and knowledge intensive. Some have even referred to *regions of learning* (Florida, 1995) that function as collectors, depositories and re-distributors of ideas and knowledge, capable of supplying and facilitating the use of new ideas and knowledge in the environment.

This perspective underlines the fact that technology is characterised by a local dimension where it forms an integrated system that, in the end, encompasses social and institutional aspects. This relation is two-way: it can also be maintained that the characteristics of the local environment (economic, social, institutional) make the technology specific and so led to its applications, results and advantages.

On the notion of technology and technology transfer in a cognitive perspective

Some conceptual and terminological differences embodied in the various theories on innovation and diffusion are, on further analysis, linked to the different meanings attributed to technology. From the economic perspective, technology has often been associated with physical assets (plant, machinery and equipment) and it is considered a capital stock that can be measured. Along side this notion of technology, many researchers have not only taken into consideration the physical dimension of technology but also the amount of knowledge involved in the use of technology. Jantsch (1967), in his definition of technology, explicitly links the hardware with software (the way of using the assets). More recently, technology has come to mean the techno-scientific content of products, and skills associated with them, or the technical and operational knowledge and skills that are embodied in technology (Rousseau and Cooke, 1984). In the same vein, some works attribute a very broad meaning to this term: the "technology of a firm" would be its entire ensemble of experience and competencies.

Even though we do not use the term so generically, a cognitive notion of technology, in which the content of the knowledge necessary is explicit, is useful and allows for a better interpretation of technological development on the local level and will be used in the research presented in this volume. In this perspective, technology has a very important contextual-behavioural dimension. Apart from the physical features of technology, it is important to consider the capacity of a subject to use technology to achieve its objectives. It is impossible to imagine that a physical object is significant or produces utility outside of a specific cognitive context. Any object or tool, in fact, assumes significance and generates economic utility only when it is "contextualised", i.e. associated with the complete set of information that allows the realisation of given objectives in a specific environment.

In general, the firm is a 'bundle' of heterogeneous resources (Penrose, 1959): physical, human and organisational assets, technologies, know-how, competencies, capabilities (Richardson, 1972), skills and routines (Nelson and Winter, 1982). Many authors have pointed out that a large part of individual knowledge is very hard to verbalise and forms a large part of all the skills embodied in the capabilities of organisations. Polanyi (1967) referred to this type of knowledge as tacit knowledge. Tacit knowledge can be acquired by individuals. It is embedded in their experience and in their ability to perceive, recognise and extrapolate patterns, and is embedded and embodied in social networks (Nightingale, 1998). Tacit knowledge is also embodied in habits and routines. A lot of the skills used in management and entrepreneurial activities have a considerable tacit component. Of course, besides the tacit component of knowledge, that part of knowledge which can be expressed in symbolic form, or codified, and easily communicated (Foray and Lundvall, 1996) has to be considered. However, currently in the real world most practical knowledge is probably tacit. Capabilities and routines are very similar concepts (Grant, 1996): they represent the way in which practical knowledge is used by individuals and organisations (sometimes without being totally re-codified and fully understood). Technology is an ensemble of physical assets and knowledge deriving from some theoretical principles and much practical experience. Technical and applied knowledge is in reality highly specific and idiosyncratic, as it is linked to the organisations where it has been elaborated and fine-tuned. In contrast to scientific knowledge, it does not have the characteristics of a public good.

The notion of technology adopted here begins with the point of view of the firm that develops and uses technology to obtain economic advantages. Technology may be considered a body of continuously evolving applied knowledge, whose potential economic utility is limited by the user's aims, which depend on the knowledge and skills previously possessed.

The term technology transfer has also been used with many different meanings. Technology transfer will here be defined as the set of efforts and deliberate actions carried out by an economic subject (a firm) to introduce a pre-existing technology into new geographic, industrial or entrepreneurial contexts of application, i.e. new cognitive environments.

These efforts, on the one hand, are to create an appropriate context for its application, that is, to develop the knowledge and complementary assets of the organisation and introduce the adjustments and new routines necessary. On the other hand, these actions are directed to adapting the technology itself so that new users can make it their own; this means making the technology congruent with their cognitive characteristics and strategic objectives. Technology transfer is in substance the complex process of adjustments required to use new technologies, developed or used elsewhere, in a new cognitive context. Of course, most difficulties occur when the transfer concerns technologies that cannot be traced back to cultural and cognitive models or the routine operations present in the new context (cfr. NIH - Not Invented Here syndrome; Katz and Allen, 1988).

Despite the great importance of the process of technology transfer, which was already emphasised by Schumpeter in his business cycles (1939), most of the studies on the generation of innovations, both from an industrial and business perspective, implicitly assume that the greatest difficulties experienced are those involved the development of new paradigms, with the arrangement of the necessary resources, and the management of R&D projects. The difficulties of transferring pre-acquired technology within firms and between firms have been underestimated in economic literature.

The costs of transfer and adoption are not irrelevant, as assumed by the orthodox (neo-classic) economic theory. On the contrary, according to some empirical studies, the transfer of a technology (and incorporated knowledge) can entail costs similar to those of its initial introduction (Nelson, 1990; Rosenberg, 1990). The orthodox approach implicitly assumes that the knowledge incorporated in a new technology can be formalised and at virtually no-cost transferred. But in reality the amount of informal and tacit knowledge necessary to use the new technology is extremely important.

The more embodied and tacit knowledge is, the more difficult it is to codify and transfer. Given that the technological patrimony of an enterprise is, on further analysis, incorporated in individuals, teams and organisation, every technology transfer involves an exchange between individuals and groups with different cultures, experiences and motivations. The problems posed by the transferability of a process are not so much related to the acquisition of new tangible assets, but to the *distance* between the cognitive models of the absorbing organisation and those of the context of origin of the new technology.

Generating technology innovation: a critical view

Economists have long been interested in the problem of measuring and identifying the effort undertaken by firms in order to have access to technological change, in terms of the resources and methods used for its implementation. But from the earliest days of the economics discipline, the entire process of the introduction of innovations in the various parts of the firms organisation has been considered in a somewhat simplistic manner.

In this context, theoretical discussion has limited the development of the firm's knowledge to a well-defined set of research activities (the already mentioned linear model of innovation). This has directed much of the analytical effort to the analysis of other concerns. As is well known, this has given rise to an international debate that has lasted for decades. It started from a meso-level of analysis, and has developed some crucial concepts related to the theories of demand pull, technology push, and technological paradigms. But these approaches have not revealed much about what happens within firms. Nor do they say anything about where the firm's principal loci of technological learning are situated.

Technology has been considered for a long time as a set of plants and equipment embodied in the capital goods portfolio of large enterprises. Consequently, innovation and technical progress have been viewed as additions to the portfolio of technologies possessed by a firm. These additions are obtained through formalised and highly planned efforts, from R&D and engineering, to industrialisation and marketing. This may be an accurate description for some forms of innovation, although the modalities with which most innovation processes are carried out are rather different. This vision of innovation processes is sketchy and inadequate. It is now widely admitted that innovation is not a linear process but a sequence of steps that may begin with R&D, as assumed in the optimistic and hyper-rationalistic vision of the orthodox approach (see e.g. Rosenberg, 1990). This has also been confirmed, for quite some time, by a large number of empirical investigations (Davies, 1979; Rogers, 1986). Kline and Rosenberg (1986) have questioned the linear model of the innovative process, where research, design, testing, production, and marketing activities are supposed to be from the top down, by arguing that dynamic feed-back and interactions give rise to innovation activities.

In fact, the results of many surveys on the innovation activity in firms and industries demonstrate that innovation is a circular process, composed of many internal cycles whose results are not easy to predict. For example, the final step, which is often indicated as the diffusion phase, is not the conclusion of the innovation cycle but is the beginning of a more advanced cycle in which new ideas and opportunities for research emerge and generate further innovations, improvements and upgrades. This circular process is also present in all the other steps, so that it is misleading to look only at its initial phases and promote the innovation cycle by supporting the initial process alone.

These policies have not always obtained positive results. Despite the high level planning for research and commercial protection for innovators, in reality it has always been difficult for subjects and private groups to appropriate completely the economic benefits of all progress in knowledge (Nelson and Rosenberg, 1993). The specific nature of the knowledge necessary for innovation involves high transaction and adaptation costs. The greatest limitation of the orthodox approaches is, considering only the most apparent aspects of innovative phenomenon, that the sources from which the practical and technological know-how emerges remain hidden. A lot of present technical change is not planned and realised by large R&D laboratories, instead it is generated as a series of small events in highly informal contexts (Gertler, 1993), emerging from a myriad of small additions within a specific environment. The knowledge that is produced is not generalised and available universally, but it is incorporated in bunches of well-defined and spatially specific relationships. Innovation is not merely scientific knowledge nor even practical know-how: it is knowledge that is put into practice, modifies existing routines and generates economic value. But, what are the boundaries of firm knowledge? Up to now economic literature has discussed the concepts of knowledge, competence and information interchangeably. We now need to make some distinctions among terms which often are used synonymously.

Let us consider in greater detail the crucial concept of firm competence and develop an appropriate analytical scheme.
1. Within the economic system, firm competence can be viewed as the firm-specific attributes which distinguish the firm's specific state of knowledge. Competencies are related to practical knowledge and not only to the scientific content of the technology used (Carlsson and Eliasson, 1994).

This regards, for instance, the way in which technologies are absorbed and re-elaborated from the external environment, the routines that are created by firms in order to maintain and reproduce the knowledge among all participants of the productive process, and the processes of organisational learning (adaptive, creative, and vicarious) that take place in firms, which vary from case to case, and which attest to the existence of different technological capabilities (Chandler, 1992).

These competencies are firm specific and they are not freely available on the market, nor can they be simply acquired because they are created in historical time; they are *attached* to the individual organisations and their members. Technologies can be sometimes imitated and copied, through reverse engineering. Competencies in order to be transferred, require a complex mix of know-how, specific information and experience. In order to resolve the problem of transferring competencies and productive knowledge, imitative behaviour is not sufficient. In the literature there are famous cases in which the transfer of knowledge related to specific patents (from German firms to American ones) has been made possible only when competence bearing actors have been employed in the US. When the process of spin-off assumes a spatial connotation this gives rise to the formation of industrial districts, where the multiplication of the number of agents possessing some common competencies (originally developed in a few *ancestor* firms) can be observed. They clearly represent a critical asset of each local system or industrial district.
2. Knowledge is a complex and interrelated set of information related to

the features of a specific technology. The boundaries of this specific knowledge in our interpretation, are defined by each product or process technology. In other words, firms in the same sector which manufacture the same family of products share this particular production know-how. This type of knowledge is partially tacit and is possessed by proprietary agents. If scientific proprieties related to specific technologies are openly available to the scientific community (here this open knowledge is a kind of general knowledge), the concrete know-how related to its use (e.g. the best way to use the necessary tools, or the capacity to implement it to begin manufacturing) is often secret and localised in nearby individual economic agents.

So, technological knowledge has two prerequisites. In some ways it can be regarded as a blueprint, freely available to all economic agents and hence easily transferable. Its adoption depends entirely on the characteristics of its diffusion process. On the other hand, technology is often tacit knowledge, which cannot be taught, articulated, or codified, as has been discussed by Polanyi (1967) and later on by Nonaka (1991). Typically in firms belonging to science-based sectors, this tacit knowledge (Senker, 1995) is most closely associated to the complex of technological activities developed in R&D departments (which often involve industrial secrets, patent protection, and short learning curves). In contrast, in skill-based sectors, production is often based on apparently staple products and process techniques, that are modified thanks to the tacit knowledge ingrained in the labour force (workers, technicians, and middle management) and inventive entrepreneurs. The areas in which these processes occur are typically the engineering departments and on the shop floor, where incremental modifications or adaptations of machinery are introduced.

3. Information is the lowest level and has to do mainly with economic signals generally available to all agents and usually involve simple decoding. Information is related to a set of messages, simple instructions or market signals (prices, economic information on the market trends, or forecasts on the availability of raw materials). It would be wrong to assume that this lower level of knowledge flows across the economic system without any barriers. First, the operations of registering, interpreting, and accessing information, must be considered as costly activities for firms. Secondly, markets are imperfect tools for the transmission of such knowledge. Prices do not carry all the relevant data that economic operators need, as is assumed by the Austrian school deriving from von Hayeck's work. Markets are often incomplete, imperfect, insufficiently transparent, etc. Clearly, they are a fundamental means for entrepreneurs to explore the *floating* knowledge and information in each economic system. However, this type of knowledge is neither instantaneously transmitted to all economic agents, nor equally accessible.

In short, in dealing with the process of information, technology, and competence absorption and creation, firms develop distinct features which differentiate one firm from another. The contextualisation of knowledge and the adaptation of technology to local conditions is at the basis of the differentiation of every local context.

Knowledge as a localised good

The perspective which is at the core of our analysis is the idea that firms have the function of being loci of productive knowledge and competence. Their knowledge can be considered a localised and not completely transferable good (Antonelli, 1996). The accumulation of productive knowledge by firms in specific geographical context is the foundation of the evolutionary patterns of local industrial systems.

In economics, the neo-classical school has ignored this issue, representing the firm as an abstraction of the production function. In this approach, firms are ruled by external signals and by economic laws: they are price-directed cogs. Broadly speaking, firms represent the fundamental microeconomic units transforming the inputs, factors of production, into outputs, goods and services; however the rules of this transformation remain an *auspicium mysteria*. The principal focus is on a distributive question, the problem of resource allocation, rather than exploring the questions found in the theory of production. It seems that this theory looks at the market as a mechanism capable of productively employing resources itself, but it ignores the creative capability of each economic agent to produce wealth. If we look at the short-term adjustments of firms, the neo-classical explanation may mirror firm behaviour realistically: quantity and price are considered the most important component which govern the firms' behaviour in response to market signals. However, this perspective is hardly suitable for assessing the long-term dynamics of firms and local industrial systems.

By contrast, in the new vision proposed here, firms are complex microcosms with autonomy, able to make decisions, formulate strategies, and create organisational routines and innovative behaviours. Moreover, firms possess productive knowledge, which is essential to activate the production process. Without this internal capability, no economic signals could make the system work. If this is the primary reason why firms exist as specialised and differentiated agents in capitalistic economies, the development of specific places where these abilities are (cumulatively) spread among the agents and are not simply transferable explains the rise of spatial specialisation and the agglomeration of industries in particular regions. The question of the spatial concentration of similar activities, a phenomenon which has attracted the attention of economists and geographers internationally, is in our view related to the mechanisms that transfer knowledge and competencies, a relatively "sticky" good (von Hippel, 1994), localised in firms and in specific local contexts. Clearly in Italy, this is the foundation of the origin of local systems, and more specifically, it helps to explain the rise of the Italian industrial district model.

The perspective adopted here regards the idea that productive knowledge and competence are not marketable factors available to everyone in the free market. The discussion leads to a positive analysis of the nature of firms and local industrial systems. They are an alternative to the market for co-ordinating productive resources, as was first proposed by Coase in 1937. However, this view differs in many ways from the Williamson analysis of transaction costs, and is more closely related to the Penrose idea of firms being the subject of managerial (organisational) rents. In developed economies, resources are not transformed by atomistic agents, but by a large variety of firms of widely differing size, partially integrated with local labour markets, with an internal capacity for research, links with other ventures, etc.

If in neo-classical theory the notion of the firm is a *black box* driven by external forces, we go inside the box in order to study the firm as an active agent of innovation, transformation and selection. The claim that firms are endowed with knowledge and competence leads to the study of endogenous learning and the acquisition of technical change.

This is particularly meaningful in the context of our analysis which focuses on the nature of localised knowledge as described by Atkinson and Stiglitz (1969), and by Stiglitz (1987). Finally, we have arrived to the core of this chapter: the notion of the firm as a locus of knowledge.[3]

By adopting this view, each firm can be distinguished from the others because of its different knowledge, competence, capabilities, skills, and know-how embodied in the human capital (shop-floor labour force or R&D laboratory personnel). Each firm can be distinguished by its strategic use of its material and non-material assets. This implies, of course, that each firm differs in the quantity and quality of resources used in innovative activities. When firms undertake a flow of innovations in products and processes, the exploitation and development of this usable and productive knowledge is fundamental.

If the firm provides the minimum know-how to allow inputs to be organised and co-ordinated, the spatial aggregation of firms in specific industrial filière is the level on which resources are organised.

Firms are also free to choose different degrees of division of labour and vertical integration, as well as their inter-firm relations, the density of links with other institutions (such as research centres).

The sum of all these individual choices gives shape to each local industrial structure. Each local system is, therefore, characterised by a different composition of firms with different modes of co-ordination, resources, competencies, innovative skills, growth propensities, etc. So, in the real world, identical firms do not exist.

Firms and local systems tend to maintain their diversity (hence, IBM is not Olivetti, and Prato has demonstrated a marked resilience throughout the 1980s, while other Italian textile districts have declined significantly).

In developing specific, proprietary knowledge, firms also advance the frontiers of the existing pool of social knowledge. In the course of doing so, often much of this knowledge and competence spill over into the surrounding nodes of the local industrial structure. Proximity allows for a leakage of knowledge and the partial appropriation of competencies by agents located in the same local industrial system or district. In the long term, this new knowledge may become useful for many agents. This starts a process of local disclosure. However, the process may end at the boundary of the local system. Distance still acts as a significant barrier when the strategic elements of local competencies and knowledge are tacit. The accumulation of such competencies is recurrent, and it provides extraordinary competitiveness to firms which belong to specific local systems in which some pieces of knowledge and competencies may be shared and socialised.

Markets, institutions and the regimes of knowledge production

If we assume, on the basis of previous considerations, that innovation is essentially knowledge (mainly practical and applicative), emerging from networks of relations and contextualised activities, then it is a question of analysing how this knowledge is really generated in specific local clusters of firms or industrial districts.

Technological change does not spring up spontaneously within an economic system. The productive use of the whole pool of available knowledge and the enhancement of general (and specific) scientific and technological knowledge in modern economies arise out of a complex set of interactions among different sources (R&D, engineering, suppliers and producers' needs, university research, etc.) and different agents (private operators, public institutions, and non-profit agencies). Deeply involved in this process, private firms play an important role, and perhaps, in contemporary market economies, an increasingly dominant one.

To increase their competitiveness firms either move along the existing trajectories currently used, or search for and discover radically new innovative solutions. Usually the patrimony of knowledge utilised to invent new solutions is not only internal, but is both internal and external. In any case, this body of knowledge, that firms make use of, produce, or transform, as Nelson (1990b) and Pavitt (1990) have argued, cannot as a rule be considered a free public good available to all economic agents, as is frequently assumed in neo-classical theory. As Nelson has shown, even if scientific knowledge has the characteristics of a public good, when referred to specific technologies, it has some characteristics of both public and private goods. Nevertheless, the more one enters the domain of technology, the more technology becomes firm-specific and ingrained in a firm's know-how.

Because firms spend resources to acquire technology (and even simply to acquire information), they will try to benefit from their efforts, by taking possession of the knowledge acquired and using it exclusively.

To improve their position, they also try to increase their stock of productive knowledge by searching for new sources of knowledge and improvements to adopt. Generally speaking, then, firm behaviour tends to minimise what they make available externally, i.e. the disclosure of their technological competence and the know-how they have acquired by direct experience to their rivals, and to maximise what they take in from outside the firm, i.e. the acquisition of knowledge and specific information usable within the production process.

Given the interplay of the firms described above, technological change occurs through a continuous process of inventing, catching up, copying, imitating, and improving. The innovative activity of firms develops through this sequence of innovative and competitive games.

In this connection, technological change can be portrayed as an equilibrium breaking mechanism, whose outcome, once activated by firms, will create an unbalanced industrial structure. At any time, in fact, some firms will be situated on the cutting edge, others behind it, some will be more innovative, others more imitative, and so on.

Given the uncertain nature of technological change, there are no standard prescriptions. Firm behaviour is characterised by a marked technological pluralism.

In any case, the result is that each firm accumulates different pieces of technological knowledge: firm specific, because it is related to the production and use of (or ability to absorb) knowledge by an individual agent; different, because there are vast possibilities for modifications or for the introduction of improvement, however small; cumulative, because what is learnt at any point in time is related to what has been learnt and experienced in the past.

It follows that, as a rule, it cannot be assumed either that technology will flow freely from one economic agent to another, or that the process of development of technology is unconditioned or random. The competitive game engaged in by firms is significantly influenced by long-term firm-specific technological accumulation.

Even in the extreme case in which firms acquire technology solely through buying new machinery and equipment from the outside, the ways in which firms use the new technology tend to differ.

What has been established so far is that the room for technological change on the firm level is unquestionably less elastic and indefinite than what is described in the textbooks of orthodox economics, and more directed and dictated by the sources, directions and determinants of technological change.

In addition, firms partially shape their technological opportunities by moving from one-product technology to a range of totally different industrial products or moving in one direction rather than another, accelerating or retarding their learning capability.

In contrast to the traditional approach, we can forecast an evolutionary pattern of firm variability, with winners and losers (thus, with *ex-post* optimisers and *ex-post* non optimisers), in which each firm adjusts its technological trajectory on the basis of its vision of the future.

Markets, in that respect, are powerful levelling tools, but inter-country differences in the economic, social and institutional context, also play a part. In similar fashion, the innovative propensity of a firm also appears to be related to these externalities, that reflect the presence of various implicit sets of rules, social behaviours, and financial attitudes regarding the economy. Pavitt and Patel (1988) have discussed these institutional determinants of innovation activity in terms of myopic or long-term strategies embodied in firm behaviour.

As discussed above, traditional economics has always treated technological change as occurring outside firms, and economists interested in technical change have concentrated their investigations exclusively on the importance of in-house R&D activity. The approach chosen by the authors of this volume is connected to the evolutionary theory of the firm (e.g. Nelson and Winter, 1982; Dosi, 1988a; Malerba, 1992). Firms are perceived as learning agents, endowed with capabilities, routines, and research procedures. The dynamics of sequential stages in innovation activity, in which a plurality of learning procedures coexists, produce a restricted sequence of imitation/innovation/imitation (or the other way around). Moreover, firms belong to very complex social and economic systems, that differ from country to country and that influence the performance of firms. Therefore, the questions to be asked are not only how technological progress is generated in firms, and what are the typical loci in firms where the creation and the transmission of knowledge are activated, but also which types of local systems and institutional contexts are more conducive to the creation of innovations.

We have to assume a wide variety of ways of producing technical change exist, that are related to the large number of actors and strategies involved (Nelson, 1993).[4] This approach is fundamental to understanding the innovative models found in different local industrial systems or districts.

The public regime of knowledge production

The first relevant distinction to establish is whether new knowledge is produced by public agents or by private operators.

The relative importance of the public compared to the private role is determined by the peculiarities of each country.

In OECD countries, detailed information is available about national differences in investment in public research, in the share of industrial R&D financed by public funds, or in the number of scientific personnel working in public institutions. These public efforts, as is widely known, are oriented mainly towards two classes of activities:
a) direct public expenditure (in R&D performed by universities, public research centres, and other institutions, such as firms in selected sectors, or mixed public and private organisations, etc.) to finance research programmes; and
b) indirect promotion of technological development through a range of

policies, such as regulations, and incentives in the public sphere. Governments influence the innovative activity of firms through industrial policies, or, more specifically, by proposing innovation oriented measures, including the introduction of specific public procurements, or, by intervention in the formation of skills in the labour market, by expanding and improving education and training, and so on. The latter does not produce any specific, clearly measurable, technological improvement, but, in spite of that, they have been considered of great importance in influencing the technological efficiency of firms—Nelson (1982), Freeman (1987), and Dosi (1988a).

As discussed in Nelson (1987), Dosi et al. (1988), and Rosenberg (1982), new pieces of knowledge are generated within the system by universities, government agencies, and non-profit research centres. They are continuously expanded. The knowledge produced by these institutions is generally available to all economic agents and everyone can benefit.

Public knowledge consists of generic universal understandings, codified in texts, and scientific magazines, that is exchanged and discussed openly in international workshops and conferences, and develops in connection with new scientific discoveries. The diffusion of public knowledge among all economic agents, and among countries, can be thought of as rather simple, except for certain constraints: languages transmission costs, and political receptiveness of different areas and countries.

However, firms located in the same country or in the physical proximity of the research institutions are clearly in a favourable position. They are the first to benefit from new discoveries or to exploit the specialised personnel who have been trained in these public centres but may be lured away by better wages or working conditions. At the same time, direct links between firms and research centres stimulate increased internal R&D efficiency. Firms may rely on university laboratories for specific tasks, such as the quality control of raw materials and finished goods, or to finance riskier research projects since public institutions are more willing to take on long-term intellectual projects. In science-based firms, these contacts may play a fundamental role and in many cases the industrial structure develops around universities and centres of research. This explains science parks, Silicon Valley, and Route 128 in Boston (Saxenian, 1994).

Both the proximity between those who transmit knowledge and those who receive it, and the reduction of the number of agents (or informational transmission nodes) involved in transactions, are directly proportional to the risks of information dissipation and degeneration (Premus, 1988).

The private regime of knowledge production

The development of technical knowledge in firms typically occurs in three distinctive ways.

1. First, it may be a result of a specific effort developed consciously by the firm to improve its knowledge of products and processes involved in its production process through R&D or other similar activities developed in a more informal context (engineering departments, the shop floor, etc.).

2. Second, it can originate in firms from a process of internal learning, both as an indirect by-product of the firm's activity (in some cases even unforeseen), or simply as a function of the time spent on using, experimenting with, and adapting a particular technology, or a firm's problem solving efforts.

3. Third, it may be produced by learning which is mainly outside the firm, concerning external sources of knowledge such as other firms, institutions, suppliers of technology, or other actors beyond the firm in question. Such external links appear to be ever more crucial in modern economies. All firms have to support their internal sources of knowledge with external learning, because of the constantly increasing costs of developing new technologies, the multidisciplinary nature of the knowledge involved, and the systemic and complex nature of the technology.

The sources of external learning are generated in four types of channels within the firm:

a) the acquisition of external technologies, usually new machinery or equipment;

b) copying and imitation;

c) interaction, along the chain of customers-suppliers-subcontractors-competitors-retailers; and

d) inter-firm co-operation.

In considering the significance of the framework it should be remembered that what is at issue is the complexity of the varied sources of firms' technological learning involved in the mastery of technology. According to this, therefore, the use of any simple indicator of innovative activity (for instance relying exclusively on the measurement of R&D activity) for the analysis of a firm's technological capability is misleading. Given that internal and external learning are experienced by firms through different channels of knowledge production, a firm's technical capability has to be evaluated in a wider context.

The internal models of knowledge production

The R&D model. It is well known that each firm can produce internally, in R&D departments, the efforts required to make advancements in technology. But they may not be able to control it exclusively. This is related, in turn, to the system to protect this intellectual property, that is, their different appropriability regimes, as described by Levin et al. (1987): patents, industrial secrecy, lead times, learning curves, marketing and service. It should be noted that firms have alternatives: they can establish more than one R&D centre in different locations, or can co-operate with other firms (both upstream and downstream in the production cycle) in strategic alliances (Mowery, 1988), or subcontract research projects externally, or acquire small innovative firms (Granstrand and Sjolander, 1988). However, the lack of internal R&D in a firm is not necessarily a sign of technological weakness. Firms can rely on external specialised centres or networking for R&D.[5]

As discussed by Cohen and Levinthal (1989), then, despite the fact that generally R&D expenditure is considered a fundamental tool for the generation of productive knowledge for firms, they have also shown that, in the firms examined, R&D played an important role in enhancing their ability to assimilate and exploit existing knowledge, including external knowledge. So R&D expenditure only measures a firm's efforts, but it does not measure the total knowledge gained by the firm (through co-operation, imitation, networking, etc.), and of course, there is no direct connection to the results in terms of its innovation and imitation capacity.

The level of technological opportunity dictates the range of probability of gaining from R&D activity and the taxonomy model indicates a wide variability among sectors. In science based sectors (Scherer, 1982; Pavitt, 1984) R&D plays a fundamental role in advancing the frontiers of knowledge, whereas in others, informal R&D, incremental improvements, and learning processes are required of the firm.

Learning processes derived from activities not related to formal R&D. As a matter of fact, the R&D proxy is probably a good macro indicator to show which countries are on the technological frontier in the production of advanced technologies. But the more one approaches the micro level of analysis, the more one needs sophisticated indicators to test the level of a firm innovativeness.

For each firm R&D activity is usually accompanied by other activities variously described as design, development or production engineering, which unsurprisingly, may be allocated to departments other than R&D. This happens more often in small firms (Kleinknecht, 1987), given that they do not have any separate functional and accounting identity for R&D (Pavitt and Patel, 1988).

R&D expenditures thus are not the only way to acquire productive knowledge, but one of the many complex options that exist within the whole range of creative strategies (see also Kay, 1985).

Learning by doing and using. The development of technology, improved efficiency the use of technology and the technological performance of a firm may derive from a more or less intentional process of learning on the factory level. For a long time this form of internal learning was scarcely considered by economists, until Arrow's (1962) seminal article, on the implications of learning by doing. Indeed, it contradicted the common neo-classical view, for which the use of identical techniques, at any point of time, implied the same level of output, since factor productivity was assumed to be fixed and unalterable. But the documentary evidence has shown that in the manufacturing stage, after a product and process have been designed, a form of learning takes place and output increases, that is, real labour costs per unit of output decrease. In Arrow's interpretation the learning consisted of developing increased skill in production, his analysis focused on factories with plants in which investment remained stable, as in the Horndal steel factory (originally studied by Lundberg in 1961, and also cited by Liebenstein) where for years after the installation of new machinery, there was a steady annual increase of labour productivity. Malerba (1988) has called this form of learning "learning through experience", and in one sense, this definition of all forms of learning by doing recognises more clearly the cognitive nature of learning applied to the productive process. He surveys a significant number of cases from the economic literature which have improved our understanding of many features of the learning processes in relation to: a) the labour process, both in assembly, and in sectors of high capital intensity; b) managerial tasks; c) the reduction of labour costs; and d) changing product characteristics.

We now turn to another aspect of the learning process. Rosenberg argues there is clear distinction between gains within the production process (doing) and gains that are generated as a result of subsequent use of that product (using), (Rosenberg, 1982, p.122). The latter, emphasised by Rosenberg, occurs when firms introduce many improvements in productivity, often small, but whose cumulative effect is very large. This is a source of technological innovation that is not usually explicitly recognised as a component of the R&D process, and receives no direct expenditure — which may be why it is ignored (*ibid.* p. 121). The focus is not on time, which may improve the performance of firms, nor on the improvement of productivity gained after starting up (each production process, like an engine, needs time to reach full speed), nor on the improved dexterity of the labour force. The point here is the introduction of incremental improvements in capital goods, in regard to design, performance, and technical characteristics. In this form of learning, what counts is the knowledge possessed by those who utilise the machine. Because in high-technology societies technical knowledge tends to be extremely specific, performance, applicability, and operating costs cannot be predicted in advance from scientific principles or methodologies, but need to be experimented with. Users, indeed, can contribute significantly to the discovery of new fields of application and new technological solutions.

The cases presented by Rosenberg offer a convincing explanation of certain determinants of technological change, and illustrate the sequences that link specialised producers of machinery and manufacturers, where improvements and new applications are applied in a framework of technological convergence and interdependence, as was the case of aircraft engines for the DC-8 and James Watt's steam engine, which to work effectively had to await Wilkinson's boring machine.

A similar framework has been proposed by von Hippel (1976, 1982, and 1988), for the analysis of innovation introduced in specialised medical equipment, and by Lundvall (1984 and 1988) in both dairy processing and clothing.

Here, too, the key to understanding the process that leads to an increase of knowledge is the users' needs (synthesised in von Hippel's words as the manufacturer and customer active paradigms and their ability to specify and elaborate their requirements).

The external models of knowledge production

Another important aspect related to the manner in which firms may acquire technological knowledge (either totally or, more frequently, partially) from the outside is external learning. As has been said above, external acquisition is often of great importance. As Dodgson (1989) has argued, contemporary technology extends the boundaries of the individual firm. Few firms, in fact, have sufficient in-house resources and expertise to generate new technologies. Frequently, technology is developed in conjunction with, or in response to, the activities of other firms. Firms resort to four types of external technological learning.

The acquisition of new machinery. In the first place, they may acquire technology by buying equipment and machinery in the marketplace or by ordering specialised customised technologies from suppliers that satisfy their specific needs, or by buying patents or licensing agreements from other firms. In this case, the prerequisite of learning activity is the availability of knowledge about these new processes or products, and above all, the availability of the financial resources internally from the owners or externally from the financial system.

Imitation and copying. While the purchase of technology is normally rather expensive, another way to acquire knowledge is by replication, imitation and copying (Teece, 1998). Imitation activity in firms sometimes leads to a very costly process of investment in new technology when the firm wishes to introduce new machinery and equipment already used by their competitors, or to the transfer of technology for which legal protection of proprietary rights exists.

But sometimes technology can be imitated at lower cost: as with product imitation, or with reverse engineering of products or processes which can be freely purchased in the marketplace. Using the same kind of reasoning, imitation activity can be a low-cost alternative if the technology transfer is the result of informal or formal exchanges of information and knowledge (among the various industrial firms of the same cluster or network). In fact, agent proximity favours imitation by rivals. Finally, the imitative activity of firms may take advantage of the mobility of labour, since firms may hire skilled blue-collar workers or technicians who previously worked for the innovative firms (both rivals and more simply experts in the technology to be imitated). In practice this behaviour is often associated with the previously described models of learning. One of the most overlooked factors is that during the adoption phase firms often improve the innovation by discovering better applications.

Learning through interactions with clients and suppliers. A third means is a process of learning through the interactions of firms. Often, technical advances are the result of the combination of more than one firm's set of experience and know-how: suppliers of parts or semi-finished goods, subcontractors, individual clients, etc., may form a dense network that promotes technological exchanges that generate new technological solutions or improvements in existing products and processes. The range of this learning is a function of the degree of product decentralisation (the more a firm is verticalised, the fewer its opportunities), and the degree of innovativeness of the economic agents in the network.

Learning through co-operation. The last kind of external learning includes the various forms of technological learning that occurs through co-operation (Axelrod, 1984).

The process is similar to the one mentioned above, but here the inter-firm interaction is intentional, stable and is manifested in formal technological collaboration, joint-ventures, co-production, etc. It has been frequently argued that the restructuring of the 1970s forced firms to develop external links to distribute the greater costs and risks involved in high technology projects.

When firms have different types of knowledge — or when they want to share the costs of investment for the development of new technological solutions — co-operation between firms may allow them to acquire complementary knowledge. Such knowledge is not freely available in the market. Given the complexity of modern technology, the high level of uncertainty, and the growing costs of developing innovative activity, learning through co-operation has become an ever more important source of innovation in the economic system. It should be mentioned that the efficacy of these co-operative agreements is influenced by a supportive inter-firm culture (Hirst and Zeitlin, 1989a and 1989b), and more generally, by the degree of co-operation exhibited in the institutional context (Sako, 1989), as occurred, for example, within the local industrial systems in Italy (You and Wilkinson, 1994).

In conclusion, in this section the various sources that stand behind the innovative dynamics of firms (and therefore related to the different local industrial systems examined) have been identified. Specifically, we have shown that technological knowledge, as it is used and generated by firms, may be drawn from two knowledge producing regimes (the public and private) and different innovative sources (both external and internal to firms). In such a complex situation, the generation of localised knowledge can no longer be considered to be the simple result of internal R&D efforts, as in standard economic theory, but is considered the result of the complex interaction of different means of knowledge absorption, use, and creation of new knowledge, based on external and internal learning, formal and informal research efforts, the interaction of agents and technological co-operation, the use of tacit and codified knowledge, and the acquisition and modification of existing on-the-shelf technologies.

Models of local systems: how diversity and path-dependency are related to evolutionary paths

Up to this point the reasons why firms exist as separate specialised agents in the market have been discussed by assuming the determining factor for their existence to be firm-specific knowledge and competence. If firms are not empty co-ordinators of inputs which could be produced by the marketplace, this means that when firms are established, they possess something not available in the marketplace. This factor is their productive capacity. Productive capacity is formed by their practical knowledge (related to their experience) and their specific competencies for dealing with technologies. This latent factor is dispersed irregularly on the territory and is dependent on past events. So, each area is characterised by the possession of certain aptitudes and the lack of others. The historical process of the accumulation of skills, abilities, and capacity for dealing with some technologies (connected to the presence of qualified (best-practice using) firms, supporting institutions and expert technicians), limits the room for subsequent development.

On territorial level this is the major cause of path-dependency in industry specialisation (Arthur, 1994; Antonelli, 1997).

Local development may be seen as a process with a long memory, whose influence persists over time. However, this historical irreversibility can be terminated when productive agents are able to activate a (costly, when intentional, or relatively cheap, if determined by historical accidents) process of learning, imitation, and acquisition of new knowledge and competencies that shifts the old pattern of economic specialisation (Audretsch, 1995; Baldwin, 1995).

How does the productive specialisation of certain geographical areas originate? And what are its connections with the productive capacity (which is not a free good), discussed above? And, what are the elements that produce the positive feed-back and the dynamics of local industrial systems?

What follows is an attempt to define more precisely the characteristics of the initial specific knowledge and competence of firms with their capacity to master technical change (innovative potential) in order to classify firms at start-up. The model may be incomplete, as all such schemes are, but it derives from the empirical analyses presented in this volume and other research work of the authors on the economy of

Northeast Italy.

On the micro level three main types of firms, classified by their specific initial knowledge and competence in the start-up phase and by their innovative strategy, are found in the local industrial systems analysed.

First, the firms may be formed by a process of expansion of the industrial structure. These firms are not created to carry out any significant novelties. However, they possess some productive capacity in traditional manufacturing. In order to enter the marketplace these firms, therefore, need to be placed in a favourable position. For instance, demand for their product is growing, or firms have some comparative advantage in terms of input costs. In this regard, Rullani (1989) and Camagni (1984) have noted, for example, that the development of Italian peripheral regions (Veneto, Emilia Romagna and Tuscany), in the 1970s, may be explained in this way. Firms located in this area had access to particularly low-cost labour from skilled labour forces. The role of market growth should be read loosely. If local firms increase the rate of subcontracting, the net effect in firm-creation may be high. Even backward producers may find a place in the market through the decentralisation of production. For instance, in all the cases presented in this volume during the 1980s, deverticalisation opened up a wide range of opportunities in subcontracting.

Strictly speaking these firms are not very innovative. In conclusion, these firms enter the market because of growing market demand (so they may be described as "market oriented" firms), or because the processes of economic decentralisation favour division of labour among firms.[6]

The second group refers to an intermediate category of product improving firms. They market products which are modified in their design, performance, applicability, etc. These firms are not very innovative in the orthodox sense. They do not perform individual R&D, nor do they exhibit strong technological performance in terms of patents. Their innovative performance is supported by varied innovative efforts, as those described above: learning processes, technological co-operation, interactions with suppliers, etc.

The market power of these firms is often very high. A rich literature in business journals, includes many striking examples. On this level the distinction between incremental technical innovations and innovations in the design sphere is often blurred (Rothwell and Gardiner, 1985). The concept of business idea, originally introduced by the Swedish economist Richard Normann (1977), is useful to describe the type of knowledge necessary to initiate this innovative process. This creation contains few technological novelties, but it is directed to create something which does not exist and which will be readily marketable. As discussed by Teece (1986), and more recently by Tellis and Golder (1996), marginal improvements applied by follower firms may put them in the position to become a dominant market leader (in terms of market share). So, often, improver firms become more profitable and powerful than early innovating firms.

Third, given the pool of knowledge of competencies already existing in the local system or industrial district, new firms are created by innovative entrepreneurs. The creation of these firms is thus based on the discovery of a truly innovative product or process. This model coincides completely with the Schumpeterian tradition of innovative firms which owes their origins to original inventions. Very often these firms perform formal R&D activities. However, their range of innovation efforts covers all forms of innovation activity described above as internal and external learning processes.

These three typologies of firms allow us to develop a framework that better differentiates and describes the main features that characterise the various local production systems and districts analysed in this volume.

On a more aggregate level of analysis, despite the Italian literature on this topic that has treated the model of industrial district as a homogeneous unit of analysis (Becattini, 1987), it is clear from the perspective of innovation there is no single model for industrial structure. On the spatial level, different local systems (or industrial districts) may be defined in the following way.

Type A. The static path. These local systems are characterised by the presence of only the first type of firms. These industrial structures are rather static. Radical changes are only introduced by external sources. The competitiveness of these local systems is limited to the absolute gap in average costs. These systems may take advantage of indirect "district" economies: economies of both scale and scope related to the "size" of the local system (measured by its share of total national or international output). Thus, each firm benefits from the fact that it is immersed in a local productive network (Grabher, 1993). The growth of subcontracting may increase the inter-firm division of labour, and thus the efficiency of the whole system.[7] Clearly the accumulation of practical knowledge and competencies is limited. In this context the mechanism for the generation of new firms is only based on the existing practical knowledge embodied in firms. As has been shown by many empirical works, new firms are founded by former employees of the more established firms in the area. The reservoir of entrepreneurship comes from the lower social strata: blue collar workers and technicians. The expansion of the system occurs mainly through the horizontal propagation of new firms. The cases of Maniago, an industrial district specialised in cutlery described in chapter 7 and the production of ceramic toilets around Civita Castellana presented in chapter 8 are in this regard typical.

Type B. The evolutionary path. These local systems include various types of firms, but they are characterised by the presence of a cluster of "improver" firms. They are typically created by the most dynamic agents (technicians, skilled blue collar workers, sales personnel). Improvements may be primarily in products or (more frequently) incremental innovations applied to the machinery used. The "industrial atmosphere" so accurately described nearly 100 years ago by Marshall describes well the social climate of emulation, envy, and co-operation that is at the basis of the "institutional model" in which the mechanism of rapid imitation and copying are part of the meta-rules that govern the behaviour of agents. Proximity acts as an accelerator of this process. So, once an incremental innovation is introduced, short diffusion curves are generally observed among firms belonging to Italian local systems within the matrix of relationships of subcontractors and suppliers, and across the *filière* upstream and downstream. In addition, the existence of economies of specialisation lead to reduced fixed costs and a high propensity to renew machinery. Frequent changes in the production cycle stimulate (and allow for) learning. This encourages the accumulation of skills and competencies within the area. In standard theory, the diffusion of an innovation is seen statically (technology is fixed), while according to evolutionary economics the diffusion and repeated use of a given technology leads to further improvement. So, the new knowledge experienced by improver and innovative firms generates continual improvement through the interaction of local agents, in a dynamic sequence which leads to increasing returns, learning, positive feed-back, and network externalities. The start-up of new firms is often stimulated by improver firms. The local diffusion of knowledge and competencies occurs as an "overflow" from the original firms, generating the dynamics for the continual improvement of technology. However, learning is temporally bounded. There is a limit (in terms of both cost reduction and product improvement) to the benefits obtained by learning and marginal improvements. Over time the implementation of learning and the possibilities of further improvements are subject to that implacable foe, the law of decreasing returns. Only when (and if) new innovations enter the cycle, is an amplifying dynamic generated. In this volume this type is described in chapter 9 by Monica Tamisari who deals with a very famous skill-based Italian industrial district: the Manzano area, which annually produces nearly 80% of the national production of chairs (and about 50% of total EU production).

Type C. Strong evolutionary path. In the last group of local systems, the presence of Schumpeterian "inventive" firms is the crucial feature that qualifies this typology.

The discovery of an innovative product (or process) may even create ex-novo[8] a new local system, but, more frequently, Schumpeterian firms are based in well established industrial structures, where innovators emerge quite randomly. These innovative local systems are characterised by the presence of strong Schumpeterian rivalry. They possess very dynamic attributes: network externalities are very significant, and normally firms within specific networks co-ordinate investment policies or share some complementary assets.

This has a strong impact on costs. The presence of very innovative firms influences the innovative performance of the entire system. Imitative behaviour firms compete, as in type B discussed above, to acquire the new knowledge and the new competencies developed by innovative firms to master their innovations. Clearly, it should be assumed that the overall impact of adopting/improving such innovations will always be stronger than in local contexts characterised by improver firms. Also the incentives to adopt them quickly are higher here. The growing competitiveness of the local system favours new start-ups. New Schumpeterian firms are only a small part of the net increase in the number of local firms. It cannot be assumed that all the new entrants have high innovative performances.

Firms which share the local culture, standards, social norms, etc., are very receptive to the flow of innovations. Dynamic local systems tend also to have more developed information channels, and institutions that evolve with them. Some institutions can play the role of global meta-organisers. Complex information channels allow for better and faster distribution of information and accumulation of knowledge. They represent (as in the Arrow view presented in his 1974 book on the limits of organisation) a large part of the social capital invested in the territory which can be characterised as an irreversible investment. A striking example of this type of local system is provided by Luciano Pilotti, in chapter 7 in which he examines the long history of growth of the Montebelluna area, specialised in boots-shoes.

The evolutionary nature of the local production systems does not mean that, once classified, their nature can be taken for granted; perhaps type A local systems may evolve into type B or C systems.

Over time, because of the declining ability of the founders (in business, it is a commonplace to say that the third generation will "fall flat on its face"), local production systems may decline. Schumpeterian firms do not always remain innovative.[9] Demand led production systems (Type A) may survive in the short term, by virtue of the deepening of their practical knowledge of the production process. However, they risk losing the initial cost advantages, as economies grow and labour costs tend to increase. The current processes of economic globalisation will undermine their competitiveness. Only systems that are able to go from Type A to Type B or C will have the opportunity to consolidate and to maintain an acceptable competitive position.

Figure 1.1

Sequence 1: static path	Type A	Type A	Type A	(Civita Castellana; Maniago)
Sequence 2: evolutionary path	Type A	Type B	Type B	(Manzano)
Sequence 3: strong evolutionary path	Type A	TypeB	Type C	(Montebelluna)

Notes

1   This was first discussed by Schumpeter. In his vision of plausible capitalism he pointed out that for innovative, and thus competitive firms, it was of limited importance knowing if in a stationary condition of perfect equilibrium they would have tended to maximise their profits (Schumpeter, 1950, ch. VI, note n. 5).

2   We owe to Schumpeter (1950) the acknowledgement that in "dealing with capitalism one is dealing with an evolutionary process" (ch VII).

3   The approach which looks at the firm's knowledge was first proposed in the works of Nelson and Winter (1982), Teece (1987), and Mowery (1988). Some elements of this new quasi-theory have been developed and specified also by others economists. As discussed by Teece (1984), firms as specialised agents endowed with knowledge exist because they provide a superior way of organising transactions in complex, multistage production systems. Firms are superior to atomistic markets because they possess a superior competence in organising economic co-ordination of dissimilar but complementary activities (Richardson, 1959 and 1972). This knowledge can be viewed as an involvement of each firm in a core business area in which the organisation has its capability. Capabilities are based on the development of information and knowledge through the firm's human capital. They are essentially dynamic (Teece, Pisano and Shuen, 1990).

4   As argued by Nelson, in capitalist economies firms are only one of the institutional actors. In the system there are universities, professional societies, and government agencies. There are public moneys as well as private. Many things that firms cannot be expected to do on their own because the returns are not readily appropriable, are picked up by the other institutions or are publicly financed or both. Also, there are a variety of modes whereby firms can do work co-operatively, rather than in rivalry (Nelson, 1987, p. 10).

5   It is difficult to calculate the contribution of R&D activity performed in firms to the growth of technological knowledge. For instance, in the 1960s Nelson, Peck and Kalachek found that within firms industrial research and development probably accounts for significantly more than half of the total national effort to advance technological knowledge (Nelson et. al., 1967, p. 45). At the same time, many books and articles survey the importance of R&D activities, see for instance: Freeman and Soete (1998), Scherer, (1984); Rosegger (1986); Coombs, Saviotti, and Walsh (1987).

6   Researchers have assumed, more generally, the total reproductive labour force costs, including: a) the access to an informal economy (see Anastasia, 1989), b) the possibility to employ flexible part-time workers which maintain ties with agriculture, or costs related to a low propensity to industrial conflicts (Camagni, 1989).

7   The increase of productive co-ordination through subcontracting is a common practice of the Japanese firms (Freeman, 1987; Arora and Gambardella, 1990).

8   As in the case of a newly created industrial district in the Murgia area around the Natuzzi firm, a firm producing leather upholstery, now covering 20% of the US market, where in the 1990s a local industrial structure of about 250 autonomous firms and 7000 employees has been set up (Belussi, 1999).

9   Each country, as Britain found a long time ago, must face the possibility of losing the vitality of its industrial districts. See for instance Elbaum and Lazonick (1985).

References

Abernathy W.J. and Utterback, J.M. (1978), "Patterns of Industrial Innovation", *Technology Review*, n.7.

Aghion P. and Howitt P. (1992), Un modèle de croissance par destruction crèatrice, in: Foray D. and Freeman C. (eds.), *Technologies et richesse des nations*, Paris, Economica.

Amendola M. and Gaffard J. (1988), The Innovative Choice, Oxford, Basil Blackwell.

Amin A. and Robins K. (1990), "The Reemergence of Regional Economies? The Mythical Geography of Flexible Accumulation", *Environment and Planning Science and Space*, n.8.

Amin A. and Robins K. (1991), "These are not marshallian times", in Camagni R. (ed.), *Innovation Networks: Spatial Perspectives*, London, Belhaven Press.

Anastasia B. (1989), *L'economia irregolare nel Veneto*, Venice, Ires Veneto.

Antonelli C. (1992), The Economics of Information Networks, Amsterdam, North-Holland.

Antonelli C. (1994), Technological districts, localised spillovers, and productivity growth. The Italian evidence on technological externalities in the core regions, *International Review of Applied Economics*, n.8.

Antonelli C. (1995), *Economia dell'innovazione*, Bari, Università Laterza-Economia.

Antonelli C. (1996), Localised knowledge, percolation processes, information networks, *Journal of Evolutionary Economics*, n.6.

Antonelli C. (1997), The economics of path-dependence in industrial organisation, *International Journal of Industrial Organisation,* n.15.

Antonelli C and Gottardi G. (1991), The interaction between the generation and diffusion of new technologies, *Economics of Innovation and New Technologies*, n. 4.

Archibugi D. and Michie J. (1997), (eds.), *Technology Globalisation and Economic Performance*, Cambridge, Cambridge University Press.

Arora A. and Gambardella A. (1989), Complementary and external linkages: the strategies of large firms in biotechnologies, *Journal of Industrial Economics,* vol. 38.

Arrow K. (1974), *The Limits of Organisation,* New York, North & Company.

Arrow K. (1962), The economic implication of learning by doing, *Review of Economic Studies*, vol. 29.

Arthur B. (1994), *Increasing Returns and Path-dependence in the Economy,* Ann Arbour, University of Michigan Press.

Archibugi D. and Pianta M. (1992), Specialisation and size of technological activities in industrial countries: the analysis of patent data, *Research Policy*, n. 21.

Atkinson J. and Stiglitz J. (1969), A new view of technological change, *Economic Journal*, vol. 78.

Audretsch B. (1995), *Innovation and Industry Evolution*, Cambridge, The MIT Press.

Audretsch D.B. and Feldman M.P. (1996), "Innovative Clusters and the Industry Life Cycle", *Review of Industrial Organisation*, n. 11.

Axelrod R. (1984), *Evolution of Co-operation*, New York, Basic Books.

Bagnasco A. (1977), *Le tre Italie: la problematica territoriale dello sviluppo*, Bologna, Il Mulino.

Baldwin J. (1995), *The Dynamics of Industrial Competition*, Cambridge, Cambridge University Press.

Becattini G. (1979), "Dal 'settore' industriale al 'distretto' industriale alcune considerazioni sull'unità di indagine", *Economia e Politica industriale*, n. 1.

Becattini G. (1987), (ed.), *Mercato e forze locali: il distretto industriale*, Bologna, Il Mulino.

Becattini G. (1989a), "Sector and/or Districts: Some Remarks on the Conceptual Foundation of Industrial Economics", in Bamford J., Saynor P., Goodman E., (eds.), *Small Firms and Industrial Districts in Italy*, New York, Routledge.

Becattini G. (1989b), *Modelli locali di sviluppo*, Bologna, Il Mulino.

Belussi F. (1999), Path-dependency vs. industrial dynamics: an analysis of two heterogeneous districts, *Human Systems Management*, forthcoming.

Camagni R. (1984), Economie di agglomerazione, investimenti e sviluppo nella recente esperienza delle regioni europee, *L'industria*, March.

Camagni R. (1989), Cambiamento tecnologico, milieu locale, e reti di impresa: verso un ateoria dinamica dello spazio economico, *Economia e Politica Industriale*, n.64.

Camagni R. (1991), "From the Local Milieu to Innovation Through Co-operation Networks", in Camagni R. (ed.), *Innovation Networks: Spatial Perspectives*, London, Belhaven.

Camagni R. (1993), "La valorizzazione dei fattori locali del processo innoivativo. Università, Imprese, Governo locale e centrale", in APSTI, *Parchi e Poli scientifici e tecnologici*, Napoli, CUEN.

Carlsson B. (1994), "Technological Systems and Economic Performance", in Rotwell M. and Dodgson R. (eds.), *The Handbook of Industrial Innovation*, Vermont Brookfield, Edward Elgar.

Carlsson B. and Eliason G. (1994), The nature and importance of economic competence, *Industrial and Corporate Change*, n. 3.

Cesaratto S., Mangano S. and Sirilli G. (1991), The innovative behaviour of Italian firms: a survey on technological innovation and R&D, *Scientometrics*, n. 21.

Chandler A. (1992), Organisational capabilities and the economic history of industrial enterprises, *Journal of Economic Perspective*, vol. 6, n. 3.

Cohen W. and Levinthal D. (1989), Innovation and learning: the two faces of R&D, *Economic Journal*, vol. 99.

Cohendet P., Llerena P, and Sorge A. (1991), Modes of usage and diffusion of science and technology, paper presented at the international Symposium Europe-USA: management of technology, Paris, May 27-28.

Cooke P. (1995), *The Rise of the Rustbelt*, New York, St. Martin's Press.

Coombs R., Saviotti P., Walsh V. (1987), *Economics and Technical Change*, London, MacMillian.

David P. and Rosenbloom J. (1990), Marshallian factor market externalities and the dynamics of industrial localisation, *Journal of Urban Economics*, vol. 28.

David P., Foray D. and Dalle M. (1997), Marshallian externalities and the emergence of spatial stability of technological enclaves, *Economics of Innovation and New Technology*, n. 5.

Davies S. (1979), *The Diffusion of Process Innovation*, Cambridge, Cambridge University Press.

Demsetz H. (1988), The theory of the firm revisited, *Journal of Law, Economics, and Organisation*, vol. 4, n. 1.

Dosi G. (1988a), Sources, procedures, and microeconomic effects of innovation, *Journal of Economic Literature*, vol. 26.

Dosi G. (1988b) Institutions and markets in a dynamic world., *The Manchester School*, vol. 56.

Dosi G. et al. (1988) (eds.) *Technical Change and Economic Theory*, London, Frances

Pinter.

Dosi G., Teece D. J., and Winter S. (1992) "Towards a Theory of Corporate Coherence: Preliminary Remarks", in Dosi G. et al., (eds.), *Technology and Enterprise in a Historical Perspective*, Oxford, Clarendon Press.

Dosi, G. (1988), "Sources, procedures and microeconomic effects of innovation", *Journal of Economic Literature* n. 25.

Edquist C. (1997), (ed.), *Systems of Innovation*, London, Pinter.

Elbaum B. and Lazonick W. (1985), *The Decline of British Economy*, Oxford, Oxford University Press.

Feldman M. (1994), *The Geography of Innovation*, Amsterdam, Kluwer Academic Press.

Florida R. (1995), "Toward the Learning Region" 1995, *Futures*. vol. 27, n. 5.

Foray D. and Lundvall B. (1996), "From the economics of knowledge to the learning economy", in *Employment and Growth in the Knowledge-based Economy*, OECD Documents, Paris.

Freeman C. (1987), *Technology Policy and Economic Performance: Lesson from Japan*, London, Pinter.

Freeman C. and Soete L. (1998), *Economics of Industrial Innovation*, London, Pinter.

Garofoli G. and Mazzoni R. (1994), (eds.) *Sistemi produttivi locali: struttura e trasformazione*, Milan, F. Angeli.

Gertler M. (1993), "Implementing advanced manufacturing technologies in mature industrial regions: towards a social model of technology production", *Regional Studies*, vol. 27, n.7.

Gibbons M. and Metcalfe J.S. (1986), Technology variety and the process of competition, *International conference on Innovation Diffusion*, Venezia, 18-21st, March.

Gottardi G. (1995), "Distretti industriali: problemi strutturali o nuove prospettive? Una riflessione in chiave evoluzionista", *Cambiamento e innovazione: Strategie e politiche per le imprese e per le aree sistema*, Como, 10 Novembre.

Gottardi G. (1996), "Technology Strategies, Innovation without R&D and the Creation of Knowledge within Industrial Districts", *Journal of Industry Studies*, Vol. 3, n. 2.

Grabher G. (1993), (ed.), *The Embedded Firm: on Socio-economics of Industrial Networks*, London, Routledge.

Granstrand O. and Sjolander S. (1988), The acquisition of technology and small firms by large firms, paper presented at the conference "*Markets for Innovation, Ownership, and Control*", Stockholm, June 12th-16th.

Grant, R.M. (1996), "Toward a knowledge based theory of the firm", *Strategic Management Journal*, v. 17, (Winter special issue), pp. 109-122.

Harrison B. (1992), Industrial Districts: Old Wine in New Bottles? *Regional Studies*, n. 25, (5).

Henderson R.M. and Clark, K.B. (1990), "Architectural innovation: the Reconfiguration of Existing Product Technologies and the Failures of the Established Firms, *Administrative Science Quarterly*, n. 29.

Hirst P. and Zeitlin J. (1989), (eds.) *Reversing Industrial Decline?, Industrial Structure and Policies in Britain and Her Competitors*, New York, St. Martins.

von Hippel E. (1976), The dominant role of users in scientific instruments innovation process, *Research Policy*, vol. 5.

von Hippel E. (1982), Appropriability in innovation benefit as a predictor of the source of innovation, *Research Policy*, vol. 11.

von Hippel E. (1988), The Sources of Innovation, Oxford, Oxford University Press.

von Hippel E. (1994), "Sticky information" and the locus of problem solving: implication for innovation, *Management Science*, vol. 40, n. 4 April.

Kay N. (1985), *The Innovating Firm,* London, MacMillian.

Katz R. and Allen T. (1988), "Investigating the Not Invented Here (NIH) Syndrome: A Look at the Performance, Tenure, and Communication Patterns of 50 R&D Projects Groups" in Tushman M. and Moore W. (eds.) *Readings in the Management of Innovation,* Cambridge, Mass, Ballinger Publishing.

Kleinknecht A. (1987), Measuring R&D in small firms: how much we are missing?, *Journal of Industrial Economics,* n. 2.

Kline S. and Rosenberg N. (1986), An overview of innovation, in Landau R. and Rosenberg N. (eds.), *The Positive Sum Strategy,* Washington, Academic of Engineering Press.

Krugman P. (1991), *Geography and Trade*, New York, The MIT Press.

Jacquemin A. (1987), *The New Industrial Organisation*, Oxford, Claredon.

Jantsch E. (1967), *Technological Forecasting in Perspectives*, OECD, Paris.

Langlois R. and Robertson P. (1995), *Firms, Markets and Economic Change*, London, Routledge.

Levin R. et. al (1987), Appropriating the return from industrial R&D, *Brooking Papers on Economic Activity,* vol. 17, n. 3.

Lucas R. (1988), On the mechanics of economic development, *Journal of Monetary Economics*, vol. 22.

Lundvall B. (1994), *National Systems of Innovation: Towards a Theory of Innovation and Interactive Learning*, London, Pinter.

Lundvall B. (1984), User-producer interaction and innovation, *TIP Workshop Paper*, Stanford, Stanford University.

Lundvall B. (1988), Innovation as an interactive process: user-producer relationships, in Dosi G. et al (1988), (eds.), cit.

Malerba F. (1988), La teoria evolutiva dell'impresa, *L'Impresa*, n.2, April.

Malerba F. (1992), Learning by firms and incremental technical change, *The Economic Journal*, vol. 102.

Malerba F., Orsenigo L., and Peretto P. (1997), Persistence of innovative activities, sectorial patterns of innovation and international technological specialisation, *International Journal of Industrial Organisation*, vol. 15.

Marcato G. (1997), L'evoluzione della struttura industriale del nord-Italia: aspetti territoriali e settoriali, paper presented at the conference on the *Multiplicity of the Growth models in the North-Italy*, Parma, November 6th-7th.

Metcalfe S. (1997), *Evolutionary Economics and Creative Destruction*, London, Routledge.

Mowery D. (1988), (ed.), *International Collaborative Ventures in US Manufacturing*, Cambridge Mass., Ballinger.

Nelson R. (1959a), "The Economics of Invention: A Survey of the Literature", *Journal of Business*, April.

Nelson R. (1959b), "The Simple Economics of Basic Scientific Research", *Journal of Political Economy*, June.

Nelson R. (1962), "The Link between Science and Invention: the Case of the Transistor", in *The Rate and Direction of Inventive Activity*, New York, NBER.

Nelson R. (1963), "Aggregate Production Function", *American Economic Review,* September.

Nelson R. (1978), R&D, knowledge, and externalities, *Yale Working Paper,* n. 787.

Nelson R. (1982), *Government and Technical Progress*, New York, Pergamon.

Nelson R. (1987), *Understanding Technological Change as an Evolutionary Process*, Amsterdam, North Holland.

Nelson R. (1990), "Capitalism as Engine of Progress", *Research Policy*, n. 19.

Nelson R. (1993), (ed.), *National Systems of Innovation*, Oxford, Oxford University Press.

Nelson R., Peck M., and Kalachek (1967), *Technology, Economic Growth and Public Policy*, London, Allen & Unwin.

Nelson R. Winter S. (1982), *An Evolutionary Theory of Economic Change*, Cambridge, Mass, Harvard University Press.

Nelson R. and Rosenberg M. (1993), "Technical innovation and national systems", in Nelson R. (ed.), *National Innovation Systems*, New York, Oxford University Press.

Nelson R. and Winter S. (1982), *An Evolutionary Theory of Economic Change*, Cambridge Mass., Harvard University Press.

Nightingale P. (1998), A cognitive model of innovation, *Research Policy*, 27.

Nonaka I. (1991), The knowledge creating company, *Harvard Business Review*, November.

Norman R. (1977), *Management for Growth*, Chicester, Wiley.

Pavitt K. (1984), Sectorial patterns of technical change: towards a taxonomy and a theory, *Research Policy*, vol. 13, n. 6

Pavitt K. (1987), "The Objectives of Technology Policy", *Science and Public Policy*, n. 14.

Pavitt K. and Patel P. (1988), The international distribution and determinants of technological activities, *Oxford Review of Economic Policy*, n. 4.

Penrose E. (1959), *The Theory of the Growth of the Firm*, London, Basil Blackwell.

Polanyi M. (1967), *The Tacit Dimension*, New York, Doubleday Anchor.

Premus R. (1988), Us technology transfer and regional policy, Paper presented at the European Summer Institute of Regional Science Association, Arco, Trent, July 17th-23.

Richardson B. (1959), Equilibrium, expectations, and information, *Economic Journal*, vol. 69.

Richardson B. (1972), The organisation of industry, *Economic Journal*, vol. 82.

Richardson H.W. (1972), *Input-Output and Regional Economics*, New York, Wiley.

Richardson H.W. (1995), "Economies and Diseconomies of Agglomeration", in Giersch H. (ed.), *Urban Agglomeration and Economic Growth*, Kiel, Springer.

Rogers E.M. (1986), "Three Decades of Research on the Diffusion of Innovation: Progress, Problems, Prospects", *Conference on Innovation Diffusion*, Venice.

Romer P. (1987), Growth based on increasing returns due to specialisation, *American Economic Review Papers and Proceedings,* vol. 77, n. 2.

Romer P. (1994), The origins of endogenous growth, *Journal of Economic Perspectives*, n. 8.

Romer P.M. (1990), "Endogenous Technological Change", *Journal of Political Economics*, n. 98(5).

Rosegger G. (1986), *The Economics of Production and Innovation*, Oxford, Pergamon.

Rosenberg N. (1982), *Inside the Black Box: Technology and Economics*, Cambridge, Cambridge University Press.

Rosenberg, N. (1990), "Why Do Firms Do Research (with Their Our Money)?", *Research Policy*, n. 19.

Rosenberg N. (1992), Economic experiments, *Industrial and Corporate Change*, vol.

1, n. 1.

Rothwell R. and Gardiner P. (1985), Invention, innovation, re-innovation and the role of users, *Technovation*, n. 3.

Rousseau D. and Cooke P. (1984), "Technology and structures", *Journal of Management*, vol. 10, n. 3.

Rullani E. (1989), Innovazione e continuità nell'industria veneta, in AA.VV. (eds.) *Anni novanta: cosa cambia nell'industria veneta*, Padua, Cedam.

Saviotti P. and Metcalfe J (1992), (eds.), *Evolutionary Theories of Economic and Technological Change*, Reading, Harwood Academic Publisher.

Saxenian A. (1994), *Regional Advantage. Culture and Competition in Silicon Valley and Route 128*, Cambridge Mass., Harvard University Press.

Senker J. (1995), Tacit knowledge and models of innovation, *Industrial and Corporate Change*, n.4.

Scherer F. (1982), Inter-industry technology flows and production growth, *Review of Economic and Statistics*, vol. 44.

Scherer F. (1984), *Innovation and Growth: Schumpeterian Perspectives*, Cambridge, The MIT Press.

Schumpeter J. (1939), *Business Cycles: A Theoretical Historical and Statistical analysis*, New York, McGraw-Hill.

Schumpeter J. (1950), *The Theory of Economic Development*, New York, Oxford University Press.

Schumpeter J. (1961), *Capitalism, Socialism and democracy*, New York, Harper Brothers.

Spender J (1996), The geography of strategic competencies, mimeo, Newark, Rutgers University.

Stiglitz J.E. (1987), "Learning to Learn Localized Learning and Technological Progress", in: Dasgupta P. and Stoneman P. (eds.), *Economic Policy and Technological Performance*, Cambridge, Cambridge University Press.

Storper M. and Harrison B. (1992), "Flessibilità, gerarchie e sviluppo regionale: la ristrutturazione organizzativa dei sistemi produttivi e le nuove forme di governance", in Belussi F. (ed.), *Nuovi modelli di impresa. Gerarchie organizzative e imprese rete*, Milan, Franco Angeli.

Storper M. and Scott A.J. (1995), "The Wealth of Regions", *Futures*, vol. 27, n. 5.

Teece D. (1984), Economic analysis and strategic management, *California Management Review*, n.3.

Teece D. (1986), Profiting from technological innovation: implication for integration, collaboration, licensing, and public policy, *Research Policy*, n. 6, vol. 5.

Teece D. (1987), (ed.), *The Competitive Challenge: Strategies for Industrial Innovation Renewal*, Cambridge Mass., Ballinger.

Teece D., Pisano G. and Shuen A. (1990), Firm capabilities, resources, and the concept of strategy, paper presented at the conference *Corporate Capabilities and Competitiveness*, Berkeley University.

Teece D. (1998), Capturing value from knowledge assets, *California Management Review*, 30.

Tellis G. and Golder P. (1996), First to market, first to fail? Real causes of enduring market leadership, *Sloan Management Review*, Winter.

Teitz, M.B. (1994), "Changes in Economic Development Theory and Practice", *International Regional Science Review*, v. 16, n. 1-2.

Varaldo E. and Ferrucci L. (1993), "La natura e la dinamica dell'impresa distrettuale",

Economia e politica industriale, n. 80.

Vet, J.M. (1993), "Globalisation and Local & Regional Competitiveness", *STI Review*, n. 13.

Winter S. (1964), "Economic Natural Selection and the Theory of the Firm", *Yale Economic Essays*, Spring.

Winter S.G. (1987), "Knowledge and Competence as Strategic Assets", in Teece D.J. (ed.), *The Competitive Challenge*, Cambridge, Ballinger.

You J. and Wilkinson F. (1994), Competition and cooperation: toward understanding industrial districts, *Review of Political Economy*, vol. 6, n. 3.

Zeitlin J. (1989), (ed.) "Local Industrial Strategies", *Economy and Society, vol.* 18, n. 4.

2 Innovation and the creation of knowledge in Italian industrial districts: A system model

GIORGIO GOTTARDI

What is the source of rapid and unexpected growth?

The most dynamic Italian industrial districts, especially those located in the Northeast of the country, have achieved good economic results for many years. In these areas the real economy has over the long run had good rates of growth with positive effects on employment and the creation of new businesses. Even during the difficulties of the nineties, the performance seems to have remained good.

Beginning after the second world war as "developing areas" peripheral to the Italian industrial triangle of Milan, Genoa and Turin, with widespread unemployment, these areas have reached high levels of prosperity in terms of added value per inhabitant and virtual full employment. A general entrepreneurial drive as a tool of economic improvement is a widely shared social value. In these areas the concentration of small businesses is extraordinary: about one for every 10 inhabitants.

Since their growth has been generally related to exports, government intervention on the exchange rate (the last in September 1992) can partially explain these performances. But clearly there are also deeper strategic and structural factors at work. Despite their considerable successes in terms of exports, innovation and employment, over the last thirty years, the Italian industrial districts have experienced a series of shocks and adjustments which have led to significant changes in their organisation and mode of operation. The strategies implemented by the enterprises as a result of the cyclical difficulties which occurred have led to gradual but effective changes in their production systems.

The history of the districts is full of information on the impact of exogenous changes and the strategies adopted by firms to adjust. For reasons of simplicity we shall limit our analysis to the nineties. Starting from an update on the performance of the most dynamic Italian districts, a general interpretation of changes affecting these structures will be developed. Their rapid evolution makes it difficult to use orthodox interpretative models derived from neo-classical or from Marshallian perspectives. In particular, it still remains difficult, from a traditional point of view, to explain the widespread creation of original knowledge that is no doubt present in these enclaves, and that has been able to bring about effective product and process innovations in order to maintain their competitiveness. Using numerous empirical examples and an evolutionary and knowledge-based interpretation, the mechanisms of knowledge generation, the learning patterns and the specialisation processes that have occurred in the dynamic Italian districts will be outlined. On this basis, a stylised model of the interactions that technical change brings about within these systems to modify their structure will be developed. One practical result from this analysis is that districts and local industrial systems are identified as a basic articulation of economic activity. From this, some considerations on industrial and innovation policies are then drawn.

What have been the sources of district growth in the recent years? The principal competitive strategies of the most dynamic districts (primarily in Northeast Italy) have been pursued by firms to meet the menacing challenge of Asian countries. These strategies can be summarised as follows (see the works of Garofoli and Mazzoni, 1994; Gottardi, 1995; Gottardi, 1996; in which other references can be found):

1. a reduction of internal costs focusing on core competencies, through more outsourcing;
2. a transition to a learning specialised organisation;
3. re-engineering of internal processes and technological enrichment;
4. a considerable rationalisation of inter-firm relationships;
5. a greater focus on the market.

The result of these actions has been the creation of more specialised economies, significant improvement in product quality, better market segmentation. On the whole, in the most dynamic districts, the internal heterogeneity (variety of products, processes and specialised firms) has grown strongly, and this has allowed a more specific and articulated penetration of local products into many countries and market areas. In part, competitiveness has been achieved through upgrading strategies and a careful choice of market segments on the global level. The rationalisation of production processes towards lean production and the adoption of strategically congruent technologies (e.g. technologies for design, and for quick response) have brought about consistent growth in capital and labour productivity.

Recent evidence, however, suggests that the most important aspect is not so much the growth in capital stock (the investment per unit of labour has increased less than in other contexts) but the improvement in the knowledge and quality of capital embodied in the processes as a consequence of the specialisation processes, the use of technologies that are congruent to the size, the inter-organisational relations and the market strategies of the firms involved, and the fine tuning of the newly created organisational routines. In these districts technological solutions such as integrated computer automation have not been successful.

Undoubtedly, there have been difficulties in the transfer of new technologies, even when they have been well received elsewhere. For example, CAD technologies, with large reductions in capital costs and the development of customised software, have only recently begun to reveal their full potential in small and medium sized enterprises within traditional sectors. In any case, in conjunction with innovation, important learning processes have taken place. They, in turn, have produced improvements and adjustments (for example, a revision of technical standards, and upgrading of hardware and software), have stimulated the introduction of other incremental and collateral innovations, and have led to a better 'appropriation/choice' of new technologies. As a result, the technological content of production processes has risen, independently from the size and position of firms within the value chain.

Due to these technical and organisational changes, many districts are undergoing significant structural evolution. Leading local firms are adopting internationalisation strategies, not only for penetrating new markets but also for the relocation of production activities; local inter-firm relations are losing some of their original informality; the typical hub-spoke network structures are becoming more formal, network hierarchies are emerging, with hub firms playing a more important role in organising the activities of intermediate producers.

In conjunction with technological innovations and the introduction of widespread organisational and structural changes within enterprises, the processes at work have the following principal features (Gottardi, 1995; 1996):

1. increases in the complexity and variety within the various districts, accompanied by internal selection processes;
2. differentiation of various districts, not only in product and process, but also in the structure of organisations;
3. due to horizontal and vertical differentiation processes, a shift of the internal value chain to a 'value-system' (Gottardi, 1998);
4. the formation of great stocks of interactive and co-operative knowledge.

Some districts have gone so far as to create an ensemble of productive competencies and capabilities that do not exist anywhere else in the world. For example, the textile-clothing areas of Treviso and Vicenza are unique in the variety and quality of their production and now supply almost all world markets.

The novelty in recent years has been that dynamic Italian districts have become a driving force for the entire national economy. Because of their ability to adapt and other characteristics of these enclaves based on a large number of small firms and on a 'heterodox' growth model (seen through classical firm theory based on the market power of large firms), the phenomenon of Italian industrial districts has attracted much scholarly interest. Is there today a general theoretical framework with which to explain this evolution of industrial districts as a model of industrial organisation? Numerous studies carried out over the last fifteen years, often referred to in other parts of this book, have clarified the role of the Marshallian externalities in the origin and development of these industrial organisational forms. However, this approach does not seem to be able to fully explain the innovation processes, the paths of growth and structural evolution that have taken place. These systems of enterprises and their performance are highly differentiated within the economic space; from a historic point of view, while production has declined in several districts, in others it has increased. The processes at work seem to differ markedly from some of the most prevalent descriptions of small firm districts, such as those included in the model of *flexible specialisation* popularised by Piore and Sabel (1984).

Various recent studies have highlighted the evolution of traditional districts (Varaldo and Ferrucci, 1993; Gandolfi, 1990; Nuti, 1992; Belussi, 1993; Garofoli and Mazzoni, 1994; Bianchi, 1994; Brusco, 1994; Bellandi and Russo, 1994; etc.), with respect to the phases of their initial development. From these new approaches, it is important to seek alternative explanatory frameworks to account for these changes, and in particular to explain the processes of organisation and technological evolution. A stylised description focusing on the principal characteristics of the innovation process, and selecting the most important variables that have triggered district evolution is developed below.

Some general interpretations from the empirical evidence on districts

To begin with, from studies on industrial districts and the findings of a large number of empirical surveys, some empirically based hypotheses on district evolution can be drawn.

The role of knowledge in growth processes. Historically, the growth of industrial districts has not depended on an increase in the quantity of factors locally available (in particular, stocks of capital and labour, according to processes as in Harrod-Domar), but rather on the improvement of their cognitive content. Many studies have found that growth seems to be based primarily on the expansion and deepening of internal knowledge. This accumulation of new knowledge is closely related to production specialisation processes that have characterised all districts and have gradually led to their internal differentiation, the formation of new activities, new sectors and, in some cases, completely new industries. These processes have in many cases determined the gradual shifting from a district to a local system, when an articulated chain of different activities using quite different technologies has developed, and intermediate producers have differentiated to such a point that they find new outlets for their products outside the original chain.

The nature of knowledge. The neo-classical assumption is that making optimal choices is related to the theoretical conception of the individual cognitive context: the individual has perfect knowledge of the external world and a complete overview of all the possible choices and of their consequences. This position is the opposite of that found in other perspectives (Hayek, Simon, the evolutionists, the Austrian school) which are based on the idea of partial ignorance and faulty knowledge, as a prerequisite to discovery and learning. According to many observations made on social and economic processes, for the most part confirmed by studies on districts, it can be assumed that knowledge is rather scarce and unequally distributed. As Hayek (1945) demonstrated, economic knowledge is always dispersed; *grass-roots* knowledge is available only to direct participants and not central organisations. So, a part of the knowledge and, as a result, a number of opportunities are missed in any centralised system, mainly due to the lack of relevant knowledge at the top of a centralised hierarchy. Much individual knowledge is very hard to express verbally and it is the basis of a number of skills. Polanyi (1967) called this type of knowledge tacit knowledge. A lot of the skills used in management and entrepreneurial activities have a sizeable tacit component. Of course, besides tacit knowledge there is also knowledge which is expressed symbolically and can be easily communicated (Teece, 1981, suggested calling it codified knowledge).

Firms as differentiated agents. The behaviour of each economic subject is highly diversified and depends not only on its history and experience but also on its 'genetic' nature (in this perspective, on its culture and its routines). So, firms are clearly differentiated agents which are able to formulate diversified strategies and follow different growth paths. They are not perfectly rational and operate within cognitive limitations and structural constraints. Their variety is essentially found in their different preferences, capabilities and cognitive proficiency, which depends on their different structures and abilities to learn and innovate, on their different stocks of accumulated knowledge. Each firm possesses a specific mixture of tangible resources, capabilities and skills that evolve in an original and unforeseen manner, within the boundaries imposed by the local environment, the market and the technological opportunities. Their diversity cannot be captured by any model which starts from the representative agent, as in the neo-classical perspective. Diversity is essential for understanding not only the structure of an industry but also its long-term development as a socio-economic process.

Localisation. The factors that influence strategic choices and innovative behaviour are not only found in structure and learning capabilities, but in local influences and externalities as well. The role of localisation is due to the fact that resources are asymmetrically distributed in an economic space, a place is characterised by assets, competencies and skills that do not exist in other contexts. So, firms belonging to a given milieu may be defined in terms of vectors of space characteristics. Firms are linked to the local environment in a twofold manner: they use local resources, and they give content and value to these resources (Belussi, 1993). In other words, the economic space represents the locus where factors and inputs are consciously organised and enriched with cognitive content. Within this space, new technological opportunities are practically developed, new capabilities and organisational routines are produced, and new paths of growth are actively explored.

Technology. Technology is an ensemble of physical assets and knowledge which derive from theoretical principles and from much practical experience. The core technology of a given firm is mostly *localised*, tacit knowledge acquired through experience. Technical and applied knowledge is highly specific and idiosyncratic, because it is linked to the organisations where it was elaborated and fine-tuned. In contrast to scientific knowledge, it does not have the characteristics of a *public good*. Therefore, the diffusion of technology, for most localised knowledge, is not a zero-cost process. In districts, the acquisition of technical capabilities and skills is the result of individual and collective efforts to learn and elaborate tacit knowledge, and cannot be separated from normal entrepreneurial activity (Antonelli, 1995). This knowledge in part is not *owned* by any particular firm, but by the district as a whole; it is one of its *intangible* productive assets.

These findings which emerge from the empirical studies on districts and recent perspectives in economic thought, clearly differ from the assumptions of conventional firm theory and the neo-classical approach. Instead, they fit the assumptions of evolutionary economic theories (Nelson and Winter, 1982; Nelson, 1990) and the 'knowledge based' theory of the firm (Barney, 1996; Grant, 1996) very well. It seems that an evolutionary approach may be more appropriate for an analysis of the temporal dynamics of districts. The role of knowledge and the concept of tacit knowledge, typically embodied in habits and routines, was employed by Nelson and Winter (1982) in their economic analysis of firm behaviour. The assumptions of evolutionary theories shift the focus away from a static equilibrium towards processes of innovation, i.e. the sources of new products, processes and knowledge used within the firms. This approach seems appropriate in our case, because it explores the effects of the speed and direction of technical change, not only on the performance of individual firms but also on modifications in the structure of industries.

Therefore, evolutionary theories seem to provide a suitable approach for describing the industrial dynamics and, in particular, the processes which operate in districts with enhanced performance. On these theoretical premises, a description of innovative processes is proposed, which emphasises the knowledge generation and learning that have supported technological innovation in the most dynamic districts. Following the precepts of evolutionary theories, the key aspects of variety generation, selection processes and transmission of favourable modifications, as well as how they have led to structural modifications are described.

How do variety and technological specialisation occur?

A wide range of literature confirms that most Italian districts were founded in conditions of favourable market demand and factor prices (above all, of labour), as well as techno-productive competence. Later, Smithian processes of division of labour, economies of specialisation and better intermediate inputs brought about considerable increases in productivity in most districts. These processes were facilitated by Weberian features (specific regional localisation factors and the gradual formation of external economies through agglomeration) and by social and territorial Marshallian factors of *atmosphere*. In many areas, division of labour and specialisation have led to the origin of complementary activities that, in some cases, have grown and, over time, gradually led to the creation of autonomous sectors.

Most Italian districts have been studied as a post-war phenomenon. But the technological premises, the accumulation of technical and productive knowledge occurred in some of them long before. For example, in the middle of the nineteenth century, the Valdagno and Schio industrial basins in the Veneto region already hosted a modern textile industry which was competitive on the European level; this industry is historically tied to the names of Lanerossi and Marzotto, the latter is today a leading firm on the international level. In these areas, the birth of a mechanised textile industry, at the beginning of this century, was a precursor of Italian industrialisation. Today, the textile-clothing industry and a number of associated activities (machinery, services) are strong, developed industries whose performance excels on the international level.

In many districts, the adoption of new technologies and the improvement of existing ones have produced incremental innovations in the value chain, the creation of new or improved intermediate inputs, the rise of new sectors and the fall of others. In other words, each area possesses the seeds of its decline and rebirth on different industrial bases. For example, the shoe district of Vigevano, which experienced decline after rapid growth in the sixties and seventies, generated a modern shoe machinery sector which today is doing well. The competitive strategies of district firms have often exploited the capabilities of existing technology, based on their in-depth practical knowledge of the production processes. Their capacity to perform well in terms of dynamic efficiency has led some districts to fully exploit internal flexibility of volume as a competitive factor. This strategy has allowed some areas to maintain their well-defined process and product specialisation (industrial districts in a narrow sense). Firms have sought high volume flexibility, but at the cost of limiting their fixed assets and so keeping their operations on a low level and excessively dependent on market forces.

In other cases, enterprises within areas characterised by greater differentiation have benefited from the effects of spillover. Diversified inter-firm relations have improved competitive capabilities and have stimulated the opening of the operations beyond the district, thereby activating production relations on the international level. This has led to more intense innovation in products and processes, and, therefore, less passive market strategies. In the same areas, small-sized enterprises have maintained direct access to the final market by successfully pursuing niche strategies. By so doing, some of these have at times achieved technological excellence on the international level.

Larger enterprises (in a relative sense) have sought better market segmentation and have improved their capacity to satisfy the country-specific characteristics of world demand. Most small, single production phase enterprises have improved their technical specialisation. This has often come about with the technical support and incentives (under the form of order guarantees) of leading local firms that want to introduce changes toward *lean production* lines. Specialisation processes, in some cases, have allowed districts to achieve such levels of excellence that they have led to the acquisition of large shares of the international market, or even world leadership status. This performance has not only affected individual enterprises but also entire areas; the examples of the eyeglasses industry in the Belluno district, and that of sport-boots in Montebelluna are only two of the best known cases. In industries like textiles-clothing, machine tools, mechanical manufacturing, shoes and furniture, local competence is so developed that they satisfy most segments of world demand. These results are often associated with large firms like Benetton, Stefanel and Marzotto in the cases of Treviso and Vicenza textile-clothing districts (Berra, Piatti and Vitali, 1992; Gottardi, 1994); but they are also found in traditional districts of very small firms. The Riviera del Brenta, for example, with about 1000 small businesses, exports over 80% of its production of high quality shoes to more than 100 countries.

Growth has generated further differentiation. Innovation has induced changes in production functions and in the mix of specialisation. This has, in turn, triggered the establishment of new businesses; districts have become more complex, and contain a large variety of firms with different structures and different combinations of resources, technologies and intangible assets. Today, the reorganisation patterns of dynamic districts can be described as the *hierarchic* evolution of local networks. This tendency has been determined by the need for effective control of new strategies, such as total quality and quick response, founded on the improvement of service content, requiring a high level of co-ordination along the value chain. So, the supply and subcontracting relationships within the area do not appear to be solely conditioned by price because other characteristics come into play, e.g. respect for quality requirements and delivery times. The principal factors that now determine the choice of supplier are quality and time which rank respectively first and second, while price only ranks third (CENSIS - Unioncamere, 1995). This means that, even without explicit co-operation agreements, these relations cannot be defined as *belonging to the market*.

Of course, internal and external district selection mechanisms are at work, but their effects on reducing variety have not delayed the growth of technological heterogeneity in products and processes. In this way, differentiation has been predominant and has gone from a vulnerable strategy of volume flexibility, to commercial differentiation and technical specialisation strategies.

The evolution we have described is highly stylised, and certainly it is not the only one possible. Most districts generally follow various growth paths. Each step emphasises a particular division of labour and use of technology related to the opportunities offered by technical change and the new requirements imposed by the final market. In general, the introduction of a radically new technology has a disruptive effect, forcing firms to adopt it or find alternative ways to compete. This was the impact, for example, of automatic cutting techniques in the clothing sector. At first, only leading firms were able to adopt this technology. But now, with the stabilisation, standardisation and cost reduction technology, cutting can once again be sub-contracted to small firms in complex inter-firm linkages.

How is endogenous knowledge created without R&D?

In this interpretative model, a fundamental question concerns the creation of new endogenous knowledge. This is a problematic issue, because firms within the districts considered make very modest investment in formal R&D. Italian R&D is very concentrated. Government, universities and government owned firms represent more than 60% of national R&D expenditures. In the private sector, the 10 largest enterprises represent about 80% of private expenditures. Moreover, total R&D is about 1.5% of GNP, as compared to 2-3% in other developed countries. Small business' share in the traditional sectors is extremely modest (Confindustria, 1994). Nevertheless these firms are clearly innovative. How can this apparent paradox be explained?

Various studies have attempted to find other sources and alternative channels for the transmission of knowledge. Most explanations concentrate on the innovative stimuli that derive from relations between machinery suppliers and buyers. However, these explanations are not totally satisfactory because they do not explain the widespread creation of *original* knowledge that has accumulated in these enclaves. The interpretation of this phenomenon is important because the accumulation of knowledge is fundamental to differentiation and growth processes, as has been recognised in several recent growth models (see e.g., Aghion and Howitt, 1992; Foray and Freeman, 1992). Evolutionary theories indicate that the motor of development is found in the application of entrepreneurial, specialised and technical knowledge (Nelson, 1990); this suggests there should be a review of the traditional view of the role of knowledge in innovation. The evolutionary approach tends to focus on the localised character of technological knowledge and the essential role that circumstances concerning conditions and location play in the paths of innovation processes. In particular, the identification of innovation with new scientific knowledge is not legitimate because new scientific knowledge does not necessarily produce economically significant innovation (as Schumpeter had already claimed about inventions; see also Rosenberg, 1982; Winter, 1987). On the contrary, the development of specific and localised know-how would allow firms to obtain significant increases in productivity, even without new scientific knowledge.

In fact, it is possible to make important economic innovations even when there is very little new scientific knowledge. The evolutionary approach insists on the significance of localised know-how (specifically related to local conditions), which is the result of processes of learning from experience, both by doing and by using. This learning is highly application-oriented, it is tacit and moulded to suit specific needs. Therefore, it is more difficult to both transfer and imitate. In contrast with scientific knowledge, which is general and held collectively, localised knowledge derives from individuals practical experience. The latter has less potential for application, and can only be used and propagated in similar areas or in those closely connected to the original ones. Nevertheless, localised knowledge may be appropriated and generate more competitive advantages than scientific knowledge. Therefore, localised knowledge is not less important than scientific knowledge in production of value by firms (see also Dasgupta and Stiglitz, 1987).

The technology derived from applied knowledge tends to be specific to the enterprise and to the subject that produces it; this means that it would be rather costly (and in some cases, impossible) to use elsewhere. Many empirical studies have outlined that the transfer of technology from one firm to another may be just as expensive as its initial production (see Mansfield, 1985; Nelson, 1990; Rosenberg, 1990). Thus, the specific nature of knowledge for technological innovation involves high transaction and adaptation costs. Contrary to the orthodox view, that assigns the task of producing the knowledge necessary for innovation to formal R&D, in the evolutionary (and neo-technological) theories, the generation of new knowledge is primarily the result of non-institutional efforts that are based on highly localised learning processes, linked to the innovator's past experience (Pavitt, 1987). R&D, the combination of resources in scientific and experimental activities, represents only one aspect, and not necessarily the most important, of the general process of learning.

So, given that the localised nature of knowledge is more important than it was traditionally thought to be, it is easy to explain why attempts to transfer innovations to small firm districts have often been slow and difficult. The reason is that these difficulties not only concern the introduction of radical innovations; but there are also problems in transferring technologies that have already been applied to other sectors. Many of these difficulties can be explained by the incompatibility or incongruity of some new technological paradigms with the new application environment. Good examples are FMS (Flexible Manufacturing Systems) and CIM (Computer Integrated Manufacturing): these systems have been designed for the highly hierarchical (Fordist) firms, creating technical flexibility without considering inter-organisational aspects. This is totally inappropriate for small district firms. Here, with respect to the CIM-based firm, where hierarchy is expensively computerised, flexibility is achieved organisationally rather than technologically.

Evolutionary hypotheses can be used to explain the mechanisms which create knowledge and innovation in dynamic districts, in which there have been long periods of growth without R&D, with few connections to the 'research sanctuaries' but with an ample generation of applied and tacit know-how, as well as channels to propagate it locally. In the evolutionary perspective, important innovations are produced by localised learning directly linked to the firm's experience. The improvement of product performance and rationalisation of production processes are, at times, decisive for competitiveness, even if they do not derive from R&D investments. Besides, for the small manufacturing firms in Italian LPSs it would be very difficult to reach the critical size to carry out effective formal R&D activities.

There are, however, resources within the district that greatly reduce this last difficulty. In fact, even if the production of innovation is difficult for individual firms, this is not true for the district as a whole. With the incremental creation of know-how, every enterprise frees positive externalities which can be appropriated by others, especially when there is physical proximity and co-operation. Therefore, even with very modest investments in research, within these systems, increasing returns in output can be achieved, through the appropriation of technological externalities which derive from the up-grades made in individual firms. Thus, we have a picture of innovation within districts that derives from local and tacit knowledge being held in common, as a common non-market asset. This lends decisive advantages to firms in districts where incremental innovations are used for market differentiation. The competitiveness of such a system is therefore based on efficient incrementalism, more than on the development of new paradigms or radical innovations, which could be created by R&D. Also in the case of the introduction of a new, not locally generated paradigm, innovation is never completely exogenous, because it still needs to be adapted to user requirements, and this entails a long and generally complex localisation process. The transfer and adoption of any innovation always requires cognitive, technical and organisational changes, both within the firm and the industry.

On learning, specialisation and co-ordination processes

A large number of empirical findings have shown that the generation and accumulation of new knowledge within districts and local systems are based on the division of labour, specialisation and learning. The origin of the advantages of specialisation and, in particular, the relationship between division of labour, productivity increases and market growth cannot be analysed from the neo-classical perspective. This has only been discussed in relatively recent studies (e.g. Rosenberg, 1976). The division of labour is the source of economies of specialisation: these derive from the simplification of firm organisation, the reduction of the scale of investments and the introduction of incremental innovations concerning intermediate inputs. The specialisation of knowledge is favoured by the fact that professional capabilities and competencies which are required in the different production phases are generally highly differentiated.

In districts, learning is mainly tacit and creates a mix of innovations, that are in part competence destroying and in part competence enhancing. The accumulation of localised and tacit knowledge is easier in the district because here two fundamental factors are present: a) models of industrial organisation that facilitate specialisation; and b) a professional labour force, within the enterprise; both of which can enhance the production of this type of knowledge. This is nearly impossible within Taylorist labour organisations and Fordist firms.

Given that localised knowledge is subject to obsolescence due to the presence of competence-destroying innovation, the accumulation of know-how and the development of new capabilities should be seen in a dynamic sense, as a flux of competencies and skills that change and are continually renewed. In a district (or branch) with multiple inter-firm links, all the subjects in their area of specialisation are committed, through learning, to keep the system's cognitive and technological stock up-to-date. A verticalised oligopolist, even with high R&D investment, hypothetically could encounter significant difficulty in maintaining its rate of innovation in all the phases of the value chain on a equivalent level to a territorial system of firms, where investment, competencies and risk are divided and shared. This point is meant to add to the criticism of the Fordist firm's difficulties in sustaining high rates of innovation. In effect, in mature oligopolistic industries the gains from R&D are falling. In many cases, like the automotive sector, producers are learning to exploit innovations introduced by suppliers. The excellence of Japanese producers is linked to their ability to lead and integrate this type of "systemic" innovation and to transfer it quickly to the market.

This model of growth, based on localised processes of technological change, specialisation, shared widespread investment in the various activities or production phases, high *internal* rates of propagation of incremental innovations due to physical proximity and their predisposition to co-operate, is a good description of evolution in a dynamic industrial district. This model can be applied in small firm areas in which complementary goods, parts and components are produced (see figure 2.1). This mechanism explains why, when there is an inter-firm division of labour, rapid propagation of know-how, specialised skills and highly differentiated final products, districts can be an efficient model for production. In this context, the growth of the system is assured by the ability to expand of the 'final' enterprises that have contact with the market, through the feedback mechanism activated by the orders of suppliers and subcontractors. On the one hand, growth makes it possible to increase investments in up-stream activities; on the other, the propagation of new methods, technologies and intermediate inputs leads to increases in the productivity of the entire system.

Figure 2.1 Evolutionary model of district competitiveness generation

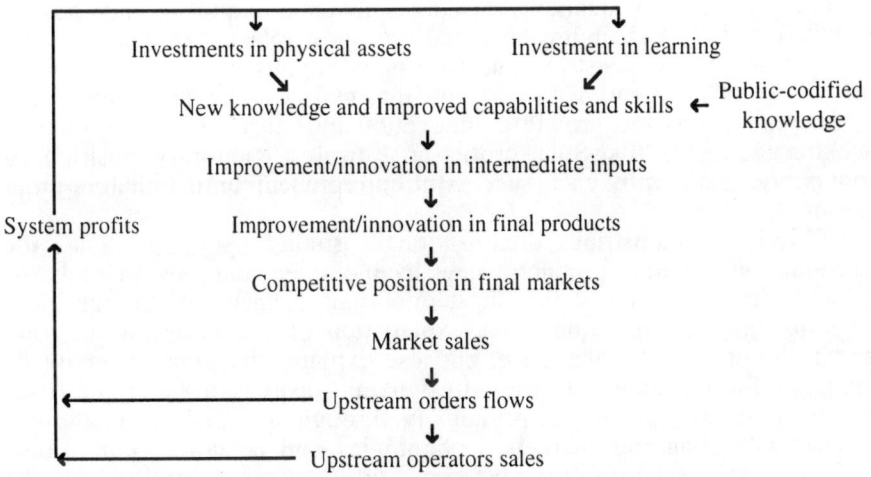

Therefore, when there is growth in demand, global competitiveness is in fact governed by the results of the down-stream enterprises that operate in the final market. But these results depend to a great extent on the capacity to innovate and on increases in productivity that are created by producers of intermediate inputs. These operators are able to generate technological and economic externalities which are useful for enterprises down-stream. Undoubtedly, 'demand pull', or Keynesian, processes have been important in the initial phases of district development, but the consolidation of their competitive capabilities in the international markets has mainly depended on the processes of learning and specialisation described above.

One of the fundamental questions in any economic theory is how coherent behaviour of economic agents results from the uncoordinated pursuit of self-interest. The conventional answer is based on the Smithian concept of *the invisible hand of the market*, but the question still needs to be addressed. The current development of evolutionary economics, by considering cognitive inter-dependencies and mutual learning processes of differentiated subjects, may throw new light on this central question.

The empirical observation of evolutionary processes (in biology as well as in economics) shows that "in the short-term perspective, systems with relatively high diversity behave worse than homogeneous systems (i.e. systems with similar *actors*), but in the long-term perspective, highly diversified systems compensate for this deficiency thanks to much greater creativity, and much more frequent emergence of innovations, resulting in much higher, long-range rates of development" (Kwasnicky, 1997, p. 79).

The empirical evidence also shows that there are forms of competition other than price-competition. Perfect (neo-classical) competition leads to an equilibrium where resources are perfectly allocated and firms have identical production functions. They therefore cannot generate any qualitative changes in their output or methods of production. But, as Schumpeter noted, the most relevant problem is how an economy creates, destroys and adjusts its organisation and structure to an incessantly changing world. In the real world, the main force underlying economic growth is innovation introduced by entrepreneurs seeking higher profits. Such profits arise from a temporary position of monopoly, attained by each successful entrepreneur until imitators enter the market.

Modern industrial organisational studies suggest that the introduction of new products, new technologies and new models of organisation are some of the most important elements of competition. This not only offers a qualitative explanation of technological progress and technological obsolescence, but also explains the great diversity of firms within the same industries. In dynamic districts, a variety of firms that is continuously created, principally through trial and error attempts to deal with changing markets, technologies and economic conditions. The solutions chosen by different firms vary according to the competencies they possess and the roles they play in the value chain. As a result, not only new competencies are incrementally developed and new technologies are adopted, but also new forms of inter-firm division of labour are introduced.

In a turbulent and constantly changing environment, it is very difficult to define a stable set of optimal solutions and practices. For this reason in the evolutionary approach *profit maximisation* is replaced by *search for profit* (Kwasnicky, 1997, p. 82). In the industrial district decisions are made continuously by firms considering their expectations of what suppliers, customers and competitors will do, as well as their perceptions of the external environment. All these decisions disrupt, directly or indirectly, each firm's routines, so that the entire set of district routines is subjected to a continuous process of adaptation. The search for profit, along the value chain, may be considered a continuous search by each intermediate supplier for the best response to the requirements of downstream operators. District competition, which may be strong, is not simply about price but predominantly about the best response to the needs of all producers.

Firm strategies, innovations and structural change: A systems model

The evolutionary approach explores the effects of the speed and direction of technological innovation on the performance of enterprises and on industrial structure. The course and direction of technological change determine the intensity of the selection, the number and variety of firms, and then the shape of the industrial structure. In the evolutionary perspective, there is a dual relationship between the direction of technical change and the evolution of market structure: on the one hand, the result of technology selection is influenced by the selection that the market exercises on firms; and on the other hand, industrial structure is mainly determined by the result of technology selection (Antonelli, 1995). The other factor that, according to this perspective, shapes growth-differentiation profiles, and, therefore, exerts influence on structure, is path dependence. In fact, all conditions and restraints throughout the course of firms histories reduce their independent choice and, therefore, limit their options.

Nevertheless, growth paths are the outcome of very deliberate strategic choices made by firms in complex and reciprocal interaction. This is also true in the case of LPSs: evolutionary paths are not predetermined, but evolve through trial and error, depending on the results of the decisions and strategies chosen. Advancement by trial and error produces a variety of experiences that on the whole enriches the local learning and pushes towards differentiation. It is firm strategic behaviour relative to technologies (their choice, development, improvement) that makes the technical change endogenous and localised.

We can formulate a stylised description (or model) of the processes operating within the district by considering the two major groups of operators: leading local firms and intermediate firms along the value chain. The activities of the latter are regulated by the leading firms through various forms of sub-contracting and co-ordination. Both sets of firms are sources of innovations: the leading firms introduce market-based innovations in product design, which can have the effect of changing production systems, while the intermediate firms are the source of productive and technical innovations in their area of specialisation. The quasi-market selection that occurs within the district influences the results of efforts to innovate and shapes the variety of paths. And, finally, there are the selective forces of the external market that has become global.

Figure 2.2 outlines the forces that play a role in district structural change. Incremental or radical exogenous innovations put into motion an initially haphazard selection process. So, only that technology which is congruent with the structural and cognitive characteristics of district firms, and compatible with the existing industrial organisation, takes root.

Starting from this initial 'localisation', selected technologies are absorbed within the district. Strategies of technical and organisational learning are activated by individual firms, to exploit opportunities for profit, and this leads to specialisation. The strategies of intermediate operators are filtered through market selection or through the governance of 'hub firms' (quasi-hierarchical), depending on the particular district's structure and organisation. Finally, only 'favourable changes' introduced by final enterprises survive the selection of the external market.

Figure 2.2   Innovation strategies and structural change in dynamic districts

District structure (t)
↓
Exogenous innovations
↓
Preliminary selection (basic capabilities)
↓
Defining strategies; learning by doing
↓
Localised innovations; differentiation variety generation
↓
Internal co-ordination—selection processes
↓
External market selection
↓
District structure (t+1)

Concluding remarks: Industrial policy and the local level

By using an evolutionary perspective, we have attempted to describe the processes of learning, variety generation, selection and structural change in districts in Northeast Italy (but the model can probably be applied to all Italian districts). In the most dynamic ones, there has been growth not only in capital stock but to an even greater extent in the enrichment of the cognitive content of capital and labour. The effects of these processes have been:

1.   an improvement in the congruity between technology and the strategy-structure of firms, and between products and markets;

2.   an increase in capital and labour productivity;
3.   the acquisition of real competitive advantages.

These processes have taken place together with adjustments and changes in firm structure and inter-organisational relations. By contributing to increased variety and differentiation in their evolutionary paths, they have also brought about changes in local industrial structure. Today district survival and growth do not appear to be linked to demand-pull phenomena and to the presence of differences in input cost (as was surely the case at the outset), but to the capacity either to operate in conditions of declining demand, or to reinvent a new market niche, to successfully face world competition. In this evolution, the most important factor seems to be the creation of local cognitive capital. From a theoretic point of view, these results may be interpreted on the basis of Saviotti's model (1996), an excellent work on the role of technological variety in economic evolution.

The orthodox theory of the firm founded on scientific Taylorism and Fordism, along with business procedures that employ a variety of techniques for the *de-coupling* of productive processes from the market, have often led to the environment being left out, which suggests the model of the firm is 'independent' of its economic and social context. Today, the limits of this view have been highlighted in post-Fordist criticism. Here, as in other places (e.g. Becattini and Rullani, 1993; Brusco, 1994; Varaldo and Ferrucci, 1993) it is held that in the future, it will be possible to have a range of production models and organisational solutions which derive from different experiences, cultures and local environments. The productive specialisation of different areas and economic regions demonstrates that they have the capacity to generate innovative responses in terms of new models of local organisation, new standards of quality, new products for the market and, above all, from the perspective of this paper, creative re-interpretations of existing knowledge.

We do not believe that these processes have pre-determined results or are purely dictated by history. Rather they are influenced by the characteristics of the environment and by the strategies adopted by enterprises. These processes are capable of creating new variety and heterogeneity in the economic space, making different interpretations and different transitions to lean production possible. The proposed model tries to highlight the complexity of the mechanisms on which these processes are founded, and underlines the improbability of equilibria in the classical sense. Even if the processes described are non-deterministic, and therefore the results are difficult to foresee, models of this type may be useful in determining policies and selecting the variables on which to act.

The first consideration regards the regional dimension of the economic activity (see also Bianchi and Giordani, 1993; Nelson and Rosenberg, 1993). From our perspective, production, technological innovation and competition are not socially decontextualized activities;

on the contrary, they are shaped by the organisational, institutional and political structures prevailing locally. Regions and local context may differ markedly from one another. Production systems are heterogeneous because resources are asymmetrically distributed in economic space and knowledge is not a universal free good. Economic subjects have different histories, competencies and skills, aims and interests, strengths and weaknesses, and, therefore, different strategies. Economic organisations are also localised, and the tools for their effective collective regulation and co-ordination are place-specific and vary over time. Finally, local environments are typically the sites of potent external economies (e.g. agglomeration) that derive from and exist as non-market spillover effects (Storper and Scott, 1995). These external economies represent the essential character of any regional industrial complex. The consequence of all this is that industrial innovation policies should also have a regional dimension.

The second consideration regards the mechanisms for generating new knowledge. Neo-classical economics sees technology as perfectly free information, concerning the production function and efficient factor combination inside the firm, while markets and competition guarantee efficient resource allocation. In this view, intervention is economically irrational, except in the rare cases where market failures occur. On the other hand, technology cannot be seen as something embodied in an options portfolio out of which manufacturers select a profit-maximising combination of machinery, equipment and products. Moreover, the introduction of innovations is rarely the result of highly formalised and planned research efforts: generally this is an inadequate model for representing the process by which new industrial technologies are generated. It hides the real nature of technology, as an ensemble of technical, practical and tacit knowledge, and the ways in which this knowledge, technological know-how and technical skills are obtained. In the real world, innovation remains a highly uncertain and risky process which emerges from a complex network of ideas and practices, from the myriad of small contributions which are added to day-by-day. The whole of these steps determines the upgrading and changes in technical solutions. At a certain point, the cumulative effects of these incremental efforts condense in a new perspective, and a new paradigm or radical innovation takes place. 'Inside the black box', the boundaries between incremental and radical innovation are not so clear (Rosenberg, 1982). These innovative ideas and efforts are localised in regional industrial complexes. Regional and local systems are repositories of specialised industrial skills and capabilities. They constitute the tangible infrastructure in which innovation is generated. Most technological change, far from being planned and carried out in large R&D sanctuaries, actually occurs as an accumulation of a large number of small-scale events in highly informal contexts.

The third consideration regards inter-firms relationships and the role of small enterprises. One of the most important mechanisms that generates product and process innovation lies in the relationships between different manufacturers: in their efforts to match output and input needs. A specific requirement related to a product or process may stimulate a machine-tool or components manufacturer to make a small but decisive improvement in its product characteristics. This learning process and technological change will obviously be accelerated where producers work together in dense, active, transactional systems. This process is totally compatible with small size. The specialisation of many different subjects is just the right condition for generating variety and triggering evolutionary processes. As we have illustrated, the successful economic performance of some regions can be explained from an evolutionary perspective, as the capacity to produce internal variety and differentiation. In these industrial systems co-operation facilitates innovation efforts (as it reduces uncertainty and risk), while competition assures the needed selection of strategies and organisational solutions.

The lesson that some dynamic Italian districts seem to teach favours new and to a degree heterodox policies, in which the regional and local dimension is significant. The focus is on production systems, industrial practices and routines, rather than on basic research and on individual firms. This means favouring the continuous adjustment of capacities on the local level, rather than the implementation of radically new technologies. A new paradigm introduces asymmetries and deep disequilibria and may have a negative impact, e.g. destroying the previously acquired competencies. It may be useful instead, to create favourable conditions for learning and adoption of selected technologies important to the existing regional structures. So, relatively small public investment, strategically targeted and focused, may have wide-ranging effects on regional development, particularly when they enhance learning and positive spillover.

By using the taxonomy suggested by Ergas (1987) these "diffusion oriented" policies are quite different from the "mission oriented" ones, whose aim is the rapid generation and transfer of advanced technologies and the creation of entry barriers. The latter are congruent for global technology-based oligopolies, and enhances the status of a few multinational firms. It is doubtful that this kind of policy can enhance competition. They may introduce deep asymmetries on the local level and have perverse effects as well. It may separate the best equipped firms from other local producers, and thereby promote the 'exit' of the latter from the LPS.

Following Storper and Scott (1995), the local or regional level is a basic level in which the economic activity is articulated. Consequently, the regional dimension of industrial policy needs to be considered. In this context the importance of regional institutions as well as technology centres, educational institutions, local training programmes, etc. must be stressed. Regional and local policies are likely to play major roles in successfully competitive economies in the next century.

References

Aghion P. and Howitt P. (1992), 'Un modèle de croissance par destruction crèatrice', in Foray D., Freeman C. (eds.), *Technologies et richesse des nations*. Paris, Economica.

Amin A. and Robins P. (1991), 'These are not Marshallian times', in Camagni R. (ed.), *Innovation Networks: Spatial Perspectives*. London, Belhaven Press.

Anastasia B. and Corò G. (1993), *I distretti industriali in Veneto*, Portogruaro, Nuova dimensione.

Antonelli C. (1995), *Economia dell'innovazione*. Bari, Università Laterza-Economia.

Antonelli C. and Gottardi G. (1991), 'The Interaction between the Generation and the Diffusion of New Technologies', *Economics of Innovation and New Technologies*, n.4.

Barney, J.B. (1996), 'The Resource-based Theory of the Firm, Organisation Science, vol. 7, n. 5.

Becattini G. and Rullani E. (1993), 'Sistema locale e mercato globale', *Economia e politica industriale*, n. 80.

Bellandi M. and Russo M. (1994), (eds.) *Distretti industriali e cambiamento economico locale*. Torino, Rosemberg e Sellier.

Belussi F (1992), (ed.) *Nuovi modelli di impresa, gerarchie organizzative e impresa rete*. Milano, F. Angeli.

Belussi F. (1993), 'Imprese e gerarchie, distretti industriali e retei globali: verso un nuovo paradigma dell'economia industriale?', in Bertini F., Belussi F. and Garibaldo F. (1993) 'Quale futuro per le piccole e medie imprese italiane?', *IRES Materiali*, n. 9.

Berra L., Piatti L. and Vitali G. (1992), 'Dimensioni di impresea e strategie di inernazionalizzazione: il caso del settore dell'Abbigliamento', *Economia e Politica Industriale*, n. 74/76.

Bertalanffy, L. von (1962), 'General System Theory - A Critical Review', *General Systems*, n. 7.

Bianchi G. (1994), 'Requiem per la terza Italia? Sistemi territoriali di piccole imprese e transizione post-industriale', in, Garofoli G. and Mazzoni R. (1994), (ed.) *Sistemi produttivi locali: struttura e trasformazione,* Milano, F. Angeli.

Bianchi P. and Giordani M.G. (1993), 'Innovation policy at the local and national level: the case of Emila-Romagna', *European Planning Studies*, vol. 1, n.1.

Brusco S. (1994), 'Sistemi gobali e sistemi locali', *Economia e politica industriale*, n. 84.

CENSIS – Unioncamere (1995), *Da protagonisti a leader: imprese e istuzioni nei distretti che cambiano*. Vicenza, Nota di sintesi.

Confindustria (1994), *La spesa dell'industria per la ricerca scientifica*, Milano, Centro Studi, Collana l'industria italiana.

Dasgupta P. and Stiglitz J.I. (1987), Learning to learn, localised knowledge, and technological progress, in Dasgupta P. and Stoneman P. (ed.), *Economic Policy and Technological Performance*, Cambridge, Cambridge University Press.

David P.A. and Rosembloom J. (1990), 'Marshallian Factor Market. Externalities and the Dynamics of Indutstrial Localization', *Journal of Urban Economics*, n.28.

Dioguardi G. (1994) (ed.), *Sistemi di imprese*, Milano, Etas Libri.

Dosi G. et al. (1988) (eds.), *Technical Change and Economic Theory,* London, Pinter.

Ergas H. (1987), The importance of technology policy, in Dasgupta P. and Stoneman P. (ed.), *Economic Policy and Technological Performance*, Cambridge, Cambridge

University Press.

Foray D. and Freeman C. (1992), (eds.) *Technologies et richesse des nations,* Paris, Economica.

Freeman C. (1982), *The Economics of Industrial Innovation,* London, Pinter.

Gandolfi V. (1990), 'Relazionalità e cooperazione nelle aree-sistema', *Economia e politica industriale,* n. 65.

Garofoli G. and Mazzoni R. (1994), (ed.) *Sistemi produttivi locali: struttura e trasformazione.* Milano, F. Angeli.

Gibbons M. and Metcalfe J.S. (1986), 'Technology variety and the process of competition', *International Conference on Innovation Diffusion,* Venezia, March 18th-21th.

Gottardi G. (1991) 'Piccole e medie imprese nella transizione tra localismo e globalità', in Filippini R., Pagliarani G. and Petroni G. (eds.): *Progettare e gestire l'impresa innovativa,* Milan, ETAS Libri.

Gottardi G. (1994), (ed.) *Da flessibilità a trasformazione. Contributi alla lettura dei percorsi di uscita dalla crisi,* Padua, CLEUP.

Gottardi G. (1995), 'Distretti industriali: problemi strutturali o nuove prospettive? Una riflessione in chiave evoluzionista', *Cambiamento e innovazione: Strategie e politiche per le imprese e per le aree sistema,* Como, 10 November.

Gottardi G. (1996), 'Technology Strategies, Innovation without R&D and the Creation of Knowledge within Industrial Districts', *Journal of Industry Studies,* Vol. 3, n. 2, December.

Gottardi G. (1998), (ed.) *Da catena del valore a sistema del valore,* Padua, CLEUP.

Grant, R.M. (1996), 'Toward a Knowledge-based Theory of the Firm', *Strategic Management Journal,* vol. 17 (Winter Special Issue).

Hanush H. (1988), (ed.) *Evolutionary Economics,* Cambridge, Cambridge University Press.

Hayek, F.A. (1945), "The Use of Knowledge in Society", *American Economic Review,* September.

Henderson R.M. and Clark K.B. (1990), 'Architectural innovation: the reconfiguration of existing products technologies and the failure of established firms', *Administrative Science Quarterly,* n. 29.

Kwasnicky W. (1996), *Knowledge, Innovation and Economy. An Evolutionary Exploration,* Cheltenham, Edward Elgar, UK.

Locke R.M. (1995), 'Una economia differenziata: politica locale e cambiamento industriale', *Stato e Mercato,* n. 43.

Lombardi M. (1994) 'L'evoluzione del distretto industriale come sistema informativo: alcuni spunti di riflessione', *L'Industria,* n. 3.

Mansfield E. (1985), 'How Rapidly Does New Industrial Technology Leak Out', *Journal of Industrial Economics,* n. 34.

Mariotti S. (1994), 'Alla ricerca di un'identità per il post-fordismo', *Economia e Politica industriale,* n. 84.

Nelson R.R.(1987), *Understanding Technological Change as an Evolutionary Process.* Amsterdam, North Holland.

Nelson R.R. (1990), 'Capitalism as Engine of Progress', *Research Policy,* n. 19.

Nelson R., Rosenberg N. (1993), 'Technical innovation and national systems' in Nelson R. (ed.) *National Innovations Systems,* New York, Oxford University Press.

Nelson R.R. and Winter S.G. (1982), *An Evolutionary Theory of Economic Change.* Cambridge, Harvard University Press.

Nomisma-Assindustria (1995), *Rapporto 1994-95 sull'industria italiana*, Bologna, Assindustria.

Nuti F. (1992), (ed.) *I distretti dell'industria manifatturiere italiana*, Milano, F. Angeli.

Onida F., Viesti G. and Falzoni A. M. (1992), (eds.) *I distretti industriali: crisi o evoluzione?* Milano: EGEA.

Pavitt K. (1984), 'Sectoral Patterns of Technology Change: Towards a Taxonomy and Theory', *Research Policy*, n. 13.

Pavitt K. (1987), 'The Objectives of Technology Policy', *Science and Public Policy*, n. 14.

Piore M. and Sabel C. (1984), *The Second Industrial Divide: Possibilities for Prosperity*, New York: Basic Books.

Polanyi M. (1967), *The Tacit Dimension*, New York, Doubleday, Anchor.

Rosenberg N. (1982), *Inside the Black Box: Technology and Economics*. Cambridge, Cambridge University Press.

Rosenberg, N. (1990), 'Why Do Firms Do Research (with Their Our Money)?', *Research Policy*, n. 19.

Saviotti P.P. (1996), *Technological Evolution, Variety and the Economy*, Cheltenham, Edward Elgar, UK.

Simon H.A. (1955), "A Behavioral Model of Rational Choice", *Quarterly Journal of Economics*, n. 69.

Scarpitti L. (1989), *Ambiti e mete di intervento di politica industriale a livello locale*, ENEA, Direzione Centrale Studi, STI/studi 3. Mimeo.

Stiglitz J.E. (1987), 'Learning to Learn. Localized Learning and Technological Progress', in Dasgupta P. and Stoneman P. (eds.), *Economic Policy and Technological Performance*, Cambridge, Cambridge University Press.

Stiglitz J.E. (1988), 'Economic Organisation, Information and Development', in, Chenery H. and Srinivasan T.S. (eds), *Handbook of Development Economics*, vol. I, London, Elsevier.

Storper M. and Harrison B. (1992), 'Flessibilità, gerarchie e sviluppo regionale: la ristrutturazione organizzativa dei sistemi produttivi e le nuove forme di governance', in Belussi F. (1992), (ed.) cit.

Storper M., Scott A.J. (1995), 'The wealth of regions. Market forces and policy imperative in local and global context', *Futures*, vol. 27, n.5.

Teece D.J. (1981), The market for knowledge and the efficient international transfer of technology, *The Annuals of the Academy of Political Social Science*, November.

Vaccà S. (1994), 'Le imprese transnazionali tra sistemi locali e sistemi globali', *Economia e politica industriale*, n. 84.

Varaldo E., Ferrucci L. (1993), 'La natura e la dinamica dell'impresa distrettuale', *Economia e politica industriale*, n. 80.

Viesti G. (1990), 'Crisi ed evoluzione dei distretti industriali', in 'L'integrazione internazionale del sistema di industria e servizi dell'Italia: mutamenti strutturali strategie verso il 1993', Onida F.(ed.), *IV Rapporto CESPRI-Bocconi per la CCIA di Milano*. Milan.

Winter S.G. (1987), 'Knowledge and Competence as Strategic Assets', in Teece D.J. (ed), *The Competitive Challenge*, Cambridge, Ballinger.

3 The cognitive approach to the study of local production systems

MAURO LOMBARDI

Introduction

Since the eighties, global economic dynamics have provoked profound transformations in the productive activities of many sectors and firms. This technological revolution, especially the transition toward what has been called a "knowledge based economy", has stimulated changes in the organisation of enterprises and in employment. Skills are bound to be radically redefined by the new technological trajectories, mainly based on "greater memory and storage, speed of transmission and easier manipulation and interpretation of data and information" (OECD, 1996, p. 13). At the same time huge improvements in transportation and communication technologies have lowered the cost and increased the speed of the flows of people, products and services throughout the world.

Knowledge based and global economics have become important characteristics of the international competitive environment. Within this kind of an environment firms are forced to change fundamentally: downsizing and flexibility seem to be the new ground rules. The debate on this is far from over, however it is plain that all components of national economies may potentially be involved in this dynamic, pervasive and apparently unceasing process.

It is interesting to analyse how, if at all, this great transformation will influence the evolutionary dynamics of local production systems, which in the 1970s and 1980s appeared in many countries and have received growing attention.

Starting from Italian studies of these systems, this essay intends to examine the features of local production systems, or industrial districts, and to assess their appropriateness to the changing environment, even if in both Italy and Europe there are many different kinds of systems (Garofoli, 1989).

The perspective adopted in the essay is primarily cognitive, so information patterns and mechanisms of information processing will be emphasised.

This essay is organised as follows: section 2 describes three

71

different approaches to the "Marshallian" industrial district, which Garofoli (1989) defines as "classical"; section 3 the systemic properties of the industrial district (a stable network of relationships, self-containment, operational flexibility); section 4 places the industrial district as a system in context; section 5 analyses its dynamics as a cognitive system and how they relate to different competitive environments; some conclusions about the new evolutionary path of local production systems are drawn in the final section.

Three approaches to the study of local production systems

Italian studies on local production systems or industrial districts (ID) utilise three different approaches.

The "Marshallian approach", developed by Becattini, Brusco and their colleagues (Goodman, Bamford, and Saynor, 1989), focuses on a "complex and tangled web of external economies and diseconomies, of joint associated costs, of historical and cultural vestiges, which envelop both inter firm and interpersonal relationships"(Becattini, 1989, p. 132). In recent years this point of view has been enriched by two main lines of research: 1) the introduction of "transaction cost analysis" (Dei Ottati, 1992; 1997) which allows one to examine trust, co-operation and investment in reputation, within the ID; 2) the analysis of knowledge processes to investigate the essential new relationships between local systems and the global market (Becattini, and Rullani, 1993; Rullani, 1997).

A second approach, proposed by Varaldo and Ferrucci (1997), based on shifting the focus of analysis from the aggregate level to the "district firm", which is the real motor of change. The logical and economic foundation of this view is that the role played by the strategies of enterprises is fundamental in order to analyse the actual evolution process of the ID, which has two important features: the emergence of leading firms and new competitive advantages.

A third approach employs "network analysis" to overcome the intrinsic limits to the aggregate or the transactional perspective, given their inability to grasp the relationships between firms which carry out different functions.

Following the three approaches different units of analysis are used: 1) ID as a collective entity (a "complex and tangled web etc."), 2) "district" firms and 3) network relationships.

Because the three approaches are not as incompatible as they seem to be at first sight, in this essay some issues are dealt with by analysing the ID in two types of competitive environments: the traditional and the new (see the introduction). Because information flows are crucial to the dynamics of whatever type of economic system (local, national), to examining the specific and general properties of the ID and to uncover its cognitive mechanisms, it is important to understand the evolutionary drives and the different organisational patterns which may arise.

Some distinctive features of the industrial districts

"The Marshallian industrial district is a localised 'thickening' (and its strength and weakness both lie in this spatial limitation) of inter industrial relationships which is reasonably stable over time" (Becattini, 1989, p. 132). One particular characteristic distinguishes the ID from the general "economic region": industrial activity predominates in the former (Becattini, 1991, p. 53). A local community, a population of firms and human resources are its three main elements which nourish a stable network of links between the ID and their clients or suppliers of technology and raw materials, etc.

Each of these elements will be explained briefly; then systemic properties like self-containment and operational flexibility will be described.

Three main elements

Local community. The local community is a rather homogeneous system of values which are shared within the local environment, its families, social and political institutions (Becattini, 1991). The interiorisation of rules implies limits on the individual behaviour reinforcing the "identity" of and the sense of belonging to the local community.

Population of firms. Brusco (1991) distinguishes three types of firms. First of all the units which produce "final products" and serve the market. A second set of firms includes units which carry out single production tasks (e.g. in the textile industry: sewing, knitting, packaging). Finally, there are firms which perform activities essential for the local production cycle, even if they are not strictly part of the distinctive sector of the local system.

The population of firms refers to the extended decomposition of the production process, so that there are many enterprises specialised in only one phase or in a limited number of phases of the process. Operating units mainly belong to the same industrial sector, which is defined broadly and includes complementary activities. The decomposition of production processes entails the formation of a local environment within which transactions develop continuously on the basis of specialised products. This type of fragmentation of a sequence of production phases is particularly suitable when final demand is varied and differentiated (Becattini, 1991), i.e. it is a non standard and fluctuating demand.

Human resources. Three principal sets of agents are considered in the literature on the ID. First of all workers, who frequently change their positions within a wide range of production activities: both with the increase of personal abilities and competence, and the pursuit of higher wages lead to a continuous search for the most appropriate and attractive role. The frequent movement among firms does not imply the loss of competence, accumulated with an operating unit; rather this movement helps to create and propagate the "industrial atmosphere" which benefits the entire local system. Indeed, this process supports a kind of "collective learning" based on extended and frequent interaction among people and firms.

"Pure entrepreneurs" belong to a second set of agents: a good example is the "impannatori" (the textile entrepreneurs of Prato) who monitor the international market to identify trends and opportunities. These "strategic" agents exercise an essential function of transforming the techno-economic capacities of the local production system into final products. Perhaps the "pure" or "strategic" entrepreneurs do not manage a firm, but they know market needs and translate these into "product design", the components of which they later assign to different "phase producers". Indeed, they know the economic and social structures well and they are able to bargain over production costs. So the strategic entrepreneurs represent the key economic units which are able to conceive "product design" and exploit local potential.

The third set of agents includes domestic workers and part-time workers; they represent the link between families and systems of firms and dampen the effects of economic cycles on the industrial structure by balancing the slow downs or speed ups of production activity (Becattini, 1991).

A stable network of relationships and systemic properties

The ID has some very interesting systemic properties based on its structural characteristics which deserve great attention. Indeed, within a stable network of relationships, self-containment, productive specialisation and a strong division of labour among the units allow for the production of a surplus of goods that the ID cannot absorb. So managing its connections to the market is fundamental.

Stable network of relationships

Marshallian scholars emphasise that the ID does not have "a centre where decisions are made" (Brusco, 1991, p. 30). The firms directly involved in the market are so numerous and independent from each other that one or more strategic centres cannot exist. Moreover the ID is based on a dynamic equilibrium between co-operation and competition, the former involving "final firms" (those which have contact with the market) and subcontractors (Sabel, 1982), the latter between units carrying out similar activities (horizontal competition).

There are three bases for co-operation: 1) the observance of unwritten rules fixing services and product standards - Becattini (1991) speaks about a kind of "local prices"; 2) the attachment to habits and local institutions (enterprises, associations, unions, local and provincial government); 3) real investments in reputation (Dei Ottati, 1997) which helps to regulate the content of the transactions (technical standards, delivery time, information exchange, etc.).

Self-containment

Another distinctive feature of the ID is self-containment which can be seen from three points of view: 1) psychologically, as a collective identity established through a long historical process; 2) politically and culturally, as a result of institutional and cultural dynamics (Trigilia, 1986); 3) technologically and economically, as a product of the intense interactions among final firms and subcontractors, "one phase" producers, technology suppliers and users. So a kind of "micro-universe" is created, within which social values, technology and economic culture (quality standards, costs of products and services) are shared.

Rullani (1997) sees all these aspects as a significant barrier between the inner and outer environments. However, while market information acquired by strategic firms (or entrepreneurs) is fundamental for such a micro-universe, many other information circuits are developed (cultural, political, technological) within the ID, which lack both strong and frequent links with the information flows from the outside. For example, Sabel (1982) analysed the relationships between final firms and one phase producers, and found that numerous incremental innovations occur because of these interactions, while innovations rarely spread to the world market.

By means of co-operation and competition, the division of the production cycle within the ID drive intense, but localised, information flows which produce interlocking behaviours.

Operational flexibility

Another important characteristic of the ID is its ability to change productive capacity according to inputs from both the market and internal sources of knowledge. The internal dynamics of knowledge involve all the technological aspects of the production phases and a widespread ability to make adjustments in order to obtain the desired mix of products. In other words, on the basis of given parameters (propagated by the strategic entrepreneurs), specialisation and knowledge are created. So the evolution of knowledge and the features of product develop together, producing a "diffused innovative capacity" (Bellandi 1989) or a "diffusion matrix-system of innovation" (Belussi, 1996). However, the fundamental limits of that knowledge must be emphasised: the central aspects of a technological path are not determined within the local system. So the ID is a technology user, even if never-ending product and process innovations are introduced. Indeed, a large number of studies (Nomisma, 1991; Lanzara, Ferrucci, 1997) have found an on-site build-up of knowledge and a low propensity to make investments in radical innovation.

This limited innovative capacity, the propensity to produce incremental innovations and to adapt to different product characteristics correspond to what Morroni (1992, p. 168) defines as "operational flexibility": "the possibility of varying the quantities produced within a given mix, using a given productive structure".

The industrial district as a system

Among the distinctive characteristics of the ID, described in the previous section, those concerning information and knowledge flows seem particularly interesting for the analysis of its evolutionary dynamics.

For this purpose, we begin from some important ideas from von Hayek, who developed his theory of economic process in many essays (1937; 1945; 1946; 1975): knowledge is always incomplete, incoherent and dispersed among economic agents; it is, therefore, impossible to concentrate in a mastermind. The division of knowledge is based on the division of labour, but it is a larger phenomenon, because it expresses the basic idea that agents face decision contexts characterised by an infinite variety of events. Thus, they must select relevant information from different and limited points of view of potentially boundless phenomena. As relevant knowledge is spread among individuals, the knowledge diffusion processes and the interactions among the agents deserve great attention. According to von Hayek, the economic process is an exploration of the unknown: economic problems arise continuously because frequent unforeseen changes require adaptation. The essential problem for the analysis is then how widespread knowledge and multiple information flows combine to produce coherent systems.

For this purpose it is useful to start by thinking of the ID as a set of entities, united by shared values, whose aggregate behaviour derives mainly from interactions among endogenous agents.

What type of system are we analysing?

Let us begin from two general statements. The fundamental characteristics of an organisation structure are "regular patterns of interlocked behaviours" (Weick, 1979, p. 90); "A systems has various fixed (or relatively slow changing) attributes that define its form, that set the scope, ground rules, and boundary conditions for the system's more variable aspects" (Langlois, 1983, p. 594).

Interlocked behaviours, relatively stable relationships and boundary conditions are inherent features of an ID, together with other properties (self-containment, operational flexibility). The division of the production cycle among many economic units, the nearly exclusive local range of co-operation (the vertical sequence of phases) and competition (horizontally), and localised information circuits, all point to self-containment as an important characteristic of local systems.

Self-containment may be defined as: "A unit is self-contained to the extent that the conditions for carrying out its activities are independent of what is done in the other organisation units" (March Simon, 1993, p. 28). We can amplify this concept by specifying some of the ID's intrinsic properties. The self-containment of the ID allows the external environment (market, technological trajectory) and internal environment (techno-economical) to be distinguished; thus, there are two types of information flows: 1) economic inflows from the outside, which are controlled and codified (transformation of demand parameters in product design); 2) localised information flows, which are informal and non codified; in other words, they are made up of very fluid knowledge (local interactions).

Besides the shared values mentioned above, which is the basis for their collective identity (or feeling of belonging), there is a clear division between the external and internal environment. Co-operation and competition occur within the local area, but two types of information exist: system and task information.

System information is related to market demand (needs, features, contacts with the final customers). The final entrepreneurs must acquire this information and then distribute the work orders; in other words, they must decide the production capacity to be used and which firms will be involved.

Task information concerns the task environment, a term from Newell and Simon, (1992, p. 56) that refers "to an environment coupled with a goal, problem, or task—the one for which the motivation of the subject is assumed". Indeed, technological and production information is based on widespread specialisation and incremental innovation, which are the result of the activity of the agents, who increase their knowledge locally and frequently interact with each other. In this way, non codified knowledge flows are continuously created around technical aspects of products or the production cycle.

The differences between system and task information mean that an *information hierarchy* exists and is articulated on two levels. The first concerns the transformation of market signals into behaviour parameters for economic units of the ID. They are selected by the final entrepreneurs who know the distribution of the competencies within the internal environment. The second concerns the widespread accumulation of "on site knowledge" by single agents (who change jobs) or by economic micro units.

So, system information is fundamental for establishing important relationships (work orders, division of labour) among the endogenous agents, while the task information stimulates further development of the productive capacity. The information hierarchy implies that definite asymmetries exist and the final entrepreneurs can be conceived as the critical subsystem in the decision-making process. They elaborate strategies concerning the fundamental aspects of work orders and co-ordination of the production cycle and, finally, placing products on the market (Bellandi and Trigilia, 1991).

So there is a clear division between the relationships with the market and those within the internal micro universe. Internally, the decomposability of the production process and the increased division of labour supply almost continuous sources of knowledge. So, the ID is an original mix of inner dynamics and environmental inputs, even if the external environment is not immediately apparent; final entrepreneurs act as a filtering screen and as "transducers" of external stimuli. They are a kind of "gatekeeper" for the information system.

Dynamics of an ID as a cognitive system

The analysis above demonstrates that local production systems adapt to the external environment by never ending changes in their accumulated knowledge: specific parts of the ID receive fundamental parameters for how the production cycle should perform from outside it, i.e. market needs or features of demand (which are translated into product design). On the basis of these fundamental parameters, many components throughout the local micro universe interact with each other, according to a diversified set of behaviours: imitation, innovation, persistence. This picture illustrates how the ID acts as a cognitive system, which can be described as a set of information processing units and mechanisms which can learn and adapt to a changing environment (Lombardi, 1996). Cognitive systems and IDs, from this point of view, are inherently dynamic and based on a mix of learning and recomposition of diffuse information in coherent sets of knowledge. There are two main sources of novelties in IDs: external inputs, encoded by the final entrepreneurs (acting as gatekeepers); endogenous evolutionary changes, activated by the exogenous stimuli and frequent interactions.

By drawing from the studies in Artificial Intelligence and cognitive psychology, there are two principal types of cognitive systems: information processing systems (IPS) and connectionist systems (CS). The first (Newell and Simon, 1972) elaborate information according to what is called the classical approach to Artificial Intelligence, based on processing symbols or structures, according to previous established instructions or explicit rules. IPSs are inferential machines, because the rules enable desired results to be reached thanks to ordered steps. The rationality of the system rests in the formal rules and in following them during the inferential process. IPSs have two characteristic features (Clark, 1991): 1) a clear-cut correspondence between the symbolic description of the sequence and the real sequence can be described; 2) they can be applied to specific purposes which have well structured descriptions, which are characterised by components, which are neither so numerous nor so interactive that the results are indefinite (Dreyfus and Dreyfus, 1986). Thanks to both the objective features of the task environment and the rules, classical IPSs are able to solve problems in a manner analogous to scientific discovery (Langley, Simon, et al. 1987): they use heuristic strategies to reduce the amount of information processing, so that research along different trajectories avoids "combinatorial explosion".

Instead CSs (or neural nets) are based on parallel, dispersed information processing units, which neither execute symbolic manipulation nor go through predefined sequences. On the contrary, they are made up of interacting units (or "knowledge atoms", neurons), often on stratified levels. The number and the depth of interactions depend on the frequency and the intensity of the propagation of inputs between the units. Their activation is the result of random processes: the repetition, the decrease or the end of stimuli propagation reinforce or weaken the "coalition groups" of knowledge atoms whose completion or abandonment is the result of stimuli diffusion dynamics. "The cognitive system is an engine for activating coherent assemblies of atoms and drawing inferences that are consistent with the knowledge represented by the activated atoms" (Smolensky, 1988, p. 203). The coalitions are defined schemata and their evolution is the basis of their inferences. The cognitive activity of the CS occurs on the basis of characteristic processes: environmental events determine the activation patterns of the input units, then the propagation processes produce activation patterns of other units of the system, which means that knowledge is accumulated as stable coalitions are formed. In other words, as the n-elements of the input vector are transformed in the n-elements of the output vector, CSs realise a vector transformation of information. It is important to emphasise that the new knowledge is not based on prearranged sets of instructions, but it is the result of random information flows, which reinforce or weaken the links between units, which depend on whether they are compatible or incoherent.

Looking again at IDs and the above analysis, they act as cognitive systems, because they are a set of processing information units, but their evolutionary dynamics produce a peculiar mix of cognitive systems, which are dealt with by Artificial Intelligence and cognitive psychology.

If the production cycle is seen from a different and complementary point of view, the sequence of production phases can be depicted as a sequence of discrete units, identified by specific parameters, such as, for example, the characteristics of intermediate goods components or product features. Each phase contains many operations, so the concept of *routine*, viewed as a *variable set of operations*, can be employed as the basic unit of analysis. In general, the dynamics of aggregation or decomposition of routines depends on how production phases are arranged to produce a product with given characteristics. In addition, different types of phase sequences can be constructed, according to how the various parameters are assigned to each phase. If there are one-way assignments from one phase to another, until the final product is produced, the sequence will also be one-way. The possibility of interaction among the units means that routines and phases can be arranged in various sequences based on the frequency and the intensity of interactions. In this way, the parameters for each phase are the result of a spontaneous process of unit "grouping" based on the exchange of information. In the former case, the task parameters are assigned from the top; in the latter, they are the outcome of an evolutionary process. We call the first, top-down assignment, the second, evolutionary emergence (Lombardi, 1997). Each of them corresponds to a different type of system: top-down and selective.

Top-down systems are based on the idea of analysing and decomposing problems or complex functions in different partitions, each of them performed through factorisation, that is "by factoring the problem in a hierarchical fashion" (March and Simon, 1993, p. 211). The basic procedure is to divide a goal (for instance, a final product) into sub goals, through the refinement of purposes, "the process of decision is one of successive approximation—constant refinement of purpose, closer and closer discrimination of fact—in which the march of time is essential" (Bernard, quoted in March and Simon, 1993, p. 211). *Selective systems* are aggregations of units, carrying out operations (routines) which depend on the occurrence of compatible values, selected through the evolutionary processes of the inner and external environment.

In conclusion, based on the above analysis, IDs can be thought of as an original mix of top-down and selective systems.

The information flows from the outside are framed by IPS: final demand and user needs are transformed in product models by the strategic entrepreneurs and, then, become task parameters diffused within the internal environment. While local competition and co-operation influence the "grouping" of operating units, it is formed according to the reciprocal information transfer, based on codified inputs, from the endogenous evolutionary environment. The inner distribution of work orders, therefore, does not follow fixed sequences, nor are final parameters subdivided into specific phase parameters; instead, the widespread activation of local entities is inherently random, and links between them are continuously formed, eliminated and transformed, according to the evolution of technological knowledge. This evolution, which is bound by the basic features of technological trajectories and fundamental external parameters, is like that of CS.

Such different cognitive mechanisms and processes imply that this cognitive system must have distinctive dynamics which can be made clearer through further comment.

The main characteristics of the local system are: 1) an information hierarchy; 2) a functional distinction between information input (concerning markets) controlled by the gatekeepers or technology suppliers, and inner information flows, which are spontaneous; 3) different roles performed by many agents. The ID as a system is then a combination of at least two principal subsystems: the first (relationships with the market and co-ordination of the production cycle) sets the main variables (inherent in marketable goods), so that the components of the second are then activated. Inside the latter other subsystems and circuits of local interaction propagate the stimuli and, at the same time, knowledge and specialisations are endogenously produced through continuous feedback, even if they are constrained by fixed parameters given by the system information. In other words, given the demand parameters, endogenous evolutionary mechanisms act in order to produce the suitable product mix. So described, the architecture of an ID can be defined as an example of a *multistable system*: "A multistable system consists of many ultrastable systems joined main variable to main variable.". (Ashby, 1952, p. 171). *Ultrastable systems* are characterised by behaviours which take it away from critical states. The principle of ultrastability formally states: "an ultrastable system acts selectively towards the fields of the main variables, rejecting those that lead the representative point to a critical state but retaining those that do not" (Ashby, 1952, p. 91).

In this way, subsystems evolve by adapting their main variables to that of the whole system, thus making general adaptations easier. Indeed multistable systems show interesting properties: 1) their adaptation is not general immediately, but "by part-functions", that is within "finite intervals of change and finite intervals of constancy" (Ashby, 1952, p. 173), which are expressed in many internal links between interacting units; 2) their stability depends on the interactions between subsystems, which each adapt to their own main variable; 3) in facing fragmented and variable environments, they achieve a generally ordered path of adjustment, which is realised sequentially or stage-by-stage, according to their interaction with other subsystems. This property is defined as *serial adaptation* (Ashby, 1952, p. 179).

This is just another systemic property which is the result of the selection and adaptation processes of the ID.

The four systemic properties of the ID (information hierarchy, self-containment, operational flexibility, serial adaptation) demonstrate how the patterns of behaviour are the result of both the inner evolutionary environment and the development of its inner potential. So, it is important to analyse another critical source of information flows: the external environment.

IDs and the external environment

The four properties correspond to the same number of macro behaviours, which refer to the *parametric rationality* as a fundamental feature of IDs: "parametric rationality ... implies that the agent thinks of himself as a variable and of all others as constants; or if he thinks that the others are adapting to their environment, he believes himself to be the only one to adapt to others' adaptation, and so on." (Elster, 1983,

p. 75). The ID, as a whole, takes in, through the gatekeepers, demand or market parameters, and adapts itself through serial adaptation (described above) based on interaction and local feedback.

When can it synthesise the external environment by means of parameters? And in a related question, in what conditions does this system perform best?

Italian IDs were successful in the 1970s and the early 1980s. This period was characterised by specific factors: varying exchange rates, fragmented and variable demand in markets, high exchange rates for the dollar and price competition. In this external environment a system with parametric rationality and these four properties is particularly fit, and follows an adaptive path by extracting signals from the market (i.e. selecting the demand parameters, the price and the qualitative characteristics of products). This system is able to select, within the local subsystems, the productive capacity to be employed to defeat the competition principally on the basis of cutting prices, fostered by particular information flows and agglomeration economies.

The architecture of information flows successfully matched demand typologies and commodities produced: after having determined the parameters of final demand, these inputs propagate within the local system, and routines are adjusted (production flexibility) in order to achieve the goals set. Interactions and serial adaptations are in the end co-ordinated by the gatekeepers, so products are marketable. Parametric rationality, and bounded systems, were thus particularly fit for the competitive environment prevailing until the mid 1980s (Mariotti, 1989), characterised by uncertainty and market segmentation with limited variety and small production lots.

In short, in this type of environment, the ID as a cognitive system was evolutionary fit, i.e. environmental information flows matched its systemic properties.

New evolutionary conditions

Many things have happened in the decade beginning in the late 80s. Technological discontinuities, represented by the growth of information and communication technologies (OECD, 1996; Tyson, 1992; Thurow, 1996), fixed rates of exchange, the globalisation of the economy, reduced price competition and the process of European unification have radically changed the competitive environment. The qualitative content of the product and new relationships with the market have become more important, mainly by bringing the demand change forward and leveraging qualitative components: the technological and scientific level of production cycle, product and organisational innovations (the verticalisation of the production cycle and the international dispersion of its phases), more frequent interaction with the demand, new systemic components (high level services). For instance, in the case of the Italian textile industry, new strategies have been developed by pursuing two fundamental objectives: 1) the creation of strategic alliances in order to influence fashion trends and, so, to time the production cycle and the development of the products; 2) the introduction of new technologies, so that production and co-ordination costs are minimised, thanks to a reduction of cycle time and warehouse size (Bertini, Forlai and Magnatti, 1991). In the new competitive environment the traditional parametric rationality is no longer appropriate; IDs need to adopt a different set of behaviours, based on *strategic rationality*, "defined by an axiom of symmetry: the agent acts in an environment of other actors, none of whom can be assumed to be less rational or sophisticated than he is himself. Each actor, then, needs to anticipate the decisions of others before he can make his own, and knows that they do the same in respect to each other and to him" (Elster, 1983, pp. 77).

Changes in relationships with the market, and technological or organisational choices, deeply alter traditional production and information flows. From the perspective adopted in this essay, it must be emphasised that the four systemic properties are subject to intense tensions. The strategic functions of final entrepreneurs are sharply modified: it is increasingly necessary to go beyond translating final demand parameters into production projects and distributing the orders within the local production system; the ability to win market shares by means of strategic design is critical. It means that the local production systems must acquire strategic flexibility "the ability to change production processes, production element endowment and the quality of output in relation to changes in environmental conditions" (Morroni, 1992, p. 168).

Strategic rationality and strategic flexibility are strictly connected: new strategies are elaborated, centred on scheduling production flows according to programs of penetration of markets. Therefore, more stable links between production phases are required. In addition, there is a new technological drive for changes in the routines, or groups of them, and thus towards a different grouping of units, more connected to the sequence of production phases, which realise a variable mix of products and a modifiable quantity of goods. In this way, the traditional information hierarchy and the previous information circuits are deeply transformed: self-containment becomes weaker and weaker, and is substituted by transversal/horizontal information flows, concerning technological, scientific and economic questions. The distinction between the external and internal environment becomes less and less clear. Instead of the serial adaptation between traditional subsystems, there is likely to be the formation of a more constrained sequence of units, connected with critical agents or units, which can elaborate new strategies. It is paradoxical, but the new mix of top-down and selective systems is realised within the traditional ID: groups of firms are created according to top-down procedures, but, within them, cognitive and selective mechanisms can co-evolve in order to obtain the required new type of productive capacity. Indeed, there is a growing amount of empirical evidence concerning the changing relationships between the firms within IDs: during the 1980s vertical groups were formed, as hierarchical networks or partial networks (Bursi, Marchi and Nardin, 1997); leading firms became an economic engine for local production systems (Lorenzoni, 1997; Varaldo and Ferrucci, 1997), a break down of self-containment occured (Rullani, 1997); the introduction of vertical integration (Crestanello, 1997) profoundly changed the relationships between internal and external firms.

Theoretical and empirical analysis, thus, converge in pointing to new features of local production systems.

From the point of view adopted here, the ID as a cognitive system acquires new systemic properties, related to radical change in the external and internal environment, and an analysis of information flows can help to understand its future evolutionary path.

Conclusions: some thoughts on the evolution of the ID

The new competitive environment has altered some basic properties of the ID: self-containment and information hierarchy are no longer distinctive features of a local production system, while strategic flexibility and strategic rationality have become important in more integrated groups of firms.

Insights about the real evolution of the ID, which differ from those expected from theory, have emerged in recent studies (Franchi and Rieser, 1991; Bellandi, 1997), but they are directed fundamentally to bringing these evolutionary patterns back into to the traditional analytical framework. However, it should be asked if these transformations are bringing about irreversible changes in the ID as we know it. If so, then it is likely that its behaviour parameters will be subject to radical changes, as strategic rationality becomes more and more important. Undoubtedly, without self-containment or an information hierarchy, local production systems are substantially different: new rules of behaviour and organisational patterns emerge within the local context. First of all, two changes can reasonably be forecasted: 1) the traditional bounded nature of the inner evolutionary environment may be substituted by a freer one, to the extent that traditional barriers (the distinction between internal and external environment) disappear; 2) multiple evolutionary patterns within the local production system are likely, as completely new competitive dynamics unfold, because different market potential may allow for the survival of multiple behaviour patterns, based on either parametric rationality and strategic rationality, depending on the persistence of the market niches agents hold.

At the same time, the possibility that vertical groups of firms may combine serial adaptation forms with new (more integrated) adaptation rules, cannot be excluded. Indeed, multiple evolutionary patterns do not exclude mixed organisation patterns, which may appear and thrive.

However, it is plain that the traditional "lay-out" of the ID and the "industrial atmosphere" will be radically altered. Agents will thus modify their cultures (the collective identity), the relationships among economic units, and the fundamental distinctions in subsystems. Asymmetries among agents, the fluid dynamics of groupings among units, and a blurred boundary between the internal and external environment, portray a new evolutionary horizon which everybody must face, with new and different rules which will emerge from the selective dynamics of economic processes.

References

Ashby, W. R. (1952), *Design for a Brain*, New York, John Wiley & Sons.

Becattini, G. (1989), Sectors and/or districts: some remarks on the conceptual foundations of industrial economics, in Goodman, E., Bamford, J., Saynor, P. (1989), (eds) *Small Firms and Industrial Districts*, London, Routledge.

Becattini, G. (1991), Il distretto industriale marshalliano come concetto socio-economico, *Studi e informazioni*, 34.

Becattini, G. and Rullani, E. (1993), Sistema locale e mercato globale, *Economia e Politica Industriale*, 80.

Bellandi, M. (1997), Le logiche del cambiamento nei distretti industriali, in Varaldo, R. and Ferrucci, L. (eds) *Il distretto industriale tra logiche di impresa e logiche di sistema*, Milan, Franco Angeli.

Bellandi, M. and Trigilia C. (1991), Come cambia un distretto industriale: strategie di riaggiustamento e tecnologie informatiche nell'industria tessile di Prato, *Economia e Politica Industriale*, 79.

Belussi, F. (1996), Local Systems: Industrial Districts and Institutional Networks: Towards a New Evolutionary Paradigm of Industrial Economics?, *European Planning Studies*, 1.

Bertini, S., Forlai, L. and Magnatti, P. (1991), Prato: elementi per l'analisi economica dell'area, in Nomisma (1991), *Strategie e valutazione nella politica industriale*, Milan, Franco Angeli.

Brusco, S. (1991), La genesi dell'idea di distretto industriale, *Studi e informazioni*, 34.

Bursi, T., Marchi, G., Nardin, G. (1997), Trasformazioni organizzative nell'impresa distrettuale: alcune premesse sulla definizione dell'unità di analisi, in Varaldo, R., Ferrucci, L. (eds) *Il distretto industriale tra logiche di impresa e logiche di sistema*, Milan, Franco Angeli.

Clark, A. (1991) *Microcognition: Philosophy, Cognitive Science, and Parallel Distributed Processing*, Cambridge Mass., MIT Press.

Crestanello, P. (1997) Le trasformazioni in 10 distretti industriali durante gli anni '80, in Varaldo, R., Ferrucci, L. (eds), *Il distretto industriale tra logiche di impresa e logiche di sistema*, Milan, Franco Angeli.

Dei Ottati, G. (1987), Fiducia, transazioni intrecciate e credito nel distretto industriale, *Note Economiche*,1-2.

Dei Ottati, G. (1997), Cooperazione e concorrenza nel distretto industriale come modello organizzativo, in Varaldo, R. and Ferrucci, L. (eds) *Il distretto industriale tra logiche di impresa e logiche di sistema*, Milan, Franco Angeli.

Dreyfus, H.L., Dreyfus, S. E. (1986), *Mind over machine. The Power of Human Intuition and Expertise in the Era of the Computer,* New York, Free Press.

Edelman, G. (1992) *Bright Air, Brilliant Fire. On the Matter of the Mind,* London, Penguin Books.

Elster, J. (1983), *Explaining technical Change,* Cambridge (UK), Cambridge University Press.

Franchi, M. and Rieser, V. (1991), Le categorie sociologiche nell'analisi del distretto industriale: tra comunità e razionalizzazione, *Stato e mercato,* 33.

Garofoli, G. (1989) Modelli locali di sviluppo: i sistemi di piccola impresa, in G. Becattini, (ed.) *Modelli locali di sviluppo,* Bologna, Il Mulino.

Giannetti, R. (1989), (ed.) *Nel mito di Prometeo,* Firenze, Il Ponte alle Grazie.

Goodman, E., Bamford, J., Saynor, P., (eds) *Small Firms and Industrial Districts,* London, Routledge.

von Hayek, F. A.(1937), Economics and Knowledge, *Economica,*13.

von Hayek, F. A.(1945), The Use of Knowledge in Society, *American Economic Review,* 4.

von Hayek, F. A.(1946), *The Meaning of Competition,* Stafford Little Lecture.

von Hayek, F. A.(1975), *The Pretence of Knowledge,* Nobel Lecture.

Langley P., Simon, H., Bradshaw, G. and Zytkow, J.M. (1987), (eds) *Scientific Discovery,* Cambridge Mass., MIT Press.

Langlois, R. (1983), Systems Theory, Knowledge and The Social Sciences, in Matchlup, F. and Mansfield, U. (eds), *The Study of Information,* New York, John Wiley & Sons.

Lanzara, R. and Ferrucci, L. (1997), Tecnologia e processi di innovazione nei distretti industriali, in Varaldo, R. and Ferrucci, L. (eds) *Il distretto industriale tra logiche di impresa e logiche di sistema,* Milan, Franco Angeli.

Lombardi, M. (1996), Conoscenza e innovazione, in Giannetti, R. (ed.), *Nel mito di Prometeo,* Firenze, Il Ponte alle Grazie.

Lombardi, M. (1997), Meccanismi evolutivi nella dinamica dei sistemi di imprese, *Economia Politica,* 3.

Lorenzoni, G. (1997), Imprese, relazioni fra imprese, distretti industriali nello sviluppo delle P.M.I., in Varaldo, R. and Ferrucci, L. (eds), *Il distretto industriale tra logiche di impresa e logiche di sistema,* Milan, Franco Angeli.

March, J. G. and Simon, H. (1993), *Organizations (2° ed.),* Oxford, Blackwell.

Mariotti, S. (1989), Efficienza dinamica e sistemi di imprese, *Economia e Politica Industriale,* 64.

Matchlup, F., Mansfield, U. (1983), (eds), *The Study of Information,* New York, John Wiley&Sons.

Morroni, M. (1992), *Production Process and Technical Change,* Cambridge, Cambridge University Press.

Newel, A. and Simon, H. (1972), *Human Problem Solving,* Englewood Cliffs (NJ), Prentice Hall.

Nomisma (1991), *Strategie e valutazione nella politica industriale,* Milan, Franco Angeli.

Oecd (1996), *Technology, Productivity and Job Creation,* Paris.

Rullani, E. (1997), L'evoluzione dei distretti industriali: un percorso tra decostruzione e internazionalizzazione, in Varaldo, R. and Ferrucci, L. (eds), *Il distretto industriale tra logiche di impresa e logiche di sistema,* Milan, Franco Angeli.

Rumelhart, D.E., McLelland, J.L. and PDP Research Group (1988), *Parallel Distributed Processing*, Cambridge Mass., MIT Press.

Sabel, C. (1982), *Work and Politics*, Cambridge Mass., Cambridge University Press.

Smolenky, P. (1988), Information Processing in Dynamical Systems: Foundations of Harmony Theory, in Rumelhart, D.E., McLelland, J.L. and PDP Research Group, *Parallel Distributed Processing*, Cambridge Mass., MIT Press.

Trigilia, C. (1986), *Grandi partiti e piccole imprese,* Bologna, Il Mulino.

Thurow, L. (1996), *The Future of Capitalism*, London, Brealey Publishing.

Tyson D'Andrea, L. (1992) *Trade Conflict in High-Technology Industries*, Washington DC, Institute for International Economics.

Varaldo, R. and Ferrucci, L. (1997), La natura e la dinamica dell'impresa distrettuale, in Varaldo, R. and Ferrucci, L. (eds) *Il distretto industriale tra logiche di impresa e logiche di sistema,* Milan, Franco Angeli.

Weick, K. E. (1979), *The Social Psychology of Organizing*, New York, Random House.

Part II

Knowledge as a resource and its implications for policy

4 Endogenous development of local systems of SMEs: lessons from practical experience

SILVANO BERTINI

Introduction

It is paradoxical that a country like Italy, that has demonstrated to the world the potential of the small enterprise to generate widespread industrial development, cannot assume a leading role in the international economic debate on this question. Great emphasis has been placed on the country's "innate" factors of the territory for the formation of "industrial districts", thereby preventing the development of a global vision of the mechanisms required for endogenous development.

The inability to elaborate a general approach to policy strategies for the development of SME local systems without historical-cultural contexts, e.g. the South of Italy, has been the inevitable consequence of this kind of discussion.

There is a need to make the Italian debate on SMEs and local development "practical", in order to move from a descriptive to a methodological approach. This necessity stems from the actual needs of small enterprises and of Italian local systems, as they have to increase their competitiveness. Yet the rest of the world, especially developing and ex-communist block countries, is waiting to learn from the Italian experience, in terms of policy for both the diffusion of small enterprises and for the formation of local competitive production systems that are socially sustainable.

The debate on local development in Italy

The real opening of the debate on small enterprises and local development in Italy can be attributed to the reintroduction of the concept of industrial district (Becattini, 1987).

The rediscovery of the concept of the Marshallian industrial district has been extremely fruitful for the interpretation of economic development, especially in the Italian case. In fact, with the introduction

91

of this concept:

a) geographical location was emphasised as a key variable for bottom-up economic growth and as the place where relations among firms are built, for the transmission of entrepreneurial spirit and technical know-how, as well as for the consolidation of external collective economies (industrial atmosphere);

b) culture, technical patrimony, local traditions, community regulations and social institutions, considered as obstacles in the Fordist era, are highly valued as the basis for spontaneous local development;

c) cooperation among SMEs was highlighted; firms working together and networking can successfully compete even with big enterprises.

Further progress has been made, based on these insights, that can be grouped into two main categories. The first concerns industrial organisation and the introduction of the concept of "flexible specialisation", as a new efficiency model, alternative to the Fordist model (Brusco, 1989; Sabel and Piore, 1984). The second, related to economic sociology, highlights the social aspects of the economic development of the "Third Italy", and the role of social institutions and collective regulations, which have historically developed around cities. This has determined the diffuse, egalitarian and democratic character of development in these regions (Bagnasco and Trigilia, 1984).

At the same time, the concept of "industrialisation without cleavages" (*industrializzazione senza fratture*) was also proposed. It highlighted how development influenced by SMEs could bring about a non-traumatic transition from agriculture to industry and how the institutions of the rural population (above all, the family) would not be an obstacle to this transition. Indeed, they could profitably accompany this transition (Fuà and Zacchia, 1983).

In the seventies, this generated great interest world-wide in the development pattern of the Third Italy. However, in the following decade, increasing difficulties emerged in interpreting the dynamic economies of LPSs in central and northern Italy. The phase of rapid industrialisation and stable growth, aided by the difficulties that the large enterprises experienced in the seventies, had ended. The local SME systems were forced to undergo a restructuring process, in order to increase quality levels and introduce innovations. The response of the districts to such needs varied from one to another: in some cases, there were situations of acute crisis; in others, there was a continuous transformation of the local industrial structure (Laboratorio di Politica Industriale, 1989).

This created several problems in interpreting the SME phenomenon.

While the concept of industrialisation without cleavages clearly referred to a historical process, greater difficulty emerged for industrial district theory, especially in defending such a model as an alternative paradigm to Fordism in terms of industrial organisation as was argued by Sabel and Piore in their "Second Industrial Divide".

Substantially, the concept of industrial district referred to an organisational pattern inseparable from local and social organisation, and linked to local history and culture. According to this interpretation, the district had to assume a monosectorial configuration, based only on small and micro-enterprises, working in the same production cycle fragmented into phases without leading enterprises. Moreover, it was retained that these local systems should form a sort of unchanging sector due to their interconnection with social relations.

Yet, in the eighties, there were continuous changes in Italian local systems: mergers, outside take-overs, international decentralisation and production modernisation. All these changes gradually modified the typical structure of industrial districts; those systems that were slow to make structural adjustment gradually lost their competitiveness (Nomisma, 1991; 1993).

In this context, alternative ideas of the SME phenomenon could not avoid the debate on the "pros and cons" of the district. Two main sets of arguments contested the district theorists: those of enterprise management and those of industrial policy.

The first set emphasised the organisational limitations of district enterprises, the low level of their tertiarisation and management abilities, and the inefficiencies of production organisation developed by district enterprises. According to this group of authors, the recovery of the competitiveness by local systems should be found in the re-organisation of individual firms; however, they, in part, lost sight of the importance of the territorial factor and of the relationships between enterprises.

The industrial policy set looked at local SME systems in methodological terms. On the basis of this approach, the historically developed industrial districts were only one feature of the possible pathways of local development, where specific objectives (innovation, internationalisation, quality, etc.) could be pursued. The approach to industrial policies by SMEs is therefore interpreted in a territorial sense; in other words, it is not aimed at individual enterprises or the sector's structure, but at changing relations between enterprises, at external economies and the local environment in general. In Italy, the theme of industrial policy has been manifested mostly through empirical and applied studies with insufficient academic importance.

An evolutionary view of local development has been established, thereby giving more space to industrial policy. Apart from empirical evidence, Porter's analysis on the competitive advantage of nations, based on the cluster concept (Porter, 1990), has added strength to this view. In the developmental process, favourable sector interrelations contribute to the increased competitiveness of local systems by generating reciprocal synergy. Emphasis is no longer placed solely on the static organisation of production (the fragmentation of the production cycle in order to realise the same type of product), but on the various activities that can be developed around the original competitive sector. This then allows them to become competitive and reciprocally gives reinforcement to related activities, fostering the concentration of know-how in the area. Such activities not only concern the production cycle, but also the technological *filière* (related production, specialised services, professional competencies, infrastructure, and particular institutions) or horizontal diversification in similar and possibly innovative products.

On the basis of this view, even the territorial limit of the analysis can change: it may no longer be restricted to a local area, around a small- to medium-sized city, but a more extensive area where different activities are interconnected. For example, in the Italian case, it is possible to point to the ceramics and mechanical-agricultural-industrial system along Via Emilia, the fashion system around Florence, the metallurgy sector in the valleys of Brescia and the textile system in Lombardy, etc. (Bertini, 1994).

The evolutionary view is also strengthened by contributions of the neo-institutionalist and systems theory schools for the analysis of endogenous development processes.

The neo-institutionalist approach is significant, not only because of Williamson (Williamson, 1975)—who had considerable success in the 80s and is well known for his theoretical analysis of trade-off: uncertainty-transaction costs—but within the dynamic vision that renders institutions endogenous to the development process and, at the same time, emphasises their role in promoting economic development. (North, 1990). Along this train of thought, greater importance was given to intermediate institutions operating on the local level and to associative entities, even in a context of inefficient macro-institutions, like in Italy. They had a decisive role in the development of local SME systems. In the same way, the analysis of local systems becomes important, not so much for its organisation of production but for its accumulation and diffusion of know-how (Lundvall, 1992).

The systems theory supplies a variety of instruments to explain the evolution of local SME systems, and provides key insights into a variety of questions (decline-success, concentration-fragmentation, selection-multiplication, start-up-failure, opening-closing, cost strategies-innovation strategies, etc.) that have been raised by competitive pressure and in relation to their capacity to incorporate (even, at times, generate) innovations (Bianchi and Miller, 1993).

The various developments, converging in the evolutionary view, have allowed the central strength of a local SME system to be identified less as a specific organisational form of the enterprise network, whose nature can change over time, but as the patrimony of knowledge spread throughout the geographical location. The geographical location represents the space in which innovations can be continually inserted to develop their particular advantages for the market. The accumulated know-how is a kind of public good at the disposal of individual initiatives that are generated within the system. This facilitates the specialisation and success of enterprises.

This evolutionary view has established itself very slowly in Italy. And this has been an obstacle to what can be seen as the lessons of the Italian experience that may be replicated elsewhere.

The variety of productive systems

It is useful to increase awareness of the variety of situations that have been produced by the spontaneous development of local small enterprises and to describe the differences, in qualitative terms, that exist in Italy. Indeed, the Northwest, the South and especially along the Adriatic coast seem to be following the "Third Italy" model. 199 industrial districts have been identified by ISTAT (1995), which employ 42,5% of manufacturing employees (Table 4.1).

Table 4.1   Industrial districts in Italy by location

	Number of industrial districts	Employment (thousands)	Share of manufacturing employment
Northwest	59	922	44.0
Northeast	65	836	60.6
Centre	60	406	43.7
South	15	59	7.2
ITALY	199	2,223	42.5

Source: ISTAT

However, structurally industrial districts have several different features.

First, it should not be forgotten that the regions in which the small enterprises were found are not homogeneous. In some areas, large plants in the chemical, metallurgic, or large scale manufacturing owned by the State, or large Italian or foreign firms, dominate the local economy, even though many of them are in difficulty: e. g. the northern coast of Tuscany, the central northern coast of Emilia-Romagna, and the area around Venice and Trieste; and in other cases, they share the same areas as the small enterprises, for example FIAT and state-owned manufacturing plants in Emilia-Romagna, Tuscany, Lombardy, and Veneto.

At the same time, many other areas of the Third Italy have not managed to participate in the phenomenon of SME development and have declined: northwestern and southern Tuscany, **Polesine,**[1] the hills of Veneto, large tracts of Umbria, the eastern part of Friuli, etc.

Second, the local production systems should be considered by their different sizes (Table 4.2). There are mega-districts, like Prato, that substantially **cover** an entire province, such as Carpi, Sassuolo, Empoli, Vicenza, Como, Biella, Castelgoffredo, Montebelluna, Pesaro, Civitanova Marche. There are also local areas of specialisation, that for various reasons, do not expand beyond a certain size, even though it is clearly a case of a specialisation dominating the communities where they are found. There are no specific criteria for defining the dimensions of a productive system that qualifies it as an industrial district, and it would be extremely complicated to identify these criteria; this explains why various studies on industrial districts in Italy have always yielded different results.

The reasons why these systems do not expand may be:
a) the size of the markets they work for;
b) the physical limits to expansion of the local environment and the difficulty in transferring technical and entrepreneurial resources outside the district.

Very often these SME groups operate in such specific market niches that they cannot be expanded beyond certain levels of production capacity, at least, until they can start processes of production diversification. The case of Lumezzane, in Lombardy, on the contrary, is an example of a medium sized district where the logistic and residential infrastructure are no longer capable of containing the local phenomenon of new start-ups. Whereas the case of Grottaglie in Apulia is an example of a district that did not come into being because of social obstacles in the local environment. However, in Italy, it is possible to identify a very large number of small local areas with 30 to 50 small enterprises involved in the same production process, created by endogenous phenomena but nevertheless not considered districts.

Table 4.2   Some important industrial districts in Italy

Location	Region	Sector	Enterprises	Employees
Prato	Tuscany	Textiles (wool)	11,000	45,000
Carpi	Emilia-Rom.	Knitwear	2,600	13,000
Sassuolo	Emilia-Rom.	Ceramic tiles	250	22,000
Biella	Piedmont	Textiles (wool)	2,300	29,000
Como	Lombardy	Textiles (silk)	1,800	17,000
Civitanova	Marche	Footwear	2,400	24,000
Pesaro	Marche	Furniture	1,000	10,000
Cerea	Veneto	Furniture	3,000	15,000
Santa Croce	Tuscany	Leather	900	10,000
Montebelluna	Veneto	Sport footwear	700	8,500
Carrara	Tuscany	Marble	1,200	9,000

Source: Sole 24 Ore "Gioielli, Bambole, Coltelli" (1992)

Third, the different organisational forms and relations among enterprises should be considered. In this regard there is great variety. In simplified terms, there are the following cases (Figure 4.1):

Figure 4.1   Some examples of local production systems

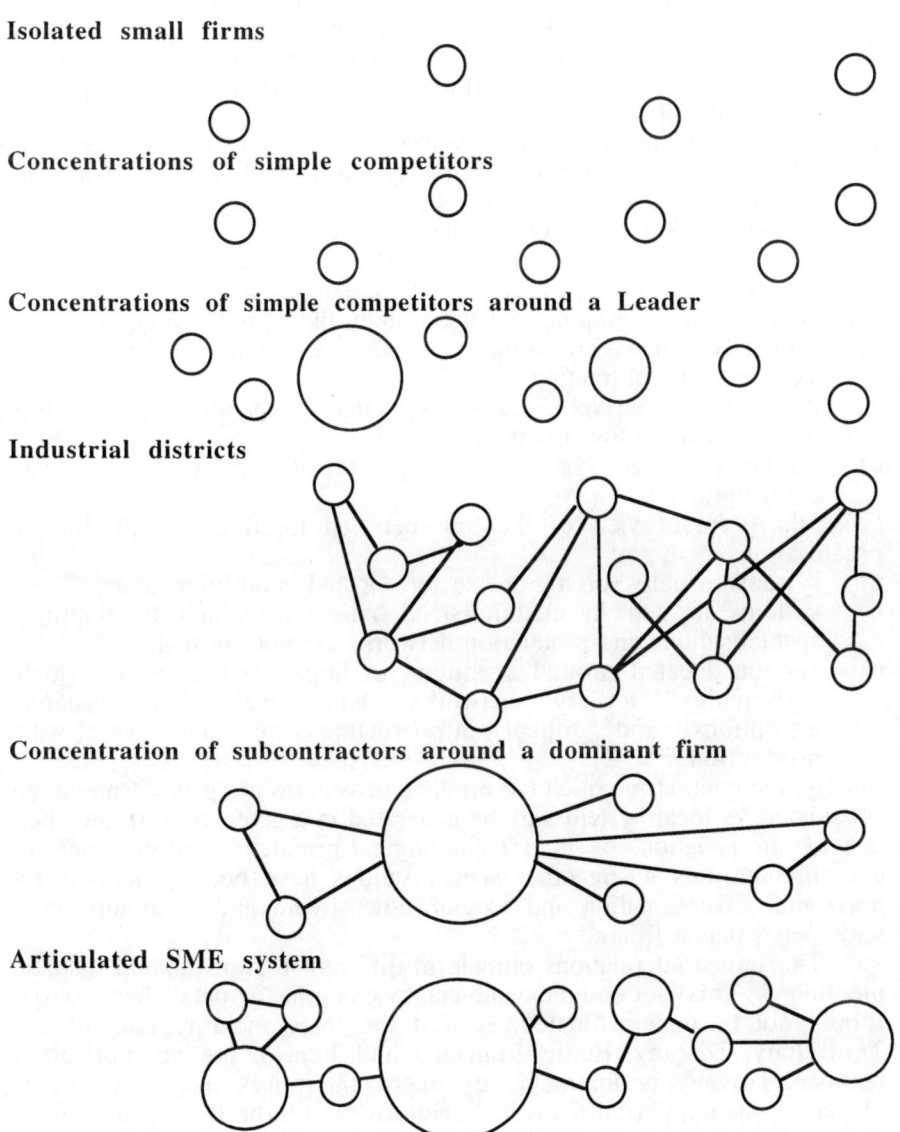

Isolated small firms

Concentrations of simple competitors

Concentrations of simple competitors around a Leader

Industrial districts

Concentration of subcontractors around a dominant firm

Articulated SME system

a) isolated small enterprises loosely linked together;
b) systems in which small enterprises have very few reciprocal relationships and compete for the same markets and for the same local production factors (craft systems, systems operating in sectors with low economies of scale);
c) similar systems based on small competing independent enterprises, but with one or several leading enterprises;
d) systems where there are small enterprises with intense co-operative and competitive relations (this is the most common type of industrial district);
e) systems of sub-contractors centred on one or more companies which control the subcontracting system and all contacts with the market;
f) systems with dynamic oligopolies of medium-sized enterprises that operate in the same sector, but in different segments and niches.

From the point of view of the model of market openness, which may be dependent on the development of the system, there are three types:

a) primarily "passive" systems which are highly dependent on external sub-contracting;
b) primarily "active" systems that operate production decentralisation towards the outside;
c) primarily closed systems, that operate principally in the local environment.

From the point of view of the link between location and productive organisation, there are:

a) systems, usually serving one sector, located in outlying areas;
b) systems located in medium sized cities, in which overlapping specialisations and production networks are not unusual;
c) systems located around medium- to large-sized cities, in which high-quality tertiary networks, educational and research institutions, and critical infrastructure are interwoven with production.

Finally, the context in which the productive systems are placed should be considered. A local system may be generated in a given context and then develop in isolation, or in a technological-productive cluster, rich in complimentarities where other specialisations have been generated by horizontal diversification and extend downstream and upstream on a wider basis than a filière.[2]

The industrial relations climate in different regions should also be mentioned. This is a complex subject to examine in detail here, but it should not be underestimated, even if the three main regions of the Third Italy, Tuscany, Emilia-Romagna and Veneto, are very different realities. Tuscany is dominated by micro enterprises, a greater role is played by medium sized firms in Veneto, while Emilia-Romagna is in an intermediate position, even if it has a higher gross industrial product per worker.

The different industrial relations models have considerable

structural effects. If workers are poorly organised, medium-sized firms operating in traditional, low value added sectors, will tend to seek efficiency and cost reduction through less favourable work contracts, extreme decentralisation towards scarcely qualified suppliers, tax evasion, etc. Sometimes, when trade unions are more powerful, enterprises may have incentives to innovate and to increase their added value; this favours specialisation and long-term competitiveness.

In brief, there is great variety among the Italian areas, in which the interaction of market and local forces have brought about endogenous development. These situations were not foreseen and can only be partly explained in retrospect. It follows that there is no sense in having a specific organisational model as the objective in the planning of local projects for development and innovation. The important thing is to create the right conditions for a variety of enterprise models, for their reproduction, growth and networking, and for establishing innovative mechanisms which can avoid the deterioration of working conditions. What can be learnt from the experience of the most advanced Italian regions? How have these favourable conditions been created? And what are the obstacles that hinder their complete realisation?

The development process of Italian SME local systems

The development of Italian SME systems in the post-war period can be seen as a paradigm for the general development process of SME systems. This paradigm is outlined below.

The origin of the systems

The development of SMEs, beginning in the fifties, originated from two kinds of human resources: those found in "old" state enterprises in crisis and those found in traditional local crafts that had improved their operating structures due to the development of more open and competitive markets.

Internal demand, linked to post-war re-construction and to the continual creation of new consumers (the exodus from the countryside), created favourable market conditions. However, the development of the small enterprise remained in the background for at least two decades because the rapid increase in demand allowed numerous Fordist integrated enterprises to reassert themselves. In the seventies, small enterprises managed to liberate themselves from their niche roles when the oil crisis and labour conflict increased costs for large enterprises, forcing them to decentralise part of production to subcontractors in order to reduce costs. At the same time, forms of de-structured production organisation seemed to be much more competitive than integrated enterprises, especially in increasingly differentiated and unstable markets.

Besides historical events that accelerated certain phenomena, the growth of SME systems followed similar historical paths, even if the history of each district is unique.

The phase of expansion

Normally, at the beginning, SMEs could sell their products outside local markets thanks to price advantages. If other advantages existed, they were usually part of the local context: quality of local raw materials, the nature of the product, technical-craft traditions, advantages of local demand.

In this first phase, the price advantage tended to increase over time in parallel with the development of the systems. This initial advantage created market opportunities; new local enterprises attempted to seize these opportunities by entering the market; other enterprises by becoming suppliers; the area became a reference point for many customers and suppliers. The main mechanisms that contributed to increasing the price advantages of SME systems were:

- growing local rivalries that forced the enterprises to look for continuous increases in productivity and efficiency in order to survive in their local environment, thereby making them competitive, even outside the system;
- the growing presence of suppliers and subcontractors in the surrounding area, making it possible to organise differentiated production cycles with minimal investment and limited adaptation costs;
- unplanned common advantages connected to local agglomerations of both customers and suppliers. In these cases, there is both a reduction in costs and in the uncertainty of access to the final market and to raw materials.

All these mechanisms together began a virtuous cycle for a certain period. How quickly systems acquired competitive advantages and grew depended on the characteristics of the final market to a great extent. Domestic demand greatly accelerated the processes of growth in competitive local systems. If there were not excessive obstacles and restrictions to setting up new enterprises, constant demand growth would quickly set the mechanisms described above in motion. The industrialisation of regions such as Tuscany, Veneto and Marche occurred much more quickly than in Northwest Italy or other European countries industrialised earlier.

Towards consolidation

Once the system achieved an important position in the market, its ability to compete in terms of flexibility and price decreased; the mechanisms of the virtuous cycle were blocked. This situation came about as a result of both internal and external dynamics. With the increase in the added value produced and distributed by the system, local inflation took hold, causing an increase in prices and pressure on salaries. The tendency towards price increases (especially in housing) was paralleled by a rise in local income and wealth. Growing flows of commuters and businessmen and even migratory pressure characterised this stage. The pressure of increased pay, as well as labour costs, thanks to the favourable conditions existing in the labour market, depended on the strong demand for labour, especially technicians.

The reduction in price advantage was also caused by two external factors: on the one hand, new competitors, often located in developing countries, with very low production costs, reduced the price advantage of the systems; on the other hand, traditionally more structured enterprises tried to re-organise themselves through product, process and organisational innovations. In this way they tried to make up for their disadvantages in terms of flexibility and, at the same time, reinforced their typical advantages: image, marketing, organisational ability, existing distribution channels, and post-sale assistance.

Therefore, several factors have forced the "mature" systems to increase the range of competitive advantages available to themselves. The ability to develop these competitive factors endogenously is not always generated automatically. In this sense, the spontaneous development of SME systems works in the opposite direction. On the one hand, there is the phenomenon of the accumulation of technical and marketing know-how, that obviously acts in favour of increasing specialisation and non-price competitiveness; on the other hand, there is resistance to some productive organisational patterns and reciprocal relationships; these are ingrained characteristics of the local social structure and culture and, therefore, possess greater inertia, which makes the transformations called for by market trends difficult to introduce. Often the traditional collective advantages that exist in industrial districts can "benefit" so many enterprises that they delay their adjustment. In the same way, excess of imitation and sharing of information can discourage investments in innovation by the more dynamic firms.

What can accelerate the structural adjustment of a SME system to "non price" and durable competitive advantages? Some factors can be mentioned:
- the presence of a leading local enterprise that guides entrepreneurial development and indirectly dictates what strategic behaviour should be followed;
- the presence on the territory of qualified human resources, connected to advanced technical schools, universities, various kinds of tertiary networks; or the presence of highly technological foreign enterprises;
- the connection of the local system with other productive systems linked to the same technological cluster;
- the activation of appropriate industrial policies at the local level.

The most successful local systems were affected by the following structural phenomena (Table 4.3):

- the average size of firms has increased, from small to medium size, because the enterprises had to adopt new technologies and equip themselves with organisational and technological knowledge;
- the human resources employed moved towards medium-high quality levels;
- the mechanism of local price competition has been increasingly substituted by monopolistic competition, based on product differentiation;
- the systems increased the number of complementary activities, especially in the sectors connected upstream and downstream (specialised engineering producers, specialised services, intermediate and complementary goods), perhaps through foreign investment;
- sub-contracting and productive decentralisation networks have gone beyond the local level, to other Italian regions or abroad;
- the level of local industrial concentration has increased through mergers and take-overs;
- the presence of foreign capital has increased, especially in leading local enterprises or specialised niche enterprises (this has occurred particularly in cases of a limited managerial capacity for globalisation).

It is clear that the typical local industrial district has become a very different and more complicated system in successful cases. The development of the system had the effect of a catalyst for entrepreneurship and institutional networks, thereby creating an extremely favourable environment for growth. The persistence of a productive system with rigidly local characteristics can no longer be justified on the basis of the production networks alone, but rather as a territorial nucleus of specialised know-how. Indeed the production networks have to become more and more innovative in order to maintain their centrality.

Obviously, the systems that are unable to produce winning structural adjustment mechanisms tend to decline and only survive if the demand remains stable or grows. However, if competitive conditions lead to price-wars and to technological lag, then the enterprises tend to downsize and sometimes even disappear.

The capacity of local systems to adjust successfully depends on local public and social institutions. But does the state play a role? The state can increase this capacity by improving the quality of national externalities: macroeconomic stability, bureaucratic efficiency, through the financial system and research institutions. The weaker these externalities are, the more local systems remain isolated and the extent of structural adjustment capacity will be limited. In the Italian case, national externalities have been of little help for the modernisation of local systems.

Table 4.3   The development phases of systems

PHASES	PHENOMENA
Starting point	A closed and static economy or one that is dependent on central government decisions. The presence of craft shops and local rural activities, and perhaps, one or more plants built with bank- or state-financed capital.
The opening up of the system	The system has the opportunity to exploit new markets and growing demand, but it is subject to greater external competition. There is a selection process that eliminates non-competitive enterprises and activities, often starting with the large enterprises. There is the risk that some fundamental technical know-how will disappear. If the system is not capable of offering at least one competitive specialisation, it risks being marginalised. The possibility of initiating a process of growth depends on the capacity to react to market forces and social cohesion.
Expansion phase	More competitive activities have the opportunity to grow and start to develop both through imitative processes and complementary integration. Production networks and rivalry increase as does the competitiveness of prices. Common advantages become more concrete and spontaneous collective initiatives (associations) are established in order to support individual needs. Basic infrastructure is created.
Maturity of the system	The system's capacity to compete in terms of price-flexibility is reduced and it has to develop non-price competitive advantages. Creative catalysts for strategic information are needed in the territory to develop and attract qualified human resources. If the system develops the characteristics to overcome these obstacles and is not completely overwhelmed by external events, then it will head towards further consolidation. If it succeeds, then it can count on the persistence of favourable demand conditions, otherwise it will head towards a phase of decline.
Decline of the system	Enterprises enter price-wars. The working conditions get worse and a tough selection process among the enterprises begins. The production apparatus is downsized and salaries are reduced. If the system survives, it will be made up of marginal enterprises. The sub-contracting network must attempt to diversify purchasers, highlighting the subordination of the area.
Consolidation	The system is increasingly oriented towards high added value activities and innovative content. The quality and wages of human resources increases. The local technical know-how becomes increasingly sophisticated. Complementary activities are set up in the local context. The infrastructure efficiency increases. Innovation is developed.

The enterprises become bigger, growing from small to medium size, reconciling the need for flexibility and the capacity to manage some strategic functions.
The system increasingly opens up through subcontracting low added value activities and strategic and technological collaboration.

The Italian lessons for development policies

In the light of local experiences and the experience of Italian development as a whole, we can attempt to reconstruct the conditions and mechanisms that have led to the formation of local competitive SME systems in Italy. In this way, we can extract a methodology for development policy in disadvantaged regions and countries.

The relevance of the Italian example, at least in the most successful areas, lies in the combination of rapid growth and high competitiveness with social and territorial balance, i.e. wealth accumulation and broad social participation in the growth process.

How was it possible to establish a process of local competitive development led by small and medium sized enterprises? Four main sets of conditions must be present for this result: the opening and liberalisation of the market, the support of demand, the territorial resources, and economic democracy.

The opening and liberalisation of the market

The opening of the market is a fundamental condition for initiating a process for improved competitiveness. Opening means the expansion of the market which, in turn, favours increased productivity, competitiveness and specialisation processes. The opening up of the market can be the result of the removal of different types of commercial barriers, especially institutional barriers (customs and tariffs, quality standards, quantitative quotas and authorisation) and infrastructure barriers (transport, telecommunications and information networks).

It is difficult to initiate the process that leads to the growth of production activities and the search for efficiency and specialisation, without opportunities to expand the market and without facing the risk of being attacked in one's own local market. The opening and liberalisation of the market needs to be managed with caution and gradualness, in order to avoid lowered expectations (opening seen as a threat). Its impact could destroy the system's productive, technological and social foundations.

The support of demand

Alongside the liberalisation and gradual opening up of markets, it is also necessary to create positive demand expectations in order to encourage the development of SMEs. The small entrepreneur is highly exposed/adverse to risk and positive demand expectations can contribute considerably to lowering their inhibitions, even compared to sophisticated financial evaluations. In addition, the prospect of increased demand can minimise financial obstacles in starting up enterprises: in part because it becomes easier to obtain loans from the credit system or from private sources, and in part because enterprises expect to be able to finance themselves through profits from sales. For this reason, they are able to obtain extensions on payment for raw materials and machinery from the suppliers.

The international financial organisms should rethink the monetary stabilisation policies imposed on developing countries. Is there any sense in zero inflation and a balanced budget in countries with a great need of growth?

This does not imply abandoning the objective of macro-economic stability in the long run; but it should be considered that emphasising this objective in the short run, without a sufficiently stable and competitive production system, can destroy the existing basis of production. It is unthinkable for a small entrepreneur to launch himself into the market spontaneously. In developing countries, "incentives" for demand need to be created by prudent Keynesian policies (based on public works or careful support given to private demand) or foreign investments that are capable of activating local supplier networks.

The resources of the territory

The presence of sound local resources, technical know-how, commercial and entrepreneurial ability, is fundamental because the opening up of the market does not only lead to a selection process among local enterprises and the decline of production in more developed areas. When faced with the opening up of the market, communities without market traditions, entrepreneurial spirit and accumulated technical know-how, risk being marginalised, resulting in high unemployment, reduction of purchasing power and emigration. Knowledge is the basis for the development of the production system; it can derive from traditional local production processes and from production plants established in the area by foreign, public, or local capital.

In the absence of these conditions, it is necessary to rapidly activate initiatives for the diffusion of new capabilities and for improving the existing ones. Building technical schools and other training initiatives often has a decisive impact on local economic development, especially when they are compatible with the vocations and characteristics of the area.

This also demonstrates that privatisation processes in transitional countries, and in many other contexts, should be an opportunity not only for selling companies, but also to generate new entrepreneurship, by dividing these companies into business units and activating networks of subcontractors and suppliers.

Economic democracy

Even in the case in which an area, faced with the challenge of the opening of the market, finds a successful response, there is no guarantee that the development process will involve a large number of entrepreneurs and affect the entire community, rather than the establishment of one or a few large integrated plants. In social and institutional contexts where the conditions for appropriating production factors (capital and loans, locations, human resources, technology, market information) are extremely selective, and it is much more probable that large integrated enterprises develop.

For the development of SME systems first of all, real democracy (that includes education levels, income distribution, legality) is necessary. In addition, there must be social institutions that lower the entrance barriers for new enterprises, generate a climate of trust and make the participation in the growth process democratic. In the case of the Central and Northern Italy, local administrations, business associations, old Chambers of Commerce and local co-operative banks, and local technical schools all have contributed greatly to lowering the entrance barriers for new enterprises.

A climate of trust is necessary for small enterprises to be created. Trust should be understood in two senses: both relations between enterprises and institutions and reciprocal relations between the enterprises.

Trust in the institutions is necessary in order to convince enterprises to abandon the informal sector and register themselves publicly as a legal entities. If the small entrepreneur operating in the informal sector whose sole aim is survival believes that the public registration of his/her firm will only expose it to taxation and restrictive rules, he/she will reluctantly change his/her opinion. If, however, public registration gives the entrepreneur access to financial services, help with taxes and bureaucratic regulations, an opportunity for well equipped locations for his/her enterprise and political protection, then he/she may decide to register. In this way, he/she gains legal protection, may offer guarantees to clients and suppliers, and develop more sophisticated relationships; the enterprise is given a opportunity to grow. Associations of entrepreneurs (especially micro-entrepreneurs), Chambers of Commerce, and local administrations have played a crucial role in ensuring this in Italy.

Institutional recognition fosters reciprocal trust between the enterprises. In the Italian experience, there are numerous cases of small enterprises that have come into being as a result of the suppliers' trust in the enterprises, by extending payments, or clients that have paid in advance so as to allow the first investments to be made in the new enterprise. In this way, the enterprises manage to overcome the shortcomings of the banking system. Reciprocal trust does not only involve relations among individuals, but it also involves the surrounding environment. An individual will trust another to behave properly, if he is certain that the environment in which these actions are carried out is ready to sanction those who do not respect the ground rules. At the same time, it is necessary to have an efficient and cheap judicial system so as to guarantee that the person who has been "wronged" can be quickly compensated. Social control of improper behaviour only exists in places where there is a civic tradition and a deep-rooted market, that has led to the acceptance of common rules to control relations among individuals. Even in this case associations are important: being a member of an association reinforces following of the rules so as avoid being ostracised. Where this does not exist and social relations are predominantly hierarchical, it is difficult that a system of SME will be developed in the short term.

Governments, especially in developing countries, should force local administrations to have a co-operative attitude towards enterprises, favour the development of direct contact between intermediate levels and entrepreneurial associations under their jurisdiction, to be aware of their problems and motivated (even for political reasons) to supply answers and solutions.

Local authorities must have the capacity to be a catalyst for other institutions and spontaneous associations, by connecting them in networks and performing their specific roles and competencies in a way to compliment and foster the local development process. This leadership role is indispensable in order to avoid uncoordinated efforts, encourage co-operation, respond to policies and offer services. The development of institutional complementarity leads to productive complementarity, thereby bringing together different types of enterprises and making the entire social environment cohesive. In the absence of an effective bottom-up policy, democratic development of small enterprises cannot take place, instead development will be led by social élites, financial groups or public investments.

The advantages of development through SMEs

When the process of local development through small enterprises is initiated, in the form of a complex system of enterprises, there are a number of advantages with respect to other social and economical models led by larger enterprises.

First of all, once the mechanism is activated, a system of small enterprises can lead to development more quickly than a system based on large enterprises and high capital investments. In a small enterprise system, emulation, imitation or product complementing processes are activated; therefore, if there are favourable market prospects, rapid industrialisation processes can occur.

Secondly, a system of small enterprises encourages the exchange of information, as it is exposed to selective phenomena determined by market competition, but at the same time, it is very open to the entrance of new enterprises. Once a compact network of local relations has been formed, the entrance barriers are lowered: entrepreneurs can enter the system with limited capital since they can participate in activity connected upstream and downstream with other complementary activities. This reduces the uncertainty and the necessity for vertical integration. The risk factor is also quite limited as it is clear what has to be done, how to do it and who to sell the product to. These conditions do not exist for enterprises operating outside the system, indeed, where the entry barriers and the necessity for vertical integration are much higher.

Thirdly, a system of small enterprises increases the collective desire to develop, including workers. Even if excessively individual management styles in small firms may lead to cases of resistance, there are not rigid relations of conflict between management and workers or dependence on decisions from above, that is typical in areas dominated by large enterprises. Instead development becomes a common interest for entrepreneurs, workers and civil institutions.

The limits of SMEs

Alongside these strengths and advantages, there are also weaknesses and disadvantages in SME systems. In particular, there may be:
- Slowness in penetrating foreign markets because of significant shortages of critical resources (managerial, technical and financial) of each small enterprise at the individual level;
- Difficulties in establishing relationships with banks, local authorities, markets and technology sources;

How can these limits be overcome? In the Italian experience, there have been three principal ways to deal with these problems:
1. Developing collective functions in areas in which small enterprises cannot create them individually due to their size;
2. Developing complementary networks between small enterprises, in other words, sharing the tasks within the same sector and production cycle and reducing the probability for fratricidal wars.
3. distributing critical information outside of informal channels.

Very particular conditions to enable these three mechanisms to function are needed. The fact that they were present in Central and Northern Italy during the development of the local systems, does not mean that they should be taken for granted. A climate of trust is necessary to encourage enterprises to enter the market and then co-operate with each other.

A lack of trust, accentuated by the problems of poverty, the certainty of rights and institutional efficiency makes it impossible for enterprises to institutionalise, co-operate with each other and with the large enterprises, and to specialise. In this case, small enterprises end up being marginal social actors that are tolerated only because they reduce the social impact of unemployment and poverty.

In short, the following outcomes should be borne in mind:

a)   the impact of opening up may lead to the economic and productive decline of areas poor in sound resources, knowledge and infrastructure;

b)   in contexts in which the appropriability of productive factors is not democratic, development and opening up the market will probably lead to a few highly integrated large enterprises or to an élite of small entrepreneurs;

c)   if there is a lack of democratic institutions and trust, it is probable that small enterprises will not be motivated to abandon the informal sector;

d)   even in cases where the opening up of the market encourages different kinds of small enterprises, it does not necessarily mean that there will be a democratic outcome which involves the entire local community.

Conclusion

The contents of this chapter lead to the conclusion that there are no ideal forms of social organisation nor of industrialisation model. Local spontaneous development depends on the capacity of local forces and institutions to confront an open economic context and to spontaneously generate autonomous and endogenous development. But the forms that this process takes on are not predetermined and depend on the capacity of the local environment to respond to the continually changing external stimuli and to adjust, when necessary, through its own internal regulatory mechanisms.

A few crucial elements in the process should be highlighted.

Firstly, there is the role of the market. The market has the function of providing opportunities for free expression of local forces, and stimulating the search for efficiency and specialisation. Naturally the process of opening up competition is extremely delicate and should be faced with caution to avoid processes destructive to the production system and to allow the local environment to prepare itself.

Secondly, there is the role of macroeconomic policy. Macroeconomic policy should have the function of guiding the process of opening the market. Initially they should avoid establishing highly restrictive demand side conditions, instead they should try to provide opportunities for growth and gradual specialisation. Only in a later stage should policy try to stabilise inflation, thereby adapting the system to open competition based on non-price advantages.

Lastly, there is the role of the territory. The territory is fundamental as the place where the values that force local individuals to conform to certain behaviours and regulations are formed, and where collective economies and public goods are available. The territory must contribute to creating relations between the enterprises, based on trust, both in the phases of price and non-price competition.

At this point, some guidelines for local policy can be inferred. A long list of alternative local policies could be made, based on numerous well-known techniques. However, it is important that they all are directed to growth in an open context and therefore foster development.

The objectives of accumulation of technical know-how (with increasingly innovative characteristics) and of adjusting the competitive response of SME to the market should be given priority. These two objectives must be pursued at the same time. Excessive emphasis on the accumulation of knowledge without paying attention to competition can generate the inappropriate use or immigration of the best qualified human resources. While solely focusing on its competitive response can push the system towards behaviours that are only aimed at the reduction of production costs.

A final observation concerns the problem of the transferability of the Italian model to other contexts, especially developing and transitional countries. We have shown that an endogenous model of industrial organisation cannot be transferred as a whole; only a few of the features that have been generated by the model can be applied to other situations.

The following principle steps can be outlined (Tab. 4.4). The first level: the introduction and fostering of a regulatory, legal and moral context that increases trust and facilitates exchange between individuals, enterprises, and the management. The gradual opening up of a local system and its regional integration. The second level: action to promote the private sector, consisting in creating basic infrastructure, offering legal and administrative services to set up enterprises, privatisation of large complexes to form micro-units, promoting the development of suppliers, eliminating every obstacle to individuals who want to become entrepreneurs (as long as they do not harm the interests of the community) and promoting associations. The third level: action aimed at strengthening enterprises, extending markets and increasing competitiveness, by facilitating the promotion of products, contact with clients and possible partners, the introduction of more modern technology, provision of services and marketing advice, the improvement of management quality and technique, training for medium and high level human resources in management, design and planning, and the promotion of joint-ventures with foreign enterprises and local networks.

All these actions put together are fundamental for a vast private sector of small and medium sized enterprises, yet in each country a different industrialisation model could emerge with different economic performance.

Table 4.4 An outline of the various aspects

	Closed Marginal Economy	The phase of opening up	Consolidation of the global market
Marco-economic context	Stable macro-economics variables Under-employment	High rate of growth Risk of inflation Risk of an increase of interest rates Public borrowing	Low rate of growth Increasing openness
National economic policies	Protection policies with a tendency to autarchy	Reinforcement of the legal and regulatory system Policies of employment stabilisation Fiscal incentives to promote investment	Monetary stabilisation Reduction of inflationary factors
National institutions	Institutions dependent on central government aimed at controlling the static situation (bureaucracy)	Large entities for research, foreign commerce, etc	Necessity of reform
Competitive context for local economies	Low competitive pressure	The opening up of local markets, increases in competitiveness	Global competition
Destination markets	Local and regional markets for SMEs Import-substitution for large plants	National market Beginnings of export activity	Foreign markets
Behaviour of the enterprises	Enterprises with little motivation towards growth, specialisation and innovation	Research into market opportunities Specialisation High rate of generating enterprises Rivalry and suppliers at the local level	High rate of specialisation Differentiation and international standards High tendency towards export Formalised relations International de-centralisation

Local institutions	Local institutions not very important	Spontaneous development of local institutions	Development of leaders and catalysts Centrality of territorial measures
Local policies	Social balance and protection of corporations	Facilitation of private initiatives Creation of promotional consortiums Basic infrastructure built	Initiatives for innovation and human resources; Measures for the accumulation, transmission and improvement of the quality of technical knowledge
Possible results	De specialisation Low degree of innovation	Formation of SME systems in terms of districts or network enterprises	Competitive clusters of medium sized enterprises
Local productive typology	Large public and private plants that are not subject to much social control De-specialised craftsmanship Rural activity	Small enterprises Sector specialisation Interrelations among enterprises	Medium sized enterprises Technological development of the filière at the international level

Notes

1 Polesine is the area along the Po river in Emilia-Romagna and Veneto.
2 Examples of such clusters can be: the agricultural-industrial cluster in Emilia-Romagna, including agriculture, breeding, milk, meat, wine, pasta, machines for agriculture and food industries, machines for food packaging, food containers, etc.; the metallurgical cluster in Lombardy, metallurgy, various intermediate and final metal products, electric materials and appliances, machines for metal working and machine tools.

References

Bagnasco A. (1977), *Tre Italie. La problematica territoriale dello sviluppo italiano*, Bologna, Il Mulino.
Bagnasco A. and Trigilia C. (1984), (eds), *Società e politica nelle aree di piccola impresa*, Venezia, Arsenale.
Becattini G. (1979), 'Dal settore industriale al distretto industriale. Alcune considerazioni sull'unità di indagine in economia industriale', in *Economia e Politica*

Industriale, n.1.

Becattini G. (1987), *Mercato e forze locali: il distretto industriale*, Bologna, Il Mulino.

Belussi F. (1992), (ed.) *Nuovi modelli di impresa, gerarchie organizzative ed imprese rete*, Milano, Angeli.

Bertini S. (1994), *SME systems and territorial development in Italy*, Bologna, Laboratorio di Politica Industriale.

Bertini S. (1995), *SMEs in the evolution of the Italian and Indian industrial systems*, Nomisma-UNIDO.

Bianchi P. and Miller L. (1993), *Collective action, strategic behavior and endogenous growth*, mimeo, Bologna, Nomisma.

Brusco S. (1989), *Piccola impresa e distretti industriali*, Turin, Rosenberg & Sellier.

Cossentino F., Pyke F., and Sengenberger W. (1996), (eds.) *Local and Regional Responses to global Pressure: the case of Italy and its industrial districts*, Geneva, ILO.

Crestanello P. (1992), The changes in 10 Industrial Districts during the Eighties: a proposal of analysis, paper presented at the Artimino conference on "Industrial district", 15th September.

Fuà G., Zacchia C. (1983), *Industrializzazione senza fratture*, Bologna, Il Mulino.

Harrison B. (1994), *Lean and mean. The changing landscape of corporate power in the age of flexibility*, New York, Basic Books.

Hirschmann A.O. (1958), *The strategy of economic development*, New Heaven, Yale University Press.

Humphrey J. and Schmitz H. (1995), *Principles for promoting clusters and networks of SMEs*, Vienna, UNIDO.

ISTAT (1995), Istituto Centrale di Statistica, *"La situazione del Paese"*, Rome.

Laboratorio di Politica Industriale (1989), Ristrutturazione industriale e piccole imprese, Bologna.

Levitsky J. (1996), *Support systems for SMEs in developing countries. A review*, Vienna, UNIDO.

Lundvall B. (1992), (ed.) *National Systems of Innovation*, London, Pinter.

Meyer-Stamer J. (1995), Governance in the post import substitution era: Perspectives for new approaches for creating systemic competitiveness in Brazil, Institute for Development Studies, Sussex University.

Nomisma (1991), *Rapporto sull'industria italiana 1991*, Bologna, Il Mulino.

Nomisma (1993), *Rapporto sull'industria italiana 1993*, Bologna, Il Mulino.

North D. (1990), *Institutions, Institutional change and economic performance*, Cambridge, Cambridge University Press.

Ouchi W.G. (1980), 'Markets, Bureaucracies and Clans', in *Administrative Science Quarterly* n.2.

Porter M.E. (1990), *The competitive advantage of nations*, New York, Free Press.

Sabel C.H., Piore M. (1984), *Second Industrial Divide. Possibilities for prosperity*, New York, Basic Books.

Scott A., Storper M. (1992), *Pathways to industrialization and regional development*, London, Routledge.

Streeten P. (1996), Globalisation and competitiveness: what are the implications for development thinking and practice?, mimeo, Washington University.

Tendler J., Alves Amorim M. (1996), 'Small firms and their helpers: lessons on demand', in *World Development* n. 3.

Williamson O.E. (1975), *Markets and Hierarchies*, New York, The Free Press.

5 Policies for the development of knowledge-intensive local production systems

FIORENZA BELUSSI

Introduction

For many years now experts in Italy have focused their attention on the increasing importance of industrial districts and local production systems in the performance of regional economies. This can be demonstrated by numerous studies conducted on the development of industrial districts. In Italy there is a vast range of literature on this argument,[1] as well as on the topic of local production networks.[2] Growing attention has been given to the phenomenon of spatial agglomeration,[3] and to the correlated intensification of innovative activities.[4]

These analyses of local production systems have shown that there is great diversity among these systems in terms of morphology (with greater or lesser concentration of industrial structures), levels of competitiveness, innovative capabilities, and above all evolutionary tendencies. Moreover institutional, cultural and social factors have been highlighted as contributing to the generation and consolidation of these structures.

This chapter intends to focus on the importance of industrial policies in supporting the local production system within the "spontaneous" effects of the market. Its aim is to propose a conceptual framework for the formulation of public policies that stresses the importance of collective learning. This is the local "value" of industrial policies which favour the adoption of innovation and the intensification of technological learning. Here the success of Italian industrial districts and local production systems is explained as a market-driven process of cumulative growth, which is loosely connected to direct industrial policies. However, the performance of the Italian model is explained in a conceptual framework where the institutions play an important role in channelling markets and supporting the positive strategies of the firms (co-operation, technology adoption, and collective learning). The Italian case provides numerous examples and, from them, a prescriptive framework can be deduced.

A partially spontaneous market driven process of collective learning

The Italian local production systems can be viewed as experimental laboratories where the so-called spontaneous working of the market is channelled, limited and/or promoted by the role of institutions, here identified as collective actors which can provide economically valuable public goods, or establish institutional models, rules, and regulations that allow a certain type of interaction among the agents operating in the local context (mainly co-operative behaviour). So, pure market outcomes are regulated by extra-economic factors.

However, the genesis of local production systems does not derive from authoritative "policy". The main concern here is that the mechanism of start-up and growth must be evaluated on the grounds of the mobilisation of "local" knowledge and collective learning, where local policies, generally speaking, have only played an important—but not an exclusive —role.

Some characteristics of the diffusion of technical change and know-how within local production systems, can clarify how growth could have taken place as an endogenous mechanism. Empirical studies indicate many factors that have contributed to the consolidation of local production systems.

Firstly, the sunk nature of the knowledge of the agents (workers and entrepreneurs) operating within a specific context (spatially delimited and concentrated in a specific sector) (Sutton, 1991; Stiglitz, 1987). This type of knowledge, especially where traditional methods of production are still important, like in the clothing, ceramics, furniture, or machinery sectors (this knowledge is often acquired through direct experience and observation, and it is often practical knowledge or tacit, uncodified knowledge), cannot be conceived *in toto* as being a public good (Becattini and Rullani, 1993). This knowledge, which characterises the specific competencies (Carlsson and Eliasson, 1994; Pavitt, 1994 and 1996), or even specific and latent resources of the enterprises that are a part of a given local context (Colletis-Wahl, 1995), is embodied in the individuals and the collective learning of organisations, and it is socialised and spread only among citizens/workers of that specific context as a free good, but is rather inaccessible to people coming from outside the area (Calza Bini and Bosco, 1996). This type of knowledge is embedded territorially and characterises the productive culture of each local production system and is cumulative over time.

Secondly, the aggregation of firms and workers, and the spatial (and social) proximity of agents, forms an integrated system where interactions are fluid. Over time, many channels (both informal and institutionalised) through which information circulates quickly, are built up. Obviously, the opportunities for all subjects to learn and know are increased (Bellandi, 1992; Gottardi, 1996).

Thirdly, the formation of local production systems allows

transaction costs related to uncertainty to be reduced. Subjects sharing the same local traditions, production culture, community regulations and communication codes, have a lower propensity towards opportunistic and free-riding behaviour, as discussed by Mutti (1987) and Dei Ottati (1994).

Fourthly, and even more importantly, within these systems, higher levels of inter firm co-operation tend to be found. This makes the possibility of implementing a higher and more efficient[5] inter-firm division of labour a reality. Therefore, in the long run, a local system made up of many small-sized firms, that can develop increasing specialisation of their activities, can achieve better performance (because of the dynamic efficiency of increased division of labour and improvement of all productive phases) than other organisational models[6] where the organisation of activities is co-ordinated by large firm-like organisations (Belussi and Arcangeli, 1998).

Fifthly, within local production systems an acceleration of technological learning may occur thanks to the large number of agents that experiment with technology. This leads to the spread of frequent incremental innovations; so, generally speaking, the introduction of radical exogenous innovations combines with a sequential production of marginal improvements (Belussi, 1988; 1994).

Sixthly, often these systems are characterised by their inability to defend an industrial secret (given the proximity of firms and the inter-firm mobility of skilled workers). This is certainly a "market failure" in a stationary world, where irreversible barriers to the acquisition of new knowledge are assumed. But, in a dynamic world of hyper-competition, the rapid spread and adoption of innovations (generated in the area by leading firms) or the acquisition of the best available off the shelf technology, is a positive feature, that reinforces incentives for continuous innovation. Competition among firms is set by the implementation of dynamic mechanisms which include lead time, accelerated product variation, and continuous product innovation.

Seventhly, a local productive system stimulates enterprises to adopt innovation processes more quickly. Because there is a considerable (and concentrated) market for technology, suppliers of machinery tend to target their marketing strategies by targeting *all* the firms belonging to the most important local production system, no matter what their size. Even the smallest enterprises have quick access to up-to-date technological innovations. Over time, in these areas, a "pool" of advanced service centres is created. In the most dynamic production systems, these tendencies have allowed for the continuous upgrading of technology and for the propagation of the best organisational practice among enterprises.

The "laws" of motion of local production systems have been discussed in another place (Belussi, 1996), focusing on three factors which influence local development patterns: a) the processes of inter-firm division of labour,[7] b) the specialisation of economic agents (Di

Bernardo, 1991; Metcalfe and De Liso, 1995; Robertson and Langlois, 1995); and, finally, c) the accumulation of knowledge in firms. A recursive sequence of a cumulative growth-inducing mechanism is found, and the various stages of growth of a typical local production system are modelled. Demand growth increases the division of labour among firms. Specialisation increases economies of scale and the generation of new knowledge (from a Smithian perspective). In turn, this renders the local production system more competitive. Its (national or international) market grows. A higher volume of production allows a greater division of labour among enterprises, and the sequence starts over. Local production systems, in which the firms are dynamic enough, are thus characterised by greater innovation incentives and by greater efficiency. In the Italian case, the predominant small size firm has allowed for a significant reduction in internal organisational costs (You, 1995).

Local policies as a mechanism for inducing collective learning

In the case of Italy, the influence of policy in determining the performance of local production systems has been mainly indirect. This is not to say that on the local level actors have not taken any action. What is stressed here is that they have not tried to substitute the spontaneous work of the market, while they have accompanied the slow but constant growth of those productive systems (Tolomelli, 1992), from time to time, by choosing a type of intervention that was regulatory or adjunctive but not a substitute to the way in which the market allocated resources. From this theoretical point of view, a line of demarcation between the prevailing explanation for the role of public intervention in the economy can be traced, in which it is the lack of private incentives for investment (Arrow's "market failures" theory) that provides the theoretical foundation that justifies, in certain specific situations, government (as opposed to market[8] intervention.

Within an evolutionary context,[9] market and non-market mechanisms (institutions and government) interact with firms and market forces, in the creation of new technological capabilities, by reinforcing collective and cumulative learning, research processes, and higher system effects. This includes locating and identifying technological opportunities, exploiting potential opportunities for investment in new technologies, developing externalities, promoting horizontal policies for firm restructuring (by focusing on lagging firms) and targeted policies, aimed at generating new and more complex technological infrastructure to increase the existing technological capabilities or to expand the innovation possibilities frontier (by focusing on innovative firms).

The operations of Italian institutions and the focus of local policy was typically set in a context in which they were supporting the firms' technological dynamics, through specific legislation (such as easier credit for small firms), the encouragement of co-operation among firms directly involved in the creation of positive externalities, and, sometimes, by providing quasi-public goods directly to the industrial environment, a policy known as *servizi reali alle imprese* (real services to firms).

Thus, both institutions and markets have played a role in determining the performance of these systems. But a genuine interpretation of these policies must stress the fact that the Italian local production systems are not the result of a "grand top-down policy plan".

In the view taken here, that traces its roots back to the institutional school and "evolutionary" thought (a typical example of the evolutionary approach can be found in the works of Gerybadze, 1992; Witt, 1992; Bellet, 1993; Bellon, 1994; Justman and Teubal, 1995; Teubal, 1997). Institutions and markets may come together in an effort that substantially improves the organisation of a given industrial sector, or the quality of human capital utilised by firms.

A good example of this comes from the implementation of law 696, that provided incentives for investment in new machinery which incorporated automated technologies in the 1980s. This law proved to be quite useful for the small firms of the Third Italy, while in the *Mezzogiorno*, the southern and less developed part of the country, it has produced little at all. Unquestionably, this seems to depend on the social nature of development, seen here as a process of social mobilisation led by the entrepreneur as the central actor. The positive role played by institutions is in vain, if the sector lacks strategic actors that can respond appropriately to market signals.

Again, in the Italian case, policies that substantially influenced efficiency were not always selected. Within local production systems, institutions and firms (or other collective actors) may pursue conflicting strategies, so, they may, at times, not be able to co-ordinate effective regulative policy between the market and the institutions. At other times, the abstract nature of the problem-solving solution of strategic decision-making actors (public institutions or private associations), may hide its implementation. Parri (1993) has studied several unsuccessful attempts to establish real services for small firms. In his research he focused his attention on four dynamic local production systems in Veneto and in Lombardy, where "policy failure" occurred. This demonstrates how procedurally complex it is to activate desirable *ad hoc* policies.

However, the Italian case can also be used to demonstrate how slightly different local policies have produced similar results in terms of economic dynamics.

In a recent survey, Freschi (1994) has described, using comparative methodology, the adoption of local policies in the regions of Tuscany, Emilia Romagna and Veneto. In the Emilia case the policy of *servizi reali alle imprese* was usually chosen (i.e., the creation of these centres was organised by Ervet, an independent institution for regional policy), while this type of intervention was rare in Tuscany and totally absent in Veneto. In other words, the three most important regions of the Third Italy model, containing many "industrial districts" and "local production systems", have been doing things quite differently (Bartolozzi, 1993). The planning of industrial sites has been very systematically pursued in Emilia Romagna (Brusco, 1993; Bartolozzi and Garibaldo, 1995), while, in Veneto, intervention has concentrated on providing credit facilities for small firms. In the South, intervention through the planning of industrial sites has been largely unsuccessful. In many regions other alternatives have been explored.

This contradictory evidence on the causal relationship between the policies adopted by institutions and performance clearly does not undermine the efficacy of the Emilia model for local policy (Cooke, 1994).

Institutional features are a central issue for many economists, such as Nelson and Winter (1982), Freeman (1987, 1992), Foray and Freeman (1993), Lundvall (1992), Lundvall and Johnson (1994), Bellet (1993), and Leoni and Mazzini (1993). In an evolutionary perspective institutions are endogenous (at least in the long term) in the context where collective actors operate. More than one alternative may survive market selection, and variation in institutional forms increases over time.

However, the essential lesson from the Italian case is that the real influence and importance of these policies rests in the provision of "real services" to firms has probably been exaggerated (Nomisma, 1991; Bellini, Giordani, Magnatti and Pasquini, 1991), while the positive impact of vocational training, based on local institutions for the development of collective learning, has been underestimated. The presence of these institutions, specialised in the sector that dominates the local industrial structure, is scattered over much of Italy. Where they exist, they have supported the propagation of practical and technical knowledge among skilled workers and potential new entrepreneurs through both teaching and experimentation with new types of machinery. For example, consider the role played by the technical institute Aldini Valeriani in Bologna in the development of the local packaging machinery district or the technical school Galileo Ferraris in Turin in the development of mechanical competencies for the automotive *filière* (AA. VV., 1980).

The existence of institutions, which create the proper conditions for matching developments in technology and the existing economic and social structure, is extremely important, and this is a positive element for enhancing the relative advantages of the local production system.

However, when using an "evolutionary" conceptual framework, the limits of possibilities available to institutions and policies need to be recognised.

In Italy, the case of the industrial district of Prato is of great significance. Over the last decade, many resources have been devoted to develop an information system to connect the small firms operating in the district together (the project was organised by Enea in Rome). The system has not been utilised much by local entrepreneurs who are proud of their independence. Generally speaking, how (and if) local policies have influenced the growth of Italian local production systems remains an unanswered question.

Figure 5.1   Local politics and mechanisms for collective learning

Levels of intervention	Concepts and processes	Outline of specific options
The mobilisation of knowledge and the creation of new knowledge	1. Focusing on interventions to maintain a high level of acquired knowledge (accumulated knowledge) in specific sectors of specialisation 2. Reinforcement of empirical learning (practical knowledge acquired through direct experience and observation) 3. Development of imitative (vicarious) learning through access to second hand experience 4. Encouragement of new connections in the local productive context: by promoting joint-ventures with external firms of strategic interest, by attracting innovative enterprises to the area, and highly specialised personnel 5. Promotion of specific research projects (R&D activity) for the implementation of innovative solutions	1. Promotion of specific training activities to spread "technological knowledge" accumulated in *depositoire* firms and organisations 2. Promotion of un-intentional and un-systematic learning opportunities (e.g. participation of local firms in fairs, conferences, debates on technology and other economic issues) 3. Promotion of reverse engineering and bench marking practices 4. Establishment of institutional channels for imitation practices: through consultants and promoting meetings between technicians 5. Shortening the learning curves of firms (financing experimentation with new technologies) 6. Establishment of centres to provide services for the advanced functions of firms 7. Promotion of specific initiatives for the competitiveness of local firms

Co-ordination and distribution of technical information	1. Use of specific structures and collective actors to intensify the distribution of information	1. Increasing the number of technical information offices 2. Promoting initiatives organised by local institutions 3. Favouring access to international data banks and to global communication networks
Producing codes and languages for interpreting knowledge Reinforcement of the local identity and production culture	1. Building communication channels for more co-operation among collective agents and the most important firms of the area 2. Reinforcement of progressive coalitions	1. Systematic control of the economic and social performance of the local system 2. Initiation of local development projects open to foreign partners 3. Promotion of social connections among collective actors
Preservation of specific accumulated knowledge		1. Financing specific cultural "depositories" (e.g. the boot museum in Montebelluna) 2. Promotion of the establishment of archives on local history 3. Promotion of research on local development

Competition as a discovery process remains the driving force behind the operation of the system. And this must occur in markets through dynamic entrepreneurs. So there are no general recipes for local policies that can be applied in less developed countries to transfer the "beauty" of the Italian model based on competitive local production systems. Policy and institutions cannot substitute the market (in Arrow's sense). And what has been successful, under certain conditions in one context, may not work in others. The essential claim of this article is that institutions can set the rules, channel and mobilise knowledge, increase the transferability of knowledge from one individual to another, but they cannot recreate or develop markets if they lack productive capacity. Consequently, the "endogenisation" of local institutions, as argued for by Vanberg (1992), Gilly and Grossetti (1993), and Kirat (1993), and their involvement (as external actors) in the market is the most obvious conclusion.

Figure 5.1 intends to develop a positive, operational approach to the setting of normative local policies. It outlines a set of related interventions and actions to increase and intensify collective learning. The process of accumulating and transmitting knowledge can be viewed as a collective process not only because it is spread over many individuals. It is collective in the sense that the storage of knowledge and experience is largely performed by collective entities (firms and institutions) within the cultural traditions of each local productive system (tacit skills, customs and habits are developed locally).

Four principal kinds of process are identified:
-   The process of mobilising knowledge and creating new knowledge;
-   The process of co-ordinating and distributing technical information;
-   The process of reinforcing the local institutional context, especially the creation of particular entities, in which common rules, loyalties, behaviours may be formed and provide a good match between innovations (which are often exogenous) and local structures;
-   The process of storing technical knowledge in their collective memory and within specific institutions such as, in services centres and museums.

Technology policies on the local level must be based on the existing pool of knowledge incorporated in local firms and entities (leading enterprises, training organisations, research centres, groups of experts and scientists employed by public institutions or as private consultants).

Projects for upgrading must be programmed. Public policies must reinforce the propagation of practical knowledge (acquired through experience) by favouring the creation of local research laboratories and technical training centres. It is also important to support other types of informal learning by promoting participation in fairs, conferences, etc. An important element in the learning process is reverse engineering and bench marking of best practices. In this context, the transfer of knowledge from the more advanced contexts must be encouraged by positive action. Finally, local policy may also try to select specific research projects and partially sponsor them in order to improve production methods used by local enterprises. Obviously, the problem of propagation of technical information must be given proper attention (access to data banks, construction of local networks, etc.).

Within this evolutionary framework, R&D policies must be combined with the learning and propagation of new routines. Technology policy needs to be evaluated, and ongoing restructuring must take place, in which new strategies are formulated, defined, and implemented, and information about the efficacy of incentives is collected.

The catalytic role of local policy should be understood as finding reasonable matches between resources and objectives, rather than as simply maximising a well-defined objective function. They must be considered as a series of experiments which the responsible government agency undertakes in order to offer a menu of choices that closely reflects local needs (Teubal, 1997).

If local policies are inserted in this context of supporting actions to insure that markets function properly, the probability that the most appropriate actions for the local environment will be selected by the firms will be higher.

Conclusion

In Italy, local institutions have played an important role in the establishment of the general rules incorporated in the local context. This has favoured creative co-operation among firms and has generated the spontaneous aggregation of firms into systems. Another important aspect has been the accumulation and mobilisation of knowledge, a process in which both markets and institutions have played a crucial role. Finally, drawing on Italian experience, an analytical framework has been outlined in which the outcomes related to markets and institutions can logically be transformed into prescriptive local policies.

Notes

1   See, for example, Becattini (1979;1987;1989), Gandolfi (1988), Brusco (1989), Gobbo (1989), Pyke, Becattini and Sengenberger (1990), Sforzi (1990; 1995), Pyke and Segenberger (1992), Moussanet and Paolozzi (1992), Falzoni Onida, and Viesti (1992), Amin and Robins (1990), Amin (1991; 1993), Schmitz (1992), Capecchi (1990), and Hirst and Zeitlin (1992), Nuti (1992), Harrison (1990), Lombardi (1994), Bellandi and Russo (1994), Gottardi (1996), Cossentino, Pyke and Sengenberger (1996), Garofoli (1978; 1983; 1992; 1995), Anastasia, Corò, and Crestanello (1993), Dei Ottati (1996); Bellandi (1993); Bramanti and Senn (1994), and Carminucci and Casucci (1995). For the international context, see Sabel and Zeitlin (1982), Sabel (1989), and Benko and Lipietz (1992).

2   For a theoretical view, see Best (1990) and Camagni (1989). For an analysis of important production networks, see, for example, Sako (1989) and Belussi (1992).

3   Studies in regional economics are essentially based on Krugman's work on the notion of increasing returns. The contributions that appeared in "Revue d'Economie Regionale et Urbaine, no. 3" (1993) are interesting in relation to the issue of the "economy of proximity".

4 See the various works of Antonelli (1986; 1994), and the comparisons of different regional innovative systems in Longhi and Quere (1993); Gordon (1992); and Audretsch and Feldman (1994).

5 As demonstrated by Rosenberg (1976) and Chandler (1990), the process of inter firm division of labour is an element that should be seen in a historical perspective.

6 A local production system based on small enterprises, may not be characterised by high levels of inter-firm division of labour, and by enterprises that co-operate with each other in a technologically dynamic context. For example, Bull, Pitt and Szarka (1991) by studying three cases of textile industrial districts in Italy, UK and France, based essentially on small-sized firms, demonstrated that only the Italian districts had these characteristics.

7 See the arguments put forward by Rullani (1993) "If the small specialised enterprise belongs to a quite large system, the relevant scope economies ... should be measured according to the size of the value-chain of the whole territorial system. In other words, what is important for the generation of value and competitive advantages, is not the size of the enterprise, but ... the level of the efficiency of the local system." (p. 35).

8 This is a typical neo-classical way of reasoning, that assumes the resolution of an allocative type of problem. Arrow has shown that the market for the development of new scientific knowledge, if left to act spontaneously, would produce a situation of under investment, deviating from the Paretian equilibrium. The most recent economic discussion has also highlighted the limitations of public intervention, introducing the theme of "government" failures (see Wolf, 1993).

9 The limitations of the market failure analysis have been widely discussed by the evolutionary school, and, particularly, the assumption that the market mechanism is always the best mechanism for innovation and technological change. In many contexts there is no clear policy guidance to account for technological externalities. The economic system is not capable of defining the optimal amount of resources to devote to innovation and learning. Policy making is often adaptive rather than optimising. Complexity and uncertainty make it impossible to identify market failure, due to inter-activity and co-evolution of the processes involved in asymmetric information and issues of the revelation of relevant information by firms. This renders the identification of projects, where market failure is significant, problematic.

References

AA. VV. (1980), *Macchine, scuola, industria*, Bologna, Il Mulino.

Amin A. and Robins K. (1990), Industrial districts and regional development: limits and possibilities, in Pyke F, Becattini G. and Sengenberger W. (eds.), *Industrial Districts and Inter-firm Co-operation in Italy*, Genevre, Ilo.

Amin A. (1991), These are not marshallian times, in Camagni (eds.), *Innovation networks: spatial perspectives*, London, Belhaven Press.

Amin A.(1993), The difficult transition from informal to Marshallian district, mimeo, University of Newcastle upon Tyne.

Anastasia B., Corò G. and Crestanello P. (1995), Problemi di individuazione dei distretti industriali, *Oltre il ponte*, n. 52.

Antonelli C., (1986), Technological districts and regional innovation capacity, *Revue d'Economie Régionale et Urbaine*, n.5.

Antonelli C. (1994), Technological districts, localised spillovers, and productivity growth. The Italian evidence on technological externalities in the core regions, *International Review of Applied Economics*, vol. 8, n. 1.

Audretsch D. and Feldman M. (1994), R&D spillover and the geography of innovation production, Discussion Paper, FS IV 94-2, Berlin, Wissenshaftszentrum.

Bartolozzi P. (1993), Le politiche industriali e di sostegno all'impresa PM-Artigianato delle Autorità regionali in Emilia Romagna, Marche, Toscana, Veneto, Friuli, mimeo, Ires Bologna, Emilia Romagna.

Bartolozzi P. and Garibaldo F. (1995), (eds.) *Lavoro creativo e impresa efficiente. Ricerca sulle piccole e medie imprese*, Rome, Esi.

Becattini G. (1979), Dal settore industriale al distretto industriale. Alcune considerazioni sull'unità di indagine in economia industriale, *Economia e Politica Industriale*, n. 1.

Becattini G. (1987), *Mercato e forze locali: il distretto industriale*, Bologna, Il Mulino.

Becattini G. (1989), *Modelli locali di sviluppo*, Bologna, Il Mulino.

Becattini G. e Rullani E. (1993), Sistema locale e mercato globale, paper presentato al convegno *Economia e politica industriale in Italia dal 1973 al 1993*, Milano 12-13 novembre.

Bellandi M. (1992), The incentives to decentralised industrial creativity in local systems of small firms, *Revue d'economie industrielle*, n. 59.

Bellandi M. (1993), Structure and change in the industrial district, *Studi e discussioni*, n. 85, Dipartimento di Scienze economiche, Università di Firenze.

Bellandi M. and Russo M (1994), (eds.), *Distretti industriali e cambiamento economico locale,* Rosenberg e Sellier, Turin.

Bellet M. (1993), Evolution de la politique technologique, et role de la proximité. Repéres sur le cas francais, *Revue d'Economie Régionale et Urbaine*, n. 3.

Bellet M., Colletis G., e Lung Y. (1993), Introduzione, *Revue d'Economie Régionale et Urbaine*, n. 3.

Bellini N., Giordani M., Magatti P., and Pasquini F. (1991), Il livello locale e la politica industriale, in Nomisma (1991), *Strategie e valutazione nella politica industriale*, Milan, Angeli.

Bellon B. (1994), L'etat et l'entreprise, in Bellon B. et al. (a cura di) *L'etat et le marché*, Paris, Economica.

Belussi F. (1988), (ed.) *Innovazione tecnologica ed economie locali*, Milan, Angeli.

Belussi F. (1992), (ed.), *Nuovi modelli di impresa, gerarchie organizzative ed imprese rete*, Milan, Angeli.

Belussi F. (1994), Industrial innovation and firm development in Italy: the Veneto case, Spru, University of Sussex, Ph. D. Thesis.

Belussi F. (1996), Local systems, industrial districts and institutional networks: towards a new evolutionary paradigm of industrial economics?, *European Planning Studies*, vol. 4, n. 3.

Belussi F. and Festa M. (1990) L'impresa rete del modello veneto: dal post-fordismo al toyotismo? Alcune note illustrative sulle strutture organizzative dell'indotto Benetton, *Oltre il Ponte*, 31.

Belussi F. and Pozzana R. (1995), Natalità e mortalità delle imprese e determinanti dell'imprenditorialità, Milan, Franco Angeli.

Belussi F. and Garibaldo F. (1996), Variety of pattern of post-Fordist economy, *Futures,* vol. 28, n. 2.

Belussi F. and Arcangeli F. (1998), A typology of networks: flexible and evolutionary firms, *Research Policy*, vol. 27, pp. 415-428.

Benko G. and Lipietz A. (1992), (eds.) *Les régions qui gagnent*, Paris, Presses Universitaires de France.

Best H. B. (1990), *The New Competition*, Cambridge, Polity Press.

Bramanti A. and Senn L. (1994), Cambiamenti strutturali, connessioni locali e strutture di governo in tre sistemi locali della lombardia del nord-ovest, Milan, Bocconi University, Quaderno Opes n. 5.

Brusco S. (1989), *Piccola impresa e distretti industriali*, Turin, Rosenberg & Sellier.

Brusco S. (1993), Il modello emiliano rivisita il distretto, *Politica ed Economia*, Luglio.

Bull A., Pitt M., and Szarka J. (1991), Small firms and industrial districts, structural explanation of small firms viability in three countries, *Entrepreneurships and Regional development*, 3.

Camagni R. (1989), Accordi di cooperazione, e alleanze strategiche: motivazioni, fattori di successo ed elementi di rischio, *Rassegna Economica Ibm*, sup. al n. 4, December.

Capecchi V. (1990), A history of flexible specialisation of industrial districts in Emilia Romagna, in Pyke F, Becattini G. and Sengenberger W., *Industrial Distinct and Inter-firm Co-operation in Italy*, Ilo, Ginevra.

Carlsson B. and Eliasson G. (1994), The nature and importance of economic competence, *Industry and Corporate Change*, vol. 3, n. 3.

Carminucci C. and Casucci S. (1995), Il ciclo di vita dei distretti industriali. Ipotesi teoriche ed evidenze empiriche, Censis, mimeo.

Chandler A. D. (1990), *Scale and Scope. The Dynamics of Capitalism*, Cambridge Mass, The Belknap Press.

Colletis-Wahl K. (1995), L'hypothèse des facteurs de concurrence spatiale, quels fondamants?, *Cahiers de recherche Adis*, n. 32, Université de Paris Sud.

Cooke P. (1994), Building a 21st century regional economy in Emilia Romagna, paper presentato al convegno "Industrial districts and local development in Italy: challenges and policy perspectives, Bologna 2nd-3nd, May.

Cossentino F., Pyke F., and Sengenberger W. (1996), (eds.), *Local regional response to global pressure: the case of Italy* Geneva, Ilo.

Dei Ottati G. (1994), Trust, interlinking transactions, and credit in the industrial districts, *Cambridge Journal of Economics*, vol. 18, n. 6.

Dei Ottati G. (1996), Economic changes in the district of Prato in the 1980s: towards a more conscious and organised industrial district, *European Planning Studies*, 4.

Di Bernardo B. (1991), *La dimensione di impresa: scala, scopo, varietà*, Angeli, Milan.

Falzoni A., Onida F., and Viesti G. (1992), (eds.), *I distretti industriali: crisi o evoluzione?*, Milan, Egea.

Freschi A.C. (1994), Istituzioni politiche e sviluppo locale nella Terza Italia, *Sviluppo Locale*, a. 1., n. 1.

Gandolfi V. (1988), *Aree sistema: internazionalizzazione e reti telematiche*, Milan, Franco Angeli.

Garofoli G. (1978), (ed.), *Ristrutturazione industriale e territorio*, Milan, Franco Angeli.

Garofoli G. (1983), Le aree-sistema in Italia, *Politica ed economia*, 11, pp. 57-70.

Garofoli G. (1992), Les systémes de petites entreprises: un cas paradigmatique de dévelopment endogène, in Benko e Lipietz (ed.), cit.

Garofoli G. (1995), (ed.), *Industrializzazione diffusa in Lombardia*, Pavia, Iuculano Editore.

Gerybadze A. (1992), The implementation of industrial policy in an evolutionary perspective, in *Explaining Process and Change*, Witt U. (ed.), Ann Arbour, The University of Michigan Press.

Gilly J.P. e Grossetti M. (1993), Organisations, individus et territoires, le cas des systemes locaux d'innovation, *Revue d'Economie Régionale et Urbaine*, n. 3.

Gobbo F. (1989), (ed.), *Distretti e sistemi produttivi alla soglia degli anni '90,* Milan, Franco Angeli.

Gordon R. (1992), State, milieu, network: systems of innovation in Silicon valley, paper presentato al workshop *Systems of Innovations*, October 5-6, Bologna.

Gottardi G. (1996), Strategie tecnologiche, innovazione senza R&D, e generazione di conoscenza nei distretti e nei sistemi locali, *Quaderni del Dipartimento di Scienze Economiche Marco Fanno*, n.63/96.

Harrison B. (1990), Industrial districts: old vine in new bottles?, Working paper n. 90, Carnegie Mellon University, Pittsburg Pa.

Harrison B. (1994), *The lean and the mean*, New York, Basic Books.

Hirst P. and Zeitlin J. (1992), Specializzazione flessibile e post-fordismo: realtà e implicazioni politiche, in Belussi (ed.), quoted.

Justman M. and Teubal M. (1995), Technological infrastructure policy (TIP): creating capabilities and building markets, *Research Policy*, vol. 24, pp. 259-281.

Kirat T. (1993), Innovation technologique et apprentissage institutionnel: institutions et proximite dans la dynamique des sytemes d'innovation territoriales, *Revue d'Economie Régionale et Urbaine*, n. 3.

Leoni R. and Mazzini M. (1993), Processi di innovazione tecnologica e istituzioni di sostegno a livello locale, *Quaderni del dipartimento di scienze Economiche*, n. 14.

Lombardi M. (1994), Meccanismi evolutivi nella dinamica dei sistemi di imprese, Ricerca di Base, *Quaderni dell'Università Bocconi,* n. 3.

Longhi C. and Quéré M. (1993), Systèmes de production et d'innovation, et dynamique des territories, *Revue économique*, vol. 44, n. 4.

Lundvall B. (1992), (ed.), *National Systems of Innovations*, London, Pinter.

Lundvall B. and Johnson B. (1994), The Learning Economy, *Industry Studies,* n. 2. pp. 23-42.

Metcalfe J. and De Liso N. (1995), Innovation, capabilities, and knowledge: the epistemic connection, mimeo, University of Manchester.

Moussanet M and Paolazzi L. (1992), (eds.), *Gioielli, bambole, coltelli. Viaggio nei distretti produttivi italiani*, Milan, Il Sole 24- Ore.

Mutti A. (1987), La fiducia un concetto fragile, una solida realtà, *Rassegna Italiana di sociologia*, 2, pp. 223-47.

Nelson R. e Winter S. (1992), *An Evolutionary Theory of Economic Change*, Belknap, Cambridge Mass.

Nomisma (1991), *Strategie e valutazione nella politica industriale*, Milan, Franco Angeli.

Nuti F. (1992) (ed.), *I distretti dell'industria manifatturiera in Italia,* vol. 1 and 2, Milan, Franco Angeli.

Parri L. (1993), I dilemmi dell'azione collettiva nell'evoluzione dei distretti industriali italiani: i casi di Cantù, Carpi ed Arzignano, *Oltre il Ponte*, 41.

Pyke F, Becattini G. and Sengenberger W., (1990), (eds.), *Industrial Districts and Inter-firm Co-operation in Italy*, Geneva, Ilo.

Pyke F. and Sengeberger W. 1992, (ed.), *Industrial Districts and Local Economic Regeneration*, Geneva, Ilo.

Revue d'Economie Régionale et Urbaine, (1993), numéro spécial, "Economie de proximités", n. 3.

Robertson P. and Langlois R. (1995), Innovation, networks and integration, *Research Policy*, vol. 24.

Rosenberg N. (1976), *Perspectives on Technology*, Cambridge, Cambridge University Press.

Rullani (1993), L'impresa minore nella teoria economica e nelle osservazioni empiriche, *Rivista italiana di economia, demografia e statistica*, 47, n. 3-4.

Sabel C. (1989), Flexible specialization and the reemergence of regional economics, in Zeitlin (eds.), Local Industrial Strategies, *Economy and Society*, vol. 18, n. 4.

Sabel C. e Zeitlin J. (1982), Alternative storiche alla produzione di massa, *Stato e Mercato*, n. 5, pp. 213-58.

Sako M. (1989), Neither markets nor hierarchies: A comparative study of the printed circuit board industry in Britain and Japan, paper presented at the conference *Comparing Capitalist Economies*, Bellagio, 29 April-2 May.

Schmitz H. (1992), Industrial districts: models and reality in Baden-Wurttemberg Germany, in Pyke F. and Sengeberger W. (eds), *Industrial Districts and Local Economic Regeneration*, Geneva, Ilo.

Sforzi F.(1990), The Italian districts in the Italian economy, in Pyke F., Becattini G. and Sengenberger W. (eds.), *Industrial Districts and Inter-firm Cooperation in Italy*, Geneva, Ilo.

Sforzi F. (1995), Elenco dei sistemi locali di piccola e media impresa 1991, paper presented at Artimino 11th September, "Lo sviluppo locale", organised by Iris.

Stiglitz, J (1987), Technological Change, Sunk costs, and competition, *Brooking Papers on Economic Activity*, n. 3.

Sutton J. (1991), *Sunk Costs and Market Structure*, Cambridge University Press, MIT Press.

Teubal M. (1997), A catalytic and evolutionary approach to horizontal technology policies, *Research Policy*, vol. 25, pp. 1161-1188.

Tolomelli C. (1992), (ed.), *Le politiche industriali regionali. Esperienze, soggetti, modelli*, Bologna, Clueb.

Vanberg V. (1992), Innovation, cultural evolution, and economic growth, in, *Explaining Process and Change*, Witt U. (ed.), The University of Michigan Press.

Witt U. (1992), (ed.), *Explaining Process and Change*, Ann Arbour, The University of Michigan Press.

Wolf C. (1993), *Markets or Governments. Choosing between imperfect alternatives*, Cambridge Mass., The MIT Press.

You J. (1995), Small firms in economic theory, *Cambridge Journal of Economics*, vol. 19.

6 Multimedia technology: An organisational challenge for small firms in industrial districts

CHRISTIAN GENTHON AND FABIO ARCANGELI

Introduction

This paper deals with some leading features of the new multimedia trends in information and communication technologies, and discusses their organisational impact for large firms, SMEs and their co-operative networks in the context of the industrial district model. They can be advantageous for the industrial district model, but also an objective limit, as will be discussed below, within the dense net of transactions, exchanges, and incremental learning which sustains the innovative process within firms.

The innovative process is stimulated by the relationships induced by the geographical proximity of agents and by the exchange of tacit knowledge. Geographical and social-cultural proximity influence the type of transactions that can be made among agents and their costs. Transactions which imply exchange of tacit knowledge might be more efficient within the industrial systems model because they are based on informal languages and on suitable communicative channels.

Despite the burdens of higher logistic and organisational costs due to the break up of production cycles within industrial districts, transactional costs are generally lower, because of the habit of co-operation, and social control mechanisms (facilitated by common codes and shared values), which eliminate the need of costly contractual solutions (with formalised content, contractual variations, etc.). As has been pointed out in other parts of this book, economically useful knowledge (pieces of knowledge that can be the basis of economic transactions) is by and large tacit. And the production and transfer of useful knowledge is a strongly localised process.

The existence of the proximity factor within the industrial district model has allowed to avoid the effort to rationalise information flows, and formalise the learning processes and accumulate a large body of knowledge by speeding up the rate of knowledge codification, as has occurred in typical Fordist firms (as well as within post-Fordist

131

organisations). This was fundamental to the long-distance transfer of knowledge and the repeated use of the same body of knowledge on the international level (first through the various management information systems, and today through the intranet and/or internet).

Formally, in the dominant organisational culture, a radical shift from informal knowledge towards a more codified knowledge has been found. This passage is detectable within large oligopolistic firms, by the introduction of much rationalisation, by making work more scientific, and by the application of quantitative methods. The formalisation of knowledge, once problems of appropriability were solved, was essentially done to allow a wider exploitation (both in space and time) of the stock of costly knowledge which needs to be less local and more global in character. On the contrary, applicative and practical knowledge is essentially tacit in nature, and is communicated primarily by observation, imitation, practical experimentation, and experience. The formalisation of production routines and decisional processes has been the pre-condition for the automation, exchange, and elaboration of information.

Nowadays, the main issue is the elaboration and transmission of tacit knowledge. New multimedia systems and new information and communication technologies seem to allow a new perspective, characterised by a new trend towards the formalisation of practical and informal knowledge. The two basic components of this technological change are: Universal Data Voice Communication (UDVC) and tele-services. The key assumption is that both technological innovations, but in particular the first (UDVC), will allow experimenting with and learning how to share tacit knowledge in co-operative activities at a distance.

The promise of multimedia and electronic commerce is to allow every agent to make low cost transactions regardless of distance and the type of knowledge. This perspective contains some destabilising elements for the model of the industrial district as a specific form of industrial organisation. Indeed, the use of information and telecommunication technologies may reduce the importance of proximity as a low cost channel for knowledge based transactions.

On the other hand, the process of the internationalisation of industrial districts has long been underway. During the 1990s, they have been very active in international commerce, and they have started to de-localise some labour-intensive production phases to the NICs (Corò and Rullani, 1998). In this perspective, the adoption of new communication technologies may even accelerate these processes.

Considering the fact that both the transactions based on cognitive content and their computer support are quite diverse, this paper explores the trends in multimedia, and their possible impact on the model of the industrial system, and more generally on economic systems based on co-operation networks characterised by geographical proximity.

The theoretical framework of this paper deals with the relationship between the application of the new (multimedia) technology and the variety of forms of knowledge used.

In one sense, the coming technological trend is considered as given. So, this article explores mainly the demand side. Tele-services and Universal Data Voice Communications (UDVC) tools are here considered as the new technologies that match and/or substitute the previous technologies based on tele-computing and on personal communication technologies. In the supply side scenario here assumed, which is still in a pre-competitive stage of the coming multimedia technologies and standards (Théry, 1994), some important new developments in the supply of information and communication technologies are portrayed. At the cross-roads of computer, telecommunications, and audio-video industries, a new set of technologies are on the way and they involve:

- either interpersonal exchanges of voice, data, sound and images (multimedia) in one channel;
- or new services (access to databases endowed with multimedia characteristics: Wright, 1993).

This introductory section deals with the following issues: the nature of economically useful knowledge and its relation to alternative communication routes. To do this a taxonomy of the four types of knowledge exchange is proposed. This taxonomy is based upon a lesson drawn from the economics of technical change: the know-how component has a different nature from the exchangeable information of technologies, therefore the map of economically useful knowledge goes well beyond the islands of "information", to the icebergs of informal knowledge.[1]

Many forms of technical, business and organisational knowledge may be treated as information, but others do not fit into this framework, and they cannot be ignored because they play an important role in the appropriability of the benefits from the use of the information itself. If the idea of tacitness in the use and generation of new knowledge is a well known concept, it is difficult to foresee the impact of new information technologies on the information-knowledge relationship.

Let us define the main forms which create the two main archetypes of human knowledge. Practical knowledge (e.g. know how, know who) is tacit in its nature and it is usually communicated through direct observation, imitation, experience, and practical example. Its "tacit" character means that economic agents find it difficult, if not impossible, to learn the complete set of information contained, and to freely use and appropriate such practical knowledge. This knowledge is typically related to skills and capabilities, thus it is embodied in different agents. Propositional knowledge (e.g. know what and why), on the contrary, has a more structured shape, allowing for its expression and translation into formal language. Therefore, it may be adequately or completely transferable and can be compressed by representation in information packages.

Montaigne had already pointed out this distinction, by arguing that the fact of knowing, when referred to a practice, does not help anyone to learn, improve and master such a practice (Bencivenga, 1990). If we look at the processes of production and transfer (communication) of these two types of knowledge, we might describe the different forms of knowledge introduced above in the following ways.

Practical knowledge is characterised by:
i)   components: sets of routines, or partially automatic answers in a given perceived framework; they are stored in an individual or an organisation's skill profile. They refer to the capability to react to different states of a known environment in order to achieve some goal;
ii)   processes: although they might be described in natural language, they include informal elements that resist being fully and unequivocally mapped in information sets written in a formal language;
iii) outcomes: tools or aids for interacting with the environment in order to reach preferred states of the world.

Propositional knowledge is made of:
i)   components: sets of propositions suitable to be stored in archives or memories;
ii)   processes: they allow for a total and unambiguous reduction to information sets, without any untranslatable residual information;
iii) outcomes: they allow a representation of precise states of the world.

Also the interpersonal or inter-organisational communication of knowledge forms a continuum of different forms: firstly, immediate perception (exchange of information even without it being expressed in formal statements); secondly, exchange of information through a formal or natural language; thirdly, exchange of information within a context in which there is a physical, cultural, or organisational distance. The obstacles to the transmission of information can be counterbalanced by the use of some media: telecommunication and inter-language translation techniques, inter-organisational codes and transactions, standards and tools, specifically prepared for knowledge transfer.

Therefore, a basic taxonomy of these two ways of communicating knowledge may be drawn. For simplicity, it is assumed that any communication has a binary form: either direct and immediate, or at a distance through media, see Table 6.1. Different kinds of communication are established for the two forms of knowledge envisaged.

The new framework of inter and intra firm relationships

In this section, some major shifts in the contemporary structure of relations within firms and between them and other agents will be described. The most likely implications of these shifts for the demand for new communication tools will also be explored. As far as forms of knowledge are concerned, there is a continuous trend in organisational cultures to go from tacit to formal knowledge over recent decades.

Schematically, a historical trend is found. Previously, "Fordist" firms were able to solve the complex problems of mass production, one by one, mainly by accumulating tacit knowledge from local learning. Late-Fordist firms have tried to rationalise flows of learning and the use of the stock knowledge, by increasing the rate of encoding, transfer and repeated use of the same knowledge systems throughout the world. The goal of this effort in formalisation has been a wider use (in space and time) of global knowledge, in order to increase productivity and eventually profitability (once the new appropriability problems of more "open" forms of knowledge have been solved).

Table 6.1   A simple taxonomy of knowledge and communication

	Propositional or formal knowledge	Practical or tacit knowledge
Direct communication (immediate)	Conferences, meetings, lectures, seminars, colleges, labs, and formal internal relations	Apprenticeships, word of mouth, clubs and professional associations, informal interviews, informal relations
Indirect communication (media)	Books and other written communication, formal networks, inter organisational relations	Telephone calls and letters, invisible colleges and informal networks, expert systems

This trend and the variety of its forms have been analysed in terms of 'algorithmising' decision-making (Zuscovitch, 1983), 'scientification' of manufacturing (Rullani and Vaccà, 1987) or an increasing use of general and abstract knowledge (Arora and Gambardella, 1994). Although it is not the subject of detailed analysis in this chapter, its existence can be outlined by a framework of facts about contemporary organisations; the persistence of the Fordist organisational paradigm in an ever more conflictual and unplanned environment leads to increasing efforts to formalise knowledge (with decreasing marginal productivity or the *productivity paradox*: see Rallet, 1995). This can be seen as a precondition for the automation of the process of knowledge-sharing within corporate information systems.

Figure 6.1   A double shift in knowledge and communication channels

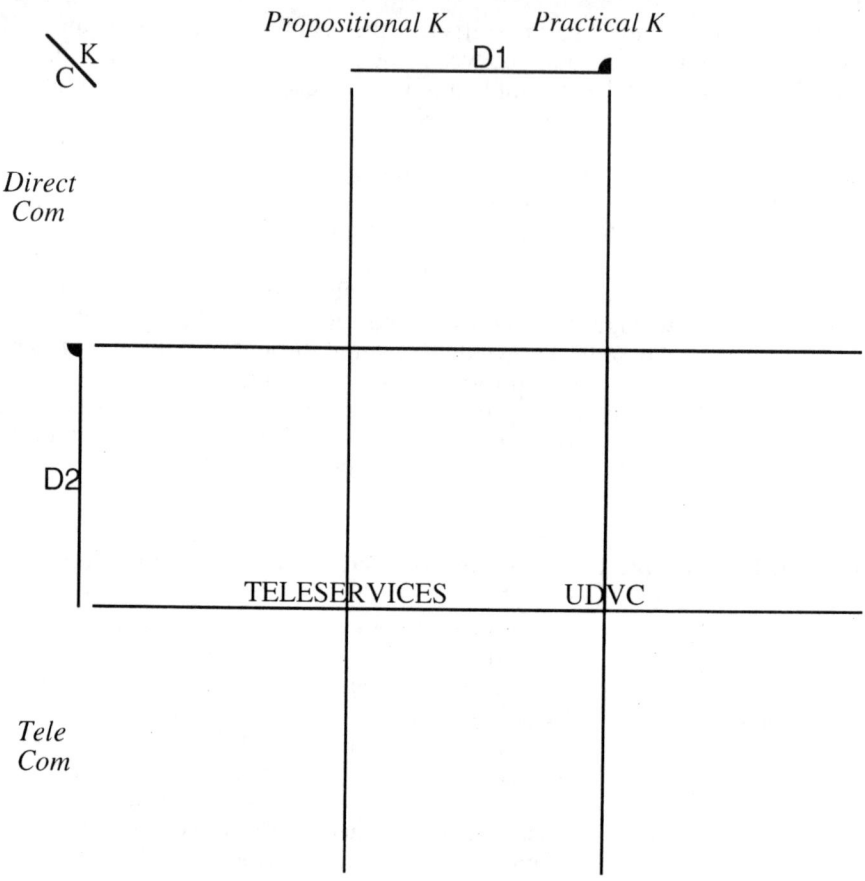

Com: communication
K: knowledge

Double diffusion and organisational change process, moving the boundaries:
Δ1: systems and tools for the formalisation of transferable knowledge
Δ2: multimedia (channelling of both propositional and tacit knowledge)

The late-Fordist organisation, which emerged in the first decades of new information technologies, might be represented by a movement from activities in the right-hand column (tacit knowledge) to the left-hand column (formal knowledge), as well as by an invasion of open or public science and knowledge into the proprietary worlds of tacit technology and organisational culture (column boundaries moving to the left: (1 in **Figure 6.1**).

An alternative characterisation of the main features of the so-called Post-Fordist firm is found in economic literature mainly in the works of Gallino (1983), Langlois (1992), and Belussi and Arcangeli (1998). They have stressed some new characteristics related to internal and external webs of relationships. They have focused their attention on "flat" organisations as a way to achieve quality. This implies:

-   a reduction of hierarchical levels;
-   increasing team co-operation (within/across projects);
-   more autonomy for workers/teams/divisions. Another important characteristic is *fuzzy* firm boundaries due to a continuous relocation of activities, for both short term (flexibility) and long term purposes (learning). This can be achieved through:
-   internal adaptability (outsourcing, tele-work, etc.);
-   external adaptability (reversibility in the make/network/buy division of labour);
-   *networking* agreements.

The organisational trends contained in this new model have profound implications for the economic treatment of knowledge within firms and networks. The need for interaction is likely to grow exponentially, and direct exchanges of tacit knowledge will continue to be very important. This is why the continuation of such organisational trends implies the search for effective ways to control costs, so as to avoid an information-based hyperinflation in terms of the global use of knowledge. With post-Fordist firms there is not only the problem of absorbing knowledge but also of economising knowledge. In order to explore the feasibility of the above mentioned *post-Fordist* characteristics of flatness and fuzziness, let us explore their implications on the need to communicate knowledge.

First, a "flat organisation" means less hierarchical control and an increasing horizontal co-operation across departments in the process of building up systems of firm-specific tacit knowledge and behavioural routines. This comes from the fact that both innovative and routine activities within the firm tend to assume a relational pattern requiring inter-departmental interactions (Kline and Rosenberg, 1986). A major consequence will be "tele-tacit" knowledge, that is the creation, sharing, recombination and exchange of tacit knowledge even among distant sites.

Second, internal adaptability is likely to imply the need for greater modularity and frequent recombination of knowledge systems among individuals, work-teams and departments within the firm and across its "borders". This implies wide-ranging effects on tacit and formal exchanges of knowledge; in particular, it will generate some sort of standardisation of firm-specific knowledge, one example of this is "tele-work", but a much more frequent one is "outsourcing".

Third, external adaptability gives rise to a continual flow of information and knowledge in both directions, between the firm and its environment. Therefore, a major consequence is an increasing demand for inter-organisational knowledge transfer. This transfer often resembles "tele-teaching" relationships.

Fourth, "network firms" are built around a broad cloth of shared knowledge, in order to allocate their activities within relatively stable networks. Many varied phenomena are involved, "tele-R&D", "telemarketing" and "tele-manufacturing". The common characteristic at the basis of all of them is the construction and use of shared knowledge in different forms: mainly propositional knowledge, databases, information, and practical knowledge.

In sum, one might argue that, even if the global stock of knowledge utilised was held constant, the new framework would imply a greater flow of knowledge to distant sites. At the same time, more tacit knowledge is required by the production systems. This knowledge may be added to the circulation as well in order to allow for the construction, maintenance, renewal and use of shared knowledge (both propositional and tacit).

Multimedia business services and the relational firm

This section applies the previous analysis to explore the possible impact of multimedia technologies. How far may new needs to communicate knowledge be satisfied by a supply of adequate tools, such as those which improve the feasibility of the new organisational paradigms?

Multimedia services may be defined, for our purposes, by two main trends in the development of communication capabilities: first, tele-services which provide access to sophisticated (audio and video) databases and services of intermediation (EDI for example), and second, what is here called Universal Data Voice Communication, the availability of data in a form similar to telephone communications. More specifically, the fields of application of these new tools are for tele-services related to information services, commercial and professional services, business intermediation, EDI applications, and for UDVC data exchange (tele-access), e-mail services, structured e-mail (cfr. Lotus Notes), groupware, and PC video-conferencing.

It should be pointed out that there is no clear demarcation between the two categories. They form a continuum. For example, an EDI transaction can be made through a third party or directly by users. In fact, the impact of the multimedia expansion of telecommunications and media capabilities may be achieved through different tools and different fields of application.

Up to this point, it has been argued that the major efforts of post-Fordist organisations were in the formalisation of procedures, transforming internal tacit knowledge into explicit knowledge. At the same time, they have also been trying to acquire environmental knowledge, absorbing the pool of existing knowledge (outside the organisation). Both technical, economic and institutional factors have promoted a *scientification* of the organisational culture. Within various corporate information systems, tele-computing has been the main tool used by firms in order to standardise their routines in different locations (Antonelli, 1986; Brousseau, 1993; Chesnais, 1994).

In the multi-plant firm, the use of telecommunications capabilities in computing has allowed for a decrease in the cost of information processing and storing. In the past, tele-computing developed during the 1970s was applied to collecting, processing and channelling information flows from the different sites of the firm towards a central point. This played a major role in the cohesion and coherence of large post-Fordist firms.

For those organisations capable of properly mastering the use of multimedia services and communications, the new opportunities opened up by applying these new technologies allow profound changes in organisations. These organisations are likely to find new ways to reduce the proportion of the more expensive informal and direct communication. In our simple scheme, this may be represented by the lower row invading the upper one (see D2 in Figure 6.1). The more powerful media will try to capture the flows of direct communication that were previously beyond their scope. Enriched computer-based tele-services will invade the upper field of lectures and interviews, while multimedia personal communications (UDVC), by incorporating the qualitative flavour and flexibility of immediate communications, will enter local learning within organisations.

Both the late-Fordist (1) and the post-Fordist (2) trends, change the relative weight of the four categories of knowledge transactions described in Table 6.1. The joint effect of these two movements is a reduction of the most expensive transactions, that is, direct/informal exchanges. Therefore, communication costs might be seen as a major incentive to organisational learning in the multimedia field; these learning curves might begin in those organisations which, because they are either more knowledge-intensive or more open to relational webs, are most sensitive to those costs.

Nonetheless, the availability of new technologies is a necessary but not yet sufficient cause for the emergence of a new model for knowledge transactions. In the previous section some trends in the demand for knowledge transactions within and among organisations have been identified, and here the emphasis is on the needs of large corporations. So, let us return to the list of organisational features of post-Fordist firms, discussed in section 2.

"Flat organisations" need tele-tacit-knowledge exchanges that can be supplied by new multimedia tools. For instance, PC video-conferencing, which allows participants to talk, see and write to each other simultaneously, will partially substitute for face-to-face meetings. More generally, UDVC tools are likely to be used in the same way as their alternative, face-to-face communication. "Internal adaptability" increases the need of formal as well as informal exchanges of knowledge, that can be met by the greater flexibility of UDVC compared to previous personal communication tools. In fact, both "tele-work" and outsourcing, two major examples in this area, could take advantage of tools that allow for the exchange of talk and data at the same time. As far as "external adaptability" and "networks" are concerned, the impact of the whole range of tele-services must also be considered. One can imagine a process of learning in both kinds of multimedia. In the case of teleservices, learning will benefit from external and network economies, while users will increase the effectiveness of UDVC through a firm-specific trial and error process.

However, the major changes will be introduced by the two driving forces of increasing communication costs and increasing multimedia users. Learning processes are likely to induce a way of dealing with knowledge exchanges. As a matter of fact, a new dynamic competition between internal "hierarchies" and external networks ("markets"), and between different organisational forms, such as large and small firms, will be activated. The major novelty in this scenario is the flow of tacit knowledge in multimedia channels, which may contribute to the acceleration of decentralisation within organisations, and the passage from hierarchical control towards flatness, self-control, and increasing autonomy of productive units (Gallino, 1983), in which the links among the various parts are characterised by relatively horizontal relations.

The fact that tacit and co-operative knowledge could also be produced and shared at a distance is the new potential of multimedia, compared to earlier communication tools; from this perspective, it is the flexibility, the physical, economic and cultural "universality" of UDVC that makes the difference. These new characteristics will allow users to share and communicate even those subsystems of knowledge that may never be suitable to complete translation and codification in an appropriate set of information. Although the upgrading of teleservices with multimedia content will also have economic potential, it is here argued that its effectiveness is restricted to those parts of knowledge systems that are suitable to being fully translated into specific information sets.

In such a framework a possible convergence of technological and organisational change can be foreseen. Within firms, the make/network/buy choices will depend upon the comparative speed of relational learning across the organisation borders, in the proximity of previously stable and definite boundaries. It is in this learning environment, that the exchange of complementary knowledge will find its proper codes, channels, conventions and regulations. This raises the question whether this multimedia standardisation process will definitely cut off SMEs, because it is neutral to firm size or perhaps even favours the shift towards smaller size organisations.

Organisational impact for SMEs

An important outcome of multimedia diffusion, learning and assimilation will be the shifting balance of competitiveness between large firms, SMEs and their networks (Genthon and Arcangeli, 1995). Let us identify the various types of small firm:

- Satellite SMEs, which are found at the end of the spokes in the hub and spoke networks created by larger firms;
- Network firms of smaller size, belonging to a variety of configurations and environments (from traditional Industrial Districts to high tech poles/regions), but with a common, Marshallian paradigm, reproducing in their peer to peer networks many of the competitive advantages internalised by large corporations (Lombardi, 1994; Dei Ottati, 1995);
- Independent SMEs as a residual class, collecting all those firms belonging neither to peer to peer nor to hub and spoke networks.

The first class will have more problems, at least in the first phase of a multimedia learning curve: therefore it might be the optimal target of diffusion and public policies, e.g. organising co-operative forms of demand for new technologies, and promoting an adequate supply of teleservices in industrial districts and in those regions with a large population of independent SMEs.

Satellite SMEs and network firms will be differentiated in terms of organisational learning in relation to their respective networks. Computer-based information systems in large corporations are a mirror and a tool of their hierarchical systems of incentives and control (Menard, 1990). Their partners will remain unpaid for externalities which will help and eventually accelerate the first phases of learning and their approach to new standards. However in the long term, they might experience some lock-in effects that could undermine their learning capabilities and impose significant constraints upon the feasible range of their relationships, unless the standards adopted (çfr. open EDI) will be sufficiently general and universal in character to allow them to shift quite freely from one network to another, which is still an unresolved and complex issue.

On the contrary, the network SMEs might shift towards multimedia communications as a continuation of their previous trend to inter-firm co-operation. Although they will have to face high initial threshold and sunk costs in order to enter the new path, the expected payoffs might be very attractive, in terms of:

- the chances of not falling behind hub-and-spoke networks, if the peer-to-peer networks will be able to diffuse quickly and efficiently their *learning on the frontier* accumulated in their faster and more advanced nodes;

- the advantages deriving from a continuous transition from traditional to advanced methods of exchanging and sharing tacit knowledge, compared to the more discontinuous trends that large corporations have to face, when they deviate from their previous formalisation and *scientification* trends, towards more flexible approaches to knowledge sharing.

Conclusions

In conclusion, it can be argued that the multimedia technologies may have interesting organisational impact on the competitiveness of SMEs. First, SMEs do not seem to facilitate the diffusion of multimedia technologies. However, in satellite and network firms a higher rate may occur because of the experiences of the most advanced firms, and from the experiments promoted by network externalities. This might be a major step towards designing the industrial districts of tomorrow.

Note

1   Since Polanyi's (1958; 1966) pioneering work, a large body of literature has examined the concept of tacit knowledge and the difference between science and technology. Among recent contributions, see Vincenti (1990; 1994) and Hicks (1995).

References

Antonelli C. (1986), Transborder Data Flows and the Structure and Strategies of TNCs, *The CTC Reporter*, n. 22, New York, United Nations.

Arora A. and Gambardella A. (1994), The changing technology of technological change: general and abstract knowledge and the division of innovative labour, *Research Policy*, 23, pp. 523-532.

Belussi F. and Arcangeli F. (1998), A typology of networks: flexible and evolutionary firms, *Research Policy* vol. 27, pp. 415-428.

Bencivenga E. (1990), *The Discipline of Subjectivity: an Essay on Montaigne,* Princeton, Princeton University Press.

Brousseau E. (1993), *L'économie des contrats, technologies de l'information et coordination inter-entreprises*, Paris, PUF.

Chesnais F. (1994), *La mondialisation du capital*, Paris, Syros.

Corò G. and Rullani E. (1998), (eds.) *Percorsi locali di internazionalizzazione*, Milan, F. Angeli.

Dei Ottati G. (1995), *Tra mercato e comunità: aspetti concettuali e ricerche empiriche sul distretto industriale*, Milan, Angeli.

Gallino L. (1983), *Informatica e qualità del lavoro*, Turin, Einaudi.

Genthon C. and Arcangeli F. (1995), Technologies multimédia et coordination inter-PME, in C. Picory and F. Rowe (eds.), Actes du Congrès *Innovation et organisation des PME*, Paris, ENST, October 25-27, pp. 457-464.

Hicks D. (1995), Published papers, tacit competences and corporate management of the public/private character of knowledge, *Industrial and Corporate Change*, 4, pp. 401-424.

Kline S.J. and Rosenberg N. (1986), An Overview of Innovation. In: National Academy of Engineering, *The Positive Sum Strategy: Harnessing Technology for Economic Growth*, Washington D.C., The National Academy Press.

Langlois R.N. (1992), Transaction-cost economics in real time, *Industrial and Corporate Change*, 1, pp. 99-127.

Lombardi M. (1994), L'evoluzione del distretto industriale come sistema informativo: alcuni spunti di riflessione, *L'Industria*, n. 3.

Menard C. (1995), *L'économie des organisations*, Paris, La Découverte.

Polanyi M. (1958), *Personal knowledge*, Chicago, Chicago University Press.

Polanyi M. (1966), *The tacit dimension*, London, Routledge & Kegan.

Rallet A. (1995), Le paradoxe de productivité à l'étape des réseaux de communication, Paper submitted at the conference *Economie de l'information*, 18-20 May, Lyon.

Rullani E. and Vaccà S. (1987), Scienza e tecnologia nello sviluppo industriale, *Economia e Politica industriale*, 53, pp. 3-41.

Théry G. (1994), *Les autoroutes de l' information*, Paris, La Documentation Française.

Vincenti W. (1990) *What engineers know and how they know it. Analytical studies from aeronautical history*, Baltimore, J. Hopkins University Press.

Vincenti W. (1994), The retractable airplane landing gear and the Northrop anomaly, *Technology and Culture*, n.1.

Wright D. (1993), *Broadband. Business Services, Technologies, and Strategic Impact*, Boston and London, Artech House.

Zuscovitch E. (1983), Informatisation, flexibilité et division du travail, *Revue d'Economie Industrielle*, 25, pp. 50-61.

Part III

The dynamics of local industrial systems: empirical evidence

7 Evolutionary and adaptive local systems in Northeast Italy: strategies of learning, leadership, and co-operation

LUCIANO PILOTTI

Introduction

The literature on industrial districts and LPSs of small and medium sized enterprises (SME) has been enriched both theoretically and empirically, by field research on the national and international level over the last twenty years (Benko and Lipietz, 1992; Amin and Robins, 1990; Pyke, Becattini and Sengenberger, 1991; Sengenberger and Pyke, 1991; David and Foray, 1993). However, it was Becattini's work in 1979 which adopted a "neo-Marshallian view" - subsequently revised in 1987 and 1989 - that gave this field a remarkable impulse and has led to considerable results, even though different approaches and conclusions are found among the various studies undertaken. The aim of this article is to indicate the common themes found in this complex range of analyses (Brusco, 1989; Sforzi, 1990; Nuti, 1992; Bramanti and Maggioni, 1997), emphasising both the spatial or local aspects of industrial development and the influence of specific institutional and, more generally, political and cultural arrangements on the development of factors of innovation and performance. The links between firms and the local environment often help to explain the different paths of innovation and the evolutionary patterns of the systems analysed. Particular attention will be given to the industrial districts of Northeast Italy.

In this paper we define the local systems in Northeast Italy[1] as Multilevel Neural Networks (MNN), characterised by specific sources, poles, nodes, and final users. This system works as a relational network with several "autonomous" states that are informatively and cognitively incomplete, but "regulated" by deeply embedded factors of self-organisation and self-co-ordination "from below" (from the bottom up). This neural network is determined by inter-firm relationships (final user/promoter of innovation) and peculiarities of the institutional context (links with public authorities, professional organisations, service infrastructure, research institutes, and non-profit organisations, including

147

voluntary groups, etc.). These actors and institutions share resources, power and decisions - consciously and unconsciously - in a complex process building a division of labour among firms and intermediary institutions (meta-organisers).

The result of these interactions is a process of collective learning that can reduce the costs of propagating information, knowledge and innovation (Winter, 1987; Torrisi, 1988; Cappello, 1994; Choi, 1994; Lombardi, 1994; Pilotti and Volpe, 1994; Audretsch and Vivarelli, 1994; Breschi, 1995; Gottardi, 1996). This context is defined as evolutionary when a new form of division of labour emerges which is characterised by cognitive variety and flexibility, which is not merely "Smithian" but "Marshallian". A Smithian division of labour, in rough terms, is characterised by very simple learning by doing in which "instructions" from a leader predominate; while, in a Marshallian division of labour there are adaptive strategies, imitation and product/process specialisation facilitated by a "district atmosphere". When the division of labour between firms assumes a cognitive nature, learning is more complex, because the key factors are the production of new knowledge, and relationships are mediated by the existing specialised network and by local institutions. In the latest stage of its evolution, meta-organisers have emerged. In some cases, they are the leading firms which have taken on new functions: they now play a more central role in the district in the propagation of knowledge, labour standards, conventions, and in absorbing outside knowledge - through the process described by Nonaka as knowledge recombination: see Nonaka (1994); Rullani (1993; 1994); Arcangeli and Gottardi (1993); and Albertini and Pilotti (1996). In others, this crucial leadership and the process of knowledge creation and propagation are handled by local associations: e.g., business associations and local institutions, be they financial, educational, research centres, quality services or laboratories (AA.VV., 1993; Anastasia and Corò, 1993; Bagnasco and Trigilia, 1984; 1985).

Then, the behaviour of firms in "well defined" contexts must also be examined: meso-economic systems in which there is considerable self-selection and transformation. In order to single out the weaknesses and strengths of the local economies in the Northeast three levels of growing complexity will be analysed:

- the static level that predominates in "Smithian" divisions of technical labour (in which local firms divide the production cycle with many subcontractors in a self-contained hierarchy);
- the adaptive or quasi-dynamic level that predominates in "Marshallian" districts in which the division of labour is among subcontracting firms which are specialised and work for many local final firms which generate incremental innovations (the local system is still hierarchical);

- the generative or creative level that predominates in a "post-Fordist local system" in which the division of labour has a cognitive nature, and it is often developed through networking relationships (sharing competencies in a community-district or through open networks). All nodes (firms) may participate in the creation of new knowledge. Here, the role of meta-organisers is essential for the development of the local system (a double institutional network – both local and regional – characterises these local industrial districts in Northeast Italy).

The industrial districts of Northeast Italy represent an original means for the generation and transfer of information and knowledge through the activities of the firms, based on communication, trust and co-operation among the firms themselves. However, there is also competition among the firms which operate in the same market niche.

This section describes the structure of a Multilevel Neural Network, with a particular emphasis on dominant innovative factors (technology, form of organisation, marketing and business strategies) of the SMEs (small and medium enterprises) in two local industrial systems located in the Northeast Italy: the evolutionary district of Montebelluna (specialised in ski boots) and the relatively static district of Maniago (specialised in cutlery) where leadership is quite limited.

Some characteristics related to the regulation of district economies and their evolution are analysed, in order to demonstrate that the Northeast's model of development is a specific form of "communitarian or social capitalism" in many ways similar to that of the Rhineland (which is a form of "corporatist capitalism"). However, this analysis demonstrates that, in some cases, local industrial districts are too static and "weak in information", or not well suited to the transfer/re-transfer of knowledge for their local small and medium size firms.

The "Communitarian Capitalism" of Northeast Italy is characterised by wide-spread entrepreneurial individualism, but the firms are enmeshed "within" a social structure dominated by a deeply rooted "culture of solidarity" in which both co-operation and competition have found "natural" conditions to evolve together in a flexible horizontal local system formed by open hierarchies and chain networks (Bianchi, 1995).

Therefore, the focus is on two kinds of conditions, which are representative of district behaviour and networking patterns. These conditions will be examined more thoroughly in the next section, both as to their evolutionary results and their legal regulation. For this reason, the two variables which seem to represent the transformational dynamics and the competitive dichotomies of the districts best are introduced:

I   learning as an evolutionary cognitive resource;
II   the institutional context, with its informative, cognitive structure (Mistri, 1993; Becattini and Rullani, 1993) that drives the local district economy towards a "relational economy", based on interdependence among competencies.

These variables often appear to combine together economic and social factors in the expansion of the cognitive division of labour among the firms, through the enhancement of the web of relationships based on trust (Dei Ottati, 1992; 1994). Patterns of co-operative behaviour do not eliminate selection and competition, but instead competition is often seen as a precondition for such relationships - see Vaccà (1989); Varaldo and Ferrucci (1997).

In the industrial districts of the Northeast, innovation occurred gradually, during the initial stages of development, and was mainly related to processes (and products of low technological content), which were transferred through "learning by doing", both temporally and spatially (Pilotti, 1990; 1996). In these early stages, technological market leadership was commonly consolidated and lead to interrelationships (Belussi and Garibaldo, 1996) between the developing district economy and the outside world according to its organisational model, which was determined by choices made by the individual leading firm, which triggered the initial phase, or by a small leadership group, which formed a centralised network, with its institutional context acting as a "passive system".

At this stage (see Figure 7.1) leadership is a proxy for the political and institutional authorities which were rather weak in the 1970s. The actors learn from the simple instructions. This acquired knowledge through learning-by-doing, which is slow and costly, was compatible with a stable competitive environment and a pervasive community identity. Industrial leadership plays a key role in forming the manufacturing area and primary skills in the new identity of the district community, hence the need for a guided transition to industrialisation. This industrialisation could have been disruptive for old "non-manufacturing" identity, because of its new needs and the development of more advanced social relationships.

However, local industrial development was influenced by the *embedded community identity*, which produced flexible, non-conflictual and co-operative arrangements among new entrepreneurs, new skills and a new spatial organisation of labour, which shared the same "moral values" and "way of life". This "continuous" sharing of values and experiences, in turn, encouraged the transfer and exchange of information and knowledge about the technical systems, often informally. The district community process of integration, mediated by the district leaders, changed midway through the 1980s due to the pressures of globalisation and internationalisation (Cer/Irs, 1993).

In the second stage, beginning in the early 1980s, firms became more dynamic as the initially slow process of increasing the technical division of labour felt the effects of the de-verticalisation of industrial district systems. During this phase network externalities were interwoven with widespread innovation in processes and products (Capello, 1994), accompanied by the reinforcement of associations and the social and economic intermediary district infrastructure, with more open and pluralistic leadership (Pilotti, 1990; 1996). Such associations and structures consolidated the pre-industrial values of trust and solidarity in new relationships, setting up a peculiar form of social capitalism within the dominant SMEs. This occurred because such relationships were deeply rooted in the local community through non self-interested individualism and were therefore less prone to ideological conflict.

Figure 7.1 The evolution of systems and actors in local systems in Northeast Italy

	Actors	Structures	Type of co-ordination	Resources
1970s	Leadership of individual firms	Quasi integrated firms	Internal market	Learning by doing
			Solidarity	
		Hierarchical networks		
1980s	Intermediate associations	Alliance networks	Relational contracts	**Learning by co-operating**
	Multiple leaders	Open networks	Co-operation/ competition	
1990s	Pluralistic leadership	Virtual firms	Innovative projects	Learning by innovating
		Open networks		
	Meta organisers		Evolutionary networks	
		Multi focal organisations		

Economic consolidation has been achieved through greater openness of small and medium-sized firms to external markets and by greater operational and strategic independence in national or international markets. The exchange of information between district firms has grown, surmounting the rigidity of the transfers through the original leaders or centralised networks. This process favours a widened leadership in processes, products, new manufacturing functions and market strategies - (see: multiple leadership in the table above) - to the advantage of both the existing leaders and growing peripheral actors. It reduces the costs of innovation by widening transactions of a co-operative nature in a more selective context for both resources and ways to adjust to change. However, a move towards more horizontal organisations (Belussi, 1992) where the management does not dominate the system, as in the early stage, when its functions of leadership were clearly identifiable, is widely felt. At the same time, network relations are able to direct individual efforts towards sustainable projects, enlarging the productive basis in the direction of multi-focal organisation (Doz, Prahalad and Hamel, 1990). The role of intermediate nodes on the Multilevel Neural Network is of great importance in this new evolutionary context, for example there are organisations which provide technical assistance in innovative projects through Business Innovation Centres, Technology Parks and Universities, Chambers of Commerce, etc., which are involved in implementing European programmes and international schemes.

This kind of institutional network plays an important role in building interfaces with other organisations on both the local and multi levels, generally by consolidating relations within the system and activating resources and structures in order to pursue four main goals:

- the introduction of flexibility in the selection of the most suitable plans (in training, R&D, internationalisation, network infrastructure and firm services);
- increasing the firms' capacity for making their own plans and re-programming on a local basis;
- searching for and creating new benefits on a global level in line with real and potential local resources;
- support for the search and selection of new alliances and agreements with internal and external firms, balancing competition and co-operation, minimising restrictions and expanding opportunities.

The Multilevel Neural Network of the Northeast: enterprises and institutions between dynamics and incomplete information

How can the innovative resources used in a complex system like Northeast Italy be described? How can the various economic, organisational, institutional and geographical levels be accounted for, without oversimplifying the picture?

First, it can be assumed that the economy of Northeast Italy evolves on the basis of differentiated learning capacities within a complex system of economic and social relations, which encourage the circulation of knowledge and information useful for economic growth and the establishment of industrial leadership. This system "without a centre" can only be understood by examining the institutional level, particularly the meta-organising institutions, which co-ordinate the exchange and increase of information and knowledge for the social actors and firms in the specific industrial context. Information and knowledge that would otherwise remain extremely fragmented and of little use.

This is the rationale of our approach to describing the economy of Northeast Italy as a Multilevel Neural Network. This approach tends to re-evaluate territorial contexts as "specific and active containers of resources for innovation", rather than simply as factors of localisation

(Becattini and Rullani, 1993). In order to understand its growth path, the innovative potential of the resources and actors involved in each local systems, as well as the interrelations between them, are examined.

An orientation towards growth and innovation should be assumed due to the particular system of relations which exist in the area, the dominant, but incomplete, system of learning and knowledge. This system is multi-purpose and multi-centred and oriented to production through self-co-ordination and self-learning. The "activators" of growth within the system have been labelled meta-organisers. There are two classes of meta-organisers: innovative firms and local institutions (both private and public, or sub-systems of institutions) involved directly or indirectly in the process of innovation.

The Multilevel Neural Network consists of four levels on each of which agents/actors, national sub-systems and local institutions enjoy considerable autonomy. They are:

1   the level of national and super-national institutions which play a role in innovation by activating specific resources (especially financial);

2   the level of nodes, formed by local institutions, or regional agencies, specifically involved in activating resources for innovation (research as well as training), or organising innovative projects (in which they act as vertical meta-organisers, integrating resources, projects and institutions);

3   the level of poles, i.e. the working structures involved in transferring resources for innovation; on this level they act as horizontal meta-organisers in the distribution of resources to users directly; they also participate in the problem-solving process of the firms belonging to the local industrial system related to innovative activity; they have the ability of contextualising and seeking out new problems to be dealt with, since they are the bridges and connectors (for the de-contextualisation or re-contextualisation of knowledge) between the district and the outside world;

4   the level of points, i.e. the final users of innovation in the area; they may be isolated organisations or a matrix of production units which connects a number of poles. Points may be identified as either suppliers or users of innovative resources. They are the agents closest to the market and they are exposed to the pressures of global competition.

The various levels of the MNN are interconnected by a complex system of links, differentiated by direction and intensity, primarily between within the system and the outside. Connections between nodes and poles may be described as strong and weak (though unconnected situations may also occur) according to:

-    direction: one-way or two-way links,
-    function: supplier or user relationships,
-    duration: the stability of the connection and its **repetition**,

- intensity: the relative importance of the exchange of information and knowledge as assigned by participants.

These connections may be classified as a series of non-alternative functions, which involve financial, technological, communicative, and organisational inputs.

The aims of the connections can be analysed by their innovative content, according to whether they are oriented towards:
- intermediary activities, i.e. inputs in other activities,
- final activities, only indirectly involved with other activities.

They may also be differentiated by their prevalent impact (or by their expected result versus actual results, consciously or unconsciously). They may involve all the firms which belong to the local industrial system (territorial impact), new relationships between industry and distribution, the provision of new services, or the new extension of existing services (functional impact). They may also have a technical-organisational impact if the technological development is directed towards the inter-organisational system (IOS), or electronic data interchange (EDI). They may also differ in the level of formalisation reached, that is in the codification and transferability of knowledge.

In our scheme a key role is clearly played by institutions, as connectors for both economic and non-economic relations. Several economists have provided theoretical insight into this crucial issue. North (1991), inspired by American institutional economists of 1930s, has described the role and scope of institutions as to create order and reduce uncertainty in exchange. Together with standard economic constraints, they define the set of choices and sometimes determine production and transaction costs, hence profitability and the possibility of initiating a given economic activity. They evolve incrementally, connecting the past with the present and future; in this sense history is largely the history of institutional evolution in which economic results can only be understood as part of sequential history.

In Arrow's view, in his famous article of 1962, the role played by economic institutions may overcome the problem of "market failure" in the creation of new scientific knowledge, by absorbing the excess risk. This occurs when institutions absorb the costs of new knowledge, rather than simply reducing the costs of non-knowledge (as in Williamson's model of contractualism). By extension, institutions may also influence the transfer of knowledge among agents and they may participate in the collective establishment of practical research projects for introducing technical change in firms. "Spontaneous order" is also reached in Hayek's "individualistic programme", which rejects explicit co-ordination and allows for effects of market mechanisms alone. However, this vision has been radically re-worked by Elster (1995, p.350-351), for whom a dynamic set of (more or less) explicit and intentional social customs and rules produce convergence and co-ordination of expectations, and hence social (and economic) order and stability. Elster associates the problem of co-operation with predictability of behaviour, and claims that disorder not only derives from lack of co-operation but also from unpredictable behaviour. Thus, co-ordination, as well as co-operation, becomes crucial. But co-operation may derive from self-interested behaviour. Self-interested individual actions evolve alongside regulations and institutions, for many different reasons, often without a single overall view of the objectives. The process of co-ordination in social systems leads to the selective creation of blocks of local- or multi-local adaptation. Such selection, however, can only be compared metaphorically to biological selection, as solutions are "locally selected" and they do not necessarily represent the most efficient choice. However, the evolution of local systems is fully in the hands of individual agents (firms). Unlike other agents, man is able to adopt indirect strategies, and not only in pursuit of his self-interest. In other words, he may act in the interest of others or the group: trust, co-operation, and social integration are the social/relational goods produced by Italian local systems. In these actions, calculation loses its importance, and learning is no longer sufficient in the face of the need for creative construction.

Clearly, on the level of the MNN, the problem of co-ordination (or inter-connectivity) rather than that of co-operation deserves the most attention, whereas, on a lower level, the analysis of co-operation prevails over co-ordination as is reflected in the literature about Italian districts.

This approach has profound consequences on the way industrial policy is depicted: incomplete information raises the problem of the convergence between two parallel paths: the strategies of innovative firms, on one hand, and public targets, on the other, thus, going from co-operation to co-ordination and vice versa. Appropriate institutions must explore a variety of solutions for transferring information and knowledge, without a pre established model.

The fundamental nature of our approach is found in the MNN. It is a complex social and economic system that allows for varying degrees of self-organisation and co-operation among agents, sub-systems, institutions and regulations (both explicit and implicit).

The MNN is not the result of a natural "social order", or an empirical fact, but describes the mechanisms that generate and influence the creation and work of specific (voluntary) institutions, their adequacy, and their contribution to social order, stability and growth.

The MNN can be compared to an institutionally based system of co-ordination that reduces transaction costs (non-knowledge costs), but it is also able to increase the advantages of co-operation (by providing new knowledge). What emerges—in a particular context of relations among subjects, systems and institutions—is a meso-system endowed with a general, developing capacity for learning at the collective level.

The dynamics of this system is described in detail, through the case-studies of two Northeast districts (ski boots in Montebelluna and knives in Maniago).

Two typical Northeast districts: Montebelluna and Maniago

Montebelluna: an evolutionary district

From original localisation to specialisation The first stage occurred between the end of the last century through the 1950s. It was characterised by a single, non standardised product: the "dalmara" until the 1920s, and the "pedula climbing" boot in the 1920s and 1930s. The commercial development of these products was largely influenced by local factors in which transport played a strategic role. In Lombardy and Piedmont (Northwest Italy), similar situations had developed, with a high concentration of shoemakers and their initial industrialisation, but they did not compete with the limited market of the Montebelluna district.

In these years, the 1920s and 1930s, the production structure of the Montebelluna area resembled a static district model: production based on craftsmanship, favoured by pre-industrial techniques and by articulated but limited demand, both quantitatively and qualitatively simply because boots were an elite consumer good through the mid 1950s.

The First World War was particularly dramatic for the growing district. During the war, some local craftsmen supplied shoes for the army, but not enough to compensate for problems of the market during and after the war, given the limited size of the firms and the weakness of management and organisations. Post-war reconstruction was long and hard and unemployment was widespread. Nevertheless, production was consolidated and the "pedula climbing" boot was a growing market. From the mid 1930s onwards, sports shoe production developed thanks to the growing popularity of skiing. In Europe, downhill skiing was the most popular mountain sport in which a range of boots were used for skiing and for walking after the skis were unfastened. In fact, until the 1960s, the boots were made entirely of water-proof leather. In this period the first process of specialisation occurred by breaking down of the boot and its production process:
- first, according to use, ski boots versus mountain boots;
- second, its component parts (soles, uppers, outer and inner body).

This technical break-down continued until recently, so a technological and planning "revolution" occurred, through the use of plastics and new raw materials and by breaking down the product into simpler and more standardised parts.

In the early 1930s, the boot went from being a multi-use to a single use product. On the one hand, the sole was flattened and hardened, while the toe was squared to bind the boot better to the ski which would allow the skier to control the ski better. This demonstrates the importance of consumers in the evolution of these boots. There followed a gradual evolution in both ski boots and pedula boots. On the other hand, the drive towards innovation favoured the first division of labour in the boot industry, the Vibram sole, inspired by a rock climber, which was introduced by Vitale Bramani (an entrepreneur from Piedmont) in 1939, and quickly adopted by all firms of the district. This sole was made of a single piece of vulcanised rubber sewn or glued to the upper (previously soles were made by sewing together various layers of leather). This innovation led to specialisation both in the division of labour and manufacturing techniques, which led to 15%-20% reduction in average labour time.

At this stage, the wide use of this production technology forced the industrialisation of the district. Before the First World War, the four biggest firms had no more than 20 employees. This trend evolved rapidly because national and international markets called for new entrepreneurs who were better prepared for large scale trade, and able to manage production on an industrial basis.

Until this time, the prevailing industrial technique was based on experience, or "the culture of practical know-how". This knowledge about the production process was ingrained in the area's labour force and potential entrepreneurs. Cultural and physical proximity allowed technical spill-over from the more consolidated firms, and an informal transfer of useful knowledge about both products and processes. In the area the technical division of labour was widely dispersed. Economic co-ordination was guaranteed, on one hand, by the attractive role played by industry leaders, and on the other hand, by community cohesion, which did not yet have institutional or political dimensions, but had "individualistic solidarity" or "communitarian identity", (for more on this subject see the works of Georg Simmel published between 1913 and 1917).

The discovery of new final markets and reworking of the product. The second stage runs from 1950 through the late 1960s and was characterised by the decision of the businessmen of Montebelluna to transform the ski boot into a single-use product. In this period the industrial structure of the local production system was consolidated, and all manufacturing was concentrated in the area. Thus, it moved towards becoming a "mature" Marshallian industrial district.

In this period many phenomena favoured the expansion of the hiking and ski boot market. Most importantly:
- favourable economic circumstances;
- steady growth in average income;
- increased consumption of sporting goods.

Other social phenomena reinforced this trend:
- the 1956 winter Olympic games in Cortina which attracted world-wide attention to the Montebelluna area, especially from Northern European and North American users and suppliers;
- the general spread of winter sports, especially skiing, which was no longer seen as an elite sport.

The firms specialised in ski boot production were few in number (about 30) at the time and only 10% of them could be considered large.

The district was formed by some leading firms (guiding a group of firms and production units, specialised in finished goods or components), and numerous subcontractors, producers of components and finished goods. The typical products manufactured in the district were, at that time, mountain boots, after-ski boots, and walking boots.

In the 1960s, ski footwear saw a real boom, with demand growing from 300,000 pairs in 1963 to 700,000 in 1969. In 1969 there were seven large leading firms which produced and marketed their own products (boots). Around them, there was a group of smaller firms which produced cheaper items for the domestic market.

The investment in ski boot production demanded financial resources which the small artisan firms and imitative enterprises, with low know-how (based exclusively on "learning by doing"), which operated in the local markets, did not possess. The leading firms were successful because they had developed formalised and transferable knowledge, by using modern techniques, developed both inside and outside the district, appropriate for operating world-wide. This is why new business took off. However, in some market niches, smaller firms could compete, with both economically and commercially simpler products, such as "light walking boots" and "after-ski boots". The last product utilised industrial and commercial know-how which was relatively accessible and appropriable through "imitative" processes, along the subcontracting production chain. In this stage of development, the decentralisation of tasks, capacity, or single phases of production, fostered local networks and built inter-district relationships.

In the Montebelluna district, this decentralisation was facilitated by the diffuse know-how of smaller firms and subcontractors, which assured the leading firms of the quality of their components and semifinished products. The district shared a common industrial atmosphere, like that described by Marshall in the English case. Transactions among agents were mediated by the "good working of the economic environment" and the transparency of the internal market. There was co-operation among the various agents. However, prices guided the local chains of partially competitive, partially collusive relationships between suppliers and sub-contractors (as compared to those outside the district). This internalised the widespread technical externalities, and socialised the costs of control through communitarian relationships.

Technological leverage: industrial transformation and quasi vertical-integration in the 1970s and 1980s. The early 1970s coincides with the creation of the plastic ski boot. In 1968, a plastics expert from Colorado, Bob Lange, made what can be truly called a revolutionary discovery, as far as ski boots are concerned. Lange made the whole external case of the boot from a very rigid synthetic material, Adiprene (a kind of polyurethane), by pouring it into a mould. Inside the case he placed a smaller soft boot for the foot. It was such an ingenious idea that all leading Italian and foreign firms adopted the method in time and perfected the injection process. Boot production was divided into the external and internal boot. The spread of plastic ski boots continued to grow from 1970 to 1975, due to growing demand, sustained by rising incomes and the popularity of downhill skiing. The success of the "blue avalanche"—the Italian national ski team—and mass media's effect on advertising created a boom in national consumption. Demand continued to increase and ski boot production in the area reached 4,100,000 pairs in 1979.

The organisation of production in the district was divided into three separate stages: leading firms set up satellite businesses, normally medium-sized firms, which, in turn, organised a putting out system to home-based workers. However, this vertical decentralisation of tasks and activities was concentrated in the district and in the nearby towns. This process proved beneficial for both leading firms and subcontractors. The large firms encouraged small firms to improve their technical skills (and hence the quality of semi-final or final goods, and components): these firms were not in fact their direct competitors; on the other side, "satellite" firms could benefit from a relationship of trust with long-term commitment from their counterparts. Such long-term relationships went beyond temporary economic convenience and, thus, promoted a climate of reciprocal trust.

At this stage the Montebelluna district was close to the third ideal-type, the "dynamic model", with the deverticalisation led by leading firms, or by those controlling access to markets. However, the division of labour within the district was still based on the technical decomposition of tasks. Considerable expansion in variety also occurred to create higher standards of quality, combined with some standardisation of basic components, and a partial rearrangement of the production cycle.

The plastic ski boot innovation brought about a radical re-shaping of the district, through processes of differentiation and diversification among the firms, modifying the technical division of labour. The reasons for diversification were obvious. The production of plastic ski boots was firmly in the hands of a few large firms, with their own proprietary know-how and large investment in machinery and distribution. Small and medium size firms had to shift to similar products, using the same kind of technology which the district already possessed. Indeed, the existence of the district encouraged the production of other sports shoes. The period saw the development of products based on creative design and commercial instinct like the Moon Boot (a plastic after-ski boot), first marketed by Tecnica, and imitated by all firms in the area. This simple to make item emphasised style, with its bright colours, and led to highly industrialised production. Many new businesses based on this product were begun because market entry was relatively easy, capital investment low, and the technology used was accessible, creating a market niche for a low-cost product.

In the Montebelluna area, firms producing ski boots before the adoption of plastics, faced a strategic decision: either to shift all their plant and machinery to the new technology, running the risk of overproduction, or to abandon their business, and shift to related products, such as after-ski boots, mountain walking boots, or other sports boots and shoes for motorcycling and cycling.

In the late 1970s and early 1980s, the district began its first period of widespread product differentiation, combined, in some cases, with aggressive marketing by a group of small firms. Alongside the core products of ski and after-ski boots manufactured by the large and middle-sized leading firms and their networks, new businesses arose. Both new products, like "high-tech" shoes and "low tech" goods, were produced, the production of which started to be decentralised to countries with lower costs.

During the 1980s, this district, with an annual production of 3,500,000 to 4,000,000 pairs of ski boots, was able to defend its leadership and international market share which is impressive at over 70% of the total market. However, in many niches, intra-district competition became more intense. In particular, two factors point to potential weaknesses: the technical evolution in raw materials and products, activities which derive from developments in large chemical firms outside the district, and the continuing evolution of marketing and distribution channels.

The complexity of technology and competition: the role of meta organisers. After twenty years of rising demand, the growth of the district came to a halt in the early 1980s. Crisis hit ski boot production mainly, but also after-ski boots were affected. The Montebelluna local system, as a whole, was expanding, while the demand for winter sports footwear was falling. The firms were faced with a severe crisis of overproduction.

The effects of the crisis were felt above all by medium and large scale enterprises, while small firms and craft shops were less affected. The recession lasted until 1982; then a period of recovery began. The crisis in the ski boots sector underlined the limits of mass markets and called for greater differentiation. The lack of differentiation was the cause of the bankruptcies of some well-known firms with established brand names (Munari and Garmont). The biggest entrepreneurs realised that to be competitive it was necessary to support sales with better distribution networks and marketing strategies. Several of them (Nordica, Lotto, Diadora, Dolomite and Tecnica), invested considerable financial resources in massive advertising campaigns. Some firms increased their product diversification and entered new markets: winter articles and all sorts of athletic shoes: trainers, tennis, jogging, volleyball, trekking, and walking shoes, as well as football boots.

Recovery, however, did not last long, and in 1987 the Montebelluna district was in recession again. The causes were similar to those of the previous crisis. The second shock, however, also affected small and very small firms and the number of craft shops in the district fell considerably.

Businesses in the area continued to have excess capacity, and high labour costs. The differentiation policies no longer seemed appropriate for the variety in demand.

In 1988 the district was still very fragmented: only 2% of firms had more than 100 employees. However, a positive sign was that a large number of district firms were producing under their own trademark. 1990 was a year of recovery for the area compared to the previous three years. The early 1990s witnessed a transformation in the product-mix of the area, led by non winter items. In these years they accounted for nearly 70% of the total production of the Montebelluna area. This is a clear sign of nearly complete re-specialisation of the district. This respecialisation compensated for the variability of demand in the "winter segment" of the market.

This last restructuring has been facilitated by local collective institutions, both public and private, within the district: the Chamber of Commerce, the museum of mountain shoes, professional and business associations, etc.

There was increased variety in both supply and demand. The respecialisation process was made possible by the interrelations created between production and distribution. The ability to interact with the final users of their products was the foundation of this process.

The evolution in production can be described as both radical and contiguous diversification, while some firms have enlarged their influence through acquisitions outside the area.

Since the mid 1980s, district leaders no longer appear to play a dominant role in the product and market strategies of district firms. In recent years, intermediate economic and industrial associations (meta-organisers) have became more important, especially for the small and medium sized firms.

The system has moved beyond the traditional forms of learning. Now many firms have access to cognitive based learning and have entered open chains of subcontractors based not only on a greater division of labour, but on the generation of new knowledge. This type of learning is connected with more formalised forms of knowledge that can be transferred into and re-transferred out of the district. If the old Marshallian district based its competitiveness on the internalisation of externalities, this new form of industrial system is able to exploit the most innovative resources, both information and knowledge, which are recombined by the various firms which populate the district.

Maniago: a static district

The district's historic origins

The original products of the Maniago district, going back to the fifteenth century, were work knives and agricultural tools; scissors, pocket and sports knives were added to the range of the district's products, beginning in the eighteenth century. The district's origins can be traced back to 1453 when Count Nicolò obtained a permit from Venice to change the course of the Colvera to form a canal along which iron works were to be built: the water provided the power to turn stone grinders. The area soon became renowned for the craftsmanship of its blacksmiths, and production was gradually enlarged from agricultural and other tools to include smaller items, such as pocket knives and scissors for the noble and free men of the area. Over the years some of the blacksmiths became specialised in the production of semi-finished blades, and beginning in the early seventeenth century the craftsmen were divided into producers of small finished items, *fabbro da fino* and those who continued to manufacture semi-finished items and larger tools, *fabbro da grosso*. This distinction may be described as the first significant specialisation in the area. In the first half of the nineteenth century, this specialisation advanced, even though the markets for their products were still local and were scarcely differentiated, serving primarily agriculture.

The history of the Maniago knife industry since the last quarter of the nineteenth century is one of oscillations between momentary successes and failures to overcome the constraints of small-scale craft production. The district has suffered from recurring crises of under-production followed by over production.

As we can see from this brief historical review, co-operation among entrepreneurs goes back to the origins of the district.

In 1870 a group of twenty entrepreneurs decided to set up a company (the *Società dei capitalisti*) to take over the entire production of several workshops. At that time, the Maniago district was under pressure because it could not satisfy the volume of orders without the risk of either delaying deliveries or reducing quality. This company became a supplier of raw materials, so that the blacksmiths began to restrict their activity to manufacturing alone. This marked the second step in specialisation towards industrial manufacturing. It was also the first sign of industrial grouping—perhaps unique in the history of the Northeast—though, as we shall see, no leading firm emerged.

Alongside the *Società dei capitalisti*, another industrial firm was founded a few years later: *Zecchin-Antonini* in 1886. In marketing its products this company used both travelling salesmen, as had been done in the past, as well as wholesalers and retailers in Italy. Specialisation bore its first fruits, in terms of new commercial outlets, and the products of Maniago's blacksmiths or "fabbri da fino" spread throughout the country. *Zecchin-Antonini* become one of the first groups in the knife industry. The craftsmen depended on the company for advance payments and supplies of raw materials. They were therefore forced to accept the firm's prices. But the workshops stopped supplying the finished products, so the company was forced to close.

In 1870, the *Società Cooperativa della Premiata Industria Fabbrile di Maniago* was established to purchase and sell raw materials, as well as to sell finished products. Over 200 master craftsmen were associated with the company of 500 workers predominantly in craft shops. Later, each associate tried to stay in business alone. In 1907, the *Società Anonima Marx e Comp. Coltellerie Riunite* took over the *Società Cooperativa della Premiata Industria Fabbrile*. This firm brought to Maniago all the equipment and techniques used in Germany and instructed the local craftsmen in the use of the machinery as a step away from traditional craft methods. During First World War, Marx was forced to abandon its activities in Italy and the factory was closed.

After the war in 1922, some local entrepreneurs set up the *Manifattura Sina e Com.* but in 1927 the company went bankrupt.

In 1929, a new *Consorzio* was founded to facilitate the purchase of raw materials, the regulation of prices and the co-ordination of production. The *Consortium* was closed four years later for political and institutional reasons.

In 1960 the *Consorzio Coltellinai* was set up for the same purpose with 70 small and medium firms taking part. The consortium's role included marketing, international markets, as well as promoting product quality (to establish guarantees and regulations of a European standard). This is the only institution still operating today. However, some entrepreneurs have used the consortium as a means of making contact with new customers, only to offer the same products sold by the consortium at lower prices afterwards. In 1972, the *Coltellerie riunite* were taken over by *S.I.A.P.* whose objective was to create a large centre for producing scissors. But a few years later, *S.I.A.P.* became part of the *Carraro* group and was forced to reconvert. Today, it produces gears, reducers and transmissions for the *Carraro* group.

The process of establishing new industrial organisations continued—despite the opposition of various groups, firms and professional associations—and, in 1983, *Sistema Maniago*, an association of 20 leading knife manufacturers was established. However, because of problems with the *Consorzio Coltellinai*, it closed two years later.

What emerges from this history is the lack of stability in the framework provided by intermediary organisations which could play the role of meta-organising institutions.

Small firms, which manufacture a few components, or carry out a few tasks, clearly cannot adapt their products to changes in demand or operate in complex, volatile markets, which often include foreign firms which enjoy more favourable labour costs. The information and technical knowledge in the district, on the other hand, is "filtered" from outside by a few agents which act as barrier.

The partial successes of the various leading firms over the years—which were based essentially on costs—were penalised by unsettling rivalries.

The leadership in the Maniago district appears to be inadequate to promote new relationships among firms to strengthen the inter-firm division of labour. The industrial structure is extremely fragmented, and the level of creativity is quite low. The district has been in decline, since the 1980s, with a decrease in employees from 3,000 to 1,200, and in the number of firms from 300 to 200.

The local production system

At the present, the average size of knife manufacturers is somewhat limited. Half of the firms consist of just one or two employees. These firms are generally family-managed.

Table 7.1 Knife manufacturers and number of employees

Employees	% Manufacturers	% Employees
Up to 2	50.6	12.1
3-5	21.5	13.8
6-10	13.4	17.7
11-20	10.4	25.4
Over 20	4.1	31.0
Total	100.0	100.0

Two different types of firms can be found in the Maniago district:
a) firms competing in national and international markets, selling under their own trade mark, and having a relatively complex structure. The firms belonging to this group can be described as "knife manufacturers". They represent 35% of the productive units within the Maniago district, employ 63% of the work force involved in knife production, and produce 80% of the turnover;
b) subcontracting firms involved prevalently in the production of semi finished goods, or producing some specific item (scissors, tweezers or tools for the construction industry).
Firms located at the end of the productive cycle have established very high qualitative standards, causing some transfer of know-how to smaller firms. Some indicators for evaluating the capacity of Maniago firms to develop can be identified by examining their sub-contracting models and co-operation strategies. Co-operation in fact is a sign of a firm's willingness to increase its division of labour.

Generally co-operation and agreements among firms in the district involve the development of a specific activity within the firm rather than the entire firm.

The knife manufacturers use their own skills, as well as those of specialised firms present in the district, to design and often to build specialised machinery: this kind of division of labour tends to be closed and circumscribed in the local system. Firms turn to the market outside the district for standard technologies and innovations.

Within the district at least three models of organisation of the production cycle can be found:

a) Integrated cycles: all the phases of the productive process are carried out internally. These are generally large producers of small kitchen knives, a field in which automated technology allows for large-batch production. However, these are firms with simple models of organisation and control over the entire cycle.

b) partial integration of the phases of the productive process with higher added value. Here deverticalisation is concentrated primarily within the local system and involves the cutting and sharpening of blades, moulding the plastic handles and labour-intensive phases, such as grinding and finishing handles. Production is decentralised among small local craft shops;

c) the third model of organisation of production is complete decentralisation: the firm does not carry out any of the productive phases. First, blades, already ground and sharpened, are bought from outside the district (generally from abroad), while assembly and packaging are performed locally. The firm is only responsible for marketing the final product. In this way skills in selecting markets upstream and downstream of the productive process have been developed. Firms in this category have better knowledge of both markets and final users than the others.

The distributive channel most often used by firms is wholesaling. Indirect channels tend to prevail over direct ones, particularly in the case of exports. This means that the manufacturers are dependent on large retailers and buyers.

Large scale retail chains (supermarkets and superstores) are rarely used. Less than 7% of the district's sales take place through this channel, which evidently offers low profit margins and requires a tightly organised production (just in time delivery, packaging suited to self-service purchases, etc.).

Over the last decade, the firms have experienced a radical extension of a Smithian (technical) division of labour.

Empirical research has shown that turnover with respect to firm size, differs in firms with more than 20 employees from those with less than 20 (the former have productivity levels 2 or 3 times greater than micro-firms). In general, average turnover per employee is higher in knife manufacture.

However, the industrial structure is fragile, the hierarchical control exercised by the few firms having direct relations with the final markets is high. Little innovation and learning has taken place over the last decade. Knife manufacturers produce for a variety of markets (kitchen, professional, pocket, multi-use and sports knives), but few firms are specialised in particular products (less than 30 firms specialise in one of these areas alone, while 23 of them specialise in pocket and sports knives). Only in the field of kitchen knives are there true leading firms which have significant, though still inadequate, market shares. In this field, legislation has prohibited the use of porous materials. This has led to the production of "technological knives" with plastic handles, produced on a large scale through automated systems. A variety of technologies are in use. In this field there are 18 firms in the area, including *Alexander, Beltrame, Di Bortolo* and *Ausonia*, even though the latter does much of its production outside the district. Local firms have lost competitiveness compared to Premana, another industrial district specialised in cutlery. Local firms have also been affected by the aggressive competition from Brasilian and Korean firms at the lower end of the quality scale, and from the French and German on higher end. In the field of professional knives, craft work is still very competitive, and is often preferred to industrial production. 15 firms work in this field, though few of them have managed to promote their products in recent years.

Finally, in the field of pocket, multi-purpose and sports knives competition among firms is based on quality and design. 38 firms work in this field, and 35 of them are specialised in pocket knives. They are generally small craft shops, which do not require large investment in machinery. All these small firms have to compete with Victorinox, a large manufacturer, which benefits from economies of scale unimaginable for district firms. There are 30 firms producing sports knives, some of which have managed to establish their name both nationally and internationally. They have based their competitive strategies on the quality of their products and face competition from American and German manufacturers. What is missing in Maniago are intermediary institutions to orient entrepreneurs on questions of quality, product innovation and distribution channels.

The absence of intermediary institutions and meta-organisers

We shall now briefly examine two simple attempts that have been made in recent years in this direction: the *Consorzio Coltellinai* and *Sistema Maniago*.

Consorzio Coltellinai, as mentioned above, was set up in 1960 by the Association of Craftsmen and the Chamber of Commerce, in order to promote the development of its members, as well as of the commercial links of the district micro firms. Now the consortium faces problems in four basic areas:
- technology transfer;
- professional and management training;
- Development and propagation of information;
- Development of specific commercial activities.

Since its establishment, the consortium has been a "hostage" of homogenous products. Moreover, the members have provided the consortium with only a small part of their products, which has distorted supply and led to price fixing. Free riding and shirking has been common among members, given the fact that there are no means for sanctioning offenders.

Sistema Maniago was set up in 1985 by a number of leading firms in the district, with the aim of combining the efforts of the top twenty manufacturers in the area in order to:

- penetrate foreign markets,
- organise the district at the major trade fairs;
- provide assistance in sales and marketing;
- conduct market research;
- promote exploitation of new technologies.

This trend could have been seen as a "natural" development of district institutions towards specialisation and complementary to the *Consorzio Coltellai*, rather than as conflicting with it.

Our analysis has shown that the system is for the most part closed: its competitiveness is almost exclusively based on the know-how available in the local context.

The district is still unable to become part of a global network in which a greater cognitive division of labour would reduce the costs of acquiring know-how produced elsewhere.

It is clear that the Maniago knife-manufacturers are unable to produce from their own resources that would give them access to the global circuits of production and circulation of knowledge: they need meta-organisations — infrastructure that provides real services and reinforces their ability to increase the cognitive division of labour. This would consist of a variety of interconnected levels in the following areas:

- research on new materials;
- Development of products for new purposes and markets;
- selection of appropriate sales channels;
- Differentiation in suppliers of materials and components;
- Consolidation of final markets;
- discovery of new final and intermediary clients.

On the one hand, there is a need to create a system of inter-firm relations within the district, permitting selective specialisation among firms. The district lacks interconnecting links with the outside world. Local development agencies could play an important role in the supply of real services, training and system infrastructure (logistic, information, professional services, etc.).

Note

1   A detailed description of institutions and processes characterising such a complex system, with reference to the Veneto region and Northeast Italy in general, can be found in the CUOA research (Covi, Gottardi, Pilotti, 1995; now also in Albertini, Pilotti, 1996).

References

AA.VV. (1993), *L'economia del Nord-Est*, Assofir - Efibanca, Padua, Cedam.

Albertini S. and Pilotti L. (1996), *Reti di reti: apprendimento, comunicazione e cooperazione nel nordest*, Padua, Cedam.

Amin A. and Robins K., (1990), Industrial Districts and regional development: limits and possibilities, in Pyke F., Becattini G. and Sengeberger W. (eds.), *Industrial Districts and Inter-firm Cooperation in Italy*, Ilo, Ginevra.

Anastasia B. and Corò G. (1993), *I distretti industriali in Veneto. Una proposta di individuazione*, Portogruaro, Ediciclo.

Arcangeli F. and Gottardi G. (1993), The Small in between traditional capabilities and new technologies, Paper presented at the workshop Innovation in the traditional sectors and the survival of old technologies, University of Venice, May, 28th-29th.

Audretsch D. and Vivarelli M. (1994), Small Firms and R&D spillovers: evidence from Italy, *Revue d'Economie Industrielle, n. 67*.

Bagnasco A. and Trigilia C. (1984), (eds.) *Società e politica nelle aree di piccola impresa. Il caso di Bassano*, Venice, Arsenale Editrice.

Bagnasco A. and Trigilia C. (1985), (eds.) *Società e politica nelle aree di piccola impresa, Il caso della Valdelsa*, Milan, F. Angeli.

Becattini G. (1979), Dal settore industriale al distretto industriale. Alcune considerazoni sull'unità di indagine in economia industriale, *Economia e Politica Industriale*, n.1.

Becattini G. (1987), *Mercato e forze locali: il distretto industriale*, Bologna, Il Mulino.

Becattini G. (1989), (ed.) *Modelli Locali di sviluppo*, Bologna, Il Mulino.

Becattini G. and Rullani E. (1993), Sistema locale e mercato globale, *Economia e Politica Industriale*, n. 80.

Bellandi M. and Russo M. (1995), (eds.) *Distretti industriali e cambiamento economico locale*, Torino, Rosenberg & Sellier.

Belussi F. (1992), (ed.) *Nuovi modelli di impresa, gerarchie organizzative e imprese rete*, Milan, F. Angeli.

Belussi F., Garibaldo F. (1996), Variety of pattern of post-fordist economy, *Futures*, vol. 28, n.2.

Benko G. and Lipietz A. (1992), (eds.) *Les regions qui gagnent*, Paris, Presses Universitaires de France.

Bianchi P. (1995), *Le politiche industriali dell'Unione Europea*, Bologna, Il Mulino.

Bramanti A. and Maggioni M. (1997), *La dinamica dei sistemi produttivi territoriali: teorie, tecniche, politiche*, Milan, F. Angeli.

Breschi S. (1995), La dimensione spaziale del mutamento tecnologico: una proposta interpretativa, *Economia e Politica Industriale*, n. 86, pp. 179-207.

Brusco S. (1989), *Piccola impresa e distretti industriali*, Turin, Rosemberg & Sellier.

Capello R. (1994), *Spatial Economics of telecommunications network externalities*, Avebury, Aldershot.

Cer-Irs (1993), (ed.) *La trasformazione difficile. VI rapporto*, Bologna, Il Mulino.

Choi J.P.(1994), Network Externalities, Compatibility Choice, and Planning Obsolescence, *The Journal of Industrial Economics*, n.2, pp. 167-182.

David P.A., Foray D. (1993), Marshallian externalities and the Emergence and Spatial stability of Technological Enclaves, Workshop on *Innovation in the traditional Sectors and the Survival of old Technologies*, Venice, May, 28th-29th.

Dei Ottati G. (1992), Fiducia, transazioni intrecciate e credito nel distretto industriale, *Note Economiche*, n.1-2, pp. 1-30.

Dei Ottati G. (1994), Trust, Interlinking transactions, and credit in the industrial districts, *Cambridge Journal of Economics*, vol. 18, n. 6.

Doz Y., Prahalad C.K. and Hamel G. (1990), Control Change and Flexibility: the Dilemma of Transnational Collaboration, in Bartlett M., Doz Y., and Hedlund L. (eds.), *Managing The Global Firm,* London, Routledge.

Elster J. (1995), *Il cemento della società. Uno studio sull'ordine sociale*, Bologna, Il Mulino.

Gottardi G. (1996), Strategie tecnologiche, innovazione senza R&D, e generazione di conoscenza nei distretti e nei sistemi locali, *Quaderni del Dipartimento di Scienze Economiche 'Marco Fanno'*, n. 63/96.

Lombardi M. (1994), L'evoluzione del distretto industriale come sistema informativo: alcuni spunti di riflessione, *L'Industria*, n. 3,

Mistri M. (1993) *Distretti Industriali e mercato unico europeo. Dal paradigma della localizzazione al paradigma dell'informazione*, Istituto Guglielmo Tagliacarne, Milan, F. Angeli.

Nonaka I. (1994), Come un'organizzazione crea conoscenza, *Economia & Management*, n.3, May.

North D.C. (1991), Institutions, *Journal of Economic Perspectives*, vol. 5, pp. 97-112.

Nuti F. (1992), (ed.) *I distretti dell'Industria manifatturiera in Italia*, vol. 1, 2, Milan, F. Angeli.

Pilotti L. (1990), Dall'impresa-struttura all'impresa-progetto: dalle transazioni ai linguaggi nelle forme di impresa a rete, *Economia e Politica Industriale*, n. 65.

Pilotti L. and Volpe M. (1994), Cluster tecnologici, domanda autospecificata e potenziale generativo, *Economia e Politica Industriale*, n. 83.

Pilotti L. (1996), (ed.), *La comunicazione in rete nelle PMI*, Milan, Edizioni Il Sole 24 ore.

Pyke F., Becattini G. and Sengenberger W. (1991), (eds.) Distretti industriali e cooperazione fra imprese in Italia, *Studi e Informazione* della Banca Toscana, Quaderno n.34.

Rullani E. (1993), *Il sistema nord est: una periferia che si fa centro* in AA. VV., Padua, Cedam.

Rullani E. (1994), Economia della conoscenza: una prospettiva emergente, *Economia e Politica Industriale*, n.82.

Sengenberger W. and Pyke F. (1991), Distretti Industriali e rinnovamento economico locale, *Il Ponte*, n.10.

Sforzi F. (1990), The Italian Districts in The Italian Economy, in Pyke F., Becattini G. and Sengeberger W. (eds.), *Industrial Districts and Inter-firm Cooperation in Italy*, Ilo, Ginevra.

Torrisi S. (1988), Apprendimento da cooperazione tra imprese e innovazione tecnologica, *Economia e Politica Industriale*, n. 59.

Vaccà S. (1989), *Scienza e Tecnologia nella Economia delle imprese*, Iefe, Milan, F. Angeli.

Varaldo R. and Ferrucci L. (1997), (eds.) *Il distretto industriale tra logiche di impresa e logiche di sistema,* Milan, F. Angeli.

Winter S. (1987), Knowledge and competence as strategic assets, in Teece D. (ed.) *The Competitive Challenge*, Cambridge Mass., Ballinger.

8 The socialisation of competencies in the development of human resources in small enterprise districts

PAOLO CALZA BINI AND M. CARMELA BOSCO

Introduction[1]

The scientific debate about the features of Italian *local production systems* or industrial districts, which developed in international economic literature over the last decade, originates from the research and studies carried out by economists and social scientists based in Central and Northeast of Italy. As early as 1969 an article pointed to the particular nature of economic development in Tuscany. It revealed that its main strength was no longer based on large industry but on small enterprises that exist in "a special climate where the technical aspects of work can be felt in the air; inventions, especially small ones, are transferred without any friction, productive ideas find attentive ears and news about markets and fashion spread very quickly" (Irpet, 1969). Several years later Becattini re-proposed the concept of the industrial district which had already been elaborated by Marshall in 1879.

From this analytical perspective, this viewpoint was extended to include the description of different systems of industrial districts (Frey 1974, Becattini 1979 and 1987), small enterprises (Brusco 1975, Favaretto 1988) and the NEC area (Balloni 1976, Calza Bini 1976 and 1989, Paci 1982). However some of the most interesting results of the research of the 1970s were ignored. In fact, these local production systems not only had a different organisation of production than in Fordism (or Taylorism), but also followed theoretical and cultural models for the development of entrepreneurship and the socialisation of practical, experience based competencies. It should be mentioned that the identity, both collective and individual, of local communities, their histories and cultural backgrounds, the ways in which their cultures are expressed and their daily life have led to particular models for the organisation of production.

Therefore the community participates, not only in the specific production activity but also in the creation of the entire environment in which it is conceived, established, organised, managed and realised. However, if this is the case, it becomes rather hazardous and scientifically incorrect to try to pinpoint "a single and representative abstract model," of this productive system (whether it be the pure model of the industrial district, or applying the looser notion of the local production system) as was done with Fordism, or to consider it as an alternative or substitute for the old optimal model (from Fordism to a kind of *industrial district flexible-specialisation model*).

This is an important point because it shifts attention from the technical and engineering aspects of the enterprise and its organisation to a social vision, emphasising the reproduction and enhancement of human resources. Quality is not built up by training techniques within firms but as a social process of mobilising human resources. In the NEC area, specific human and capital resources have been the essential factors for the social construction of the local economic model.[2] The historical accumulation of productive knowledge and information has been developed within each specific local system in connection with the organisation of the markets and of qualified workers and professionals. Many studies have also highlighted the risk of impoverishing human resources where there is a lack of activity and an inappropriate mix inhibits sufficient relational and informative interaction between the various activities.

The *socialisation of competencies* (in other words, the socialisation of knowledge and information in restricted areas) in fact facilitates a better interchange of skills and synergy that often are the key characteristics of local enterprises and economies (and not only in monocultural industrial areas, Calza Bini, 1981). The reasons for the concentration of global finance and related services in such cities as New York, London and Tokyo do not seem to be much different. In fact, the logic behind the forming of districts in a specific territory, is similar (Sassen, 1991; Mollenkopf and Castells, 1992).

Territory and the socialisation of knowledge: from the first studies to the most recent debate.

On the question of the labour market and on-the-job training, Italian research has emphasised the following elements of theory:
- The existence of different segments of the labour market, characterised by particular productive and organisational processes, for which the measurement of costs and training needs using a simple neo-classical scheme is practically impossible, given the extreme variety of labour practices (i.e. formal-informal, primary-secondary, internal-external);

- the existence of more than one "logic of rationality" (with good inclinations, according to Boudon), in different social environments;
- the variety of social models in a single country is due to the different ways in which schools and training institutions function;
- the presence/absence of interaction and social networks formed by resources, uses and customs;
- the diversity and plurality of the social construction of identities (that consequently determines different models of intentionality);
- the under evaluation of the economic value of competencies and skills acquired in the cognitive accumulation of interactive processes and every day experiences.

Today, as a consequence of these new areas of research, the literature furnishes a more complex definition of the constitution of the local productive system as an organisational model with a strong territorial basis, strong interrelations between the productive system and local institutions in the presence of external economies. This, in turn, brings about a dense interchange of goods and information in the area of production, as well as the continual generation and re-production of specific knowledge, skills and forms of local regulation. These aspects characterise the territory and are not easily exportable (Garofoli and Mazzoni, 1994).

A wealth of varied empirical findings that have emerged from the various studies on Italian local production systems has stimulated work on the construction of ideal analytical models. But, how are the processes of diffusion of existing knowledge among the different actors generated and how is new knowledge created and incorporated in innovations? How does this come about in modern contexts where more complex social systems have substituted the traditional community? The territorial dimension of development is one of the crucial aspects that explains industrial complexity (Becattini and Rullani, 1993).

The aspect we want to highlight from district studies is the shift of focus from the accumulation of material capital to that of competencies. The potential for development is essentially consolidated through the *in loco* accumulation of production competencies, or made up of production practices. Education and on-the-job training is developed through social and community relationships rather than through educational institutions (Calza Bini, 1994). In fact, the codification and de-codification of competencies means that these competencies and skills cannot be transformed into a simple standardised code. On the contrary, they are complex, often elusive and sometimes "difficult to describe precisely". They can only be acquired through first hand experience, continual use or observation by the individual.

The skills of workers and entrepreneurs, in the cases studied, are not only the result of craft traditions, but originate from a mixture of individual and collective memory, of know-how that has been acquired over a relatively long period (which varies according to skills and length of memory) and of knowledge and problems that come up in everyday life and are socialised in social relations in well-defined environments. In such cases, on-the-job learning grows, by combining community or family know-how, where lessons of knowing what to do (and not to do) are socialised.[3]

The socialisation of professional knowledge in industrial districts and in local production systems

In the 1980s, the academic debate denied or greatly underestimated the significance of human resources in the competitive effectiveness of district and network enterprises. The predominant point of view was that the reasons for the competitiveness of the economy were thought to be found on the level of the management of the enterprise. This approach did not give enough attention to the contribution to competitiveness which derived from labour resources of the local pool of labour and professional skills. In other words, the substantial competitive advantage of enterprises in Italian districts or systems of production because of the existence of a skilled and competent labour force was underestimated. This success was built on the accumulation of information and experience, but the same aspects can also lead to crisis and market turbulence. The lack of awareness of the importance of the process of enhancing human resources also prevented adequate studies to determine and demonstrate how this happened, and if it would be possible to reproduce this accumulation of professional competencies (learning by doing, using and interacting) within other less developed areas *artificially*.

In local production systems, daily life produces individual and social accumulation of knowledge, information and experience (that Marx had already seen as the basis for the appropriation and expropriation of skills, connected to the division of labour). The more "skilled" work is, the greater the impulse for cognitive learning develops. In turn, human resources are enhanced and the products of that given area become more attractive. This environment that Marshall had already called, as Becattini highlighted, an *industrial atmosphere* must, however, be produced in some way and must be able to reproduce itself in order to last.

This was not given sufficient consideration in some interpretations of the phenomenon of the so-called Third Italy model - see for instance the theories of flexible specialisation (Sabel, 1987), which were based, by contrast, on the importance of the firm flexibility.

But what makes the territory of an industrial district an area where the socialisation of competencies can take place? The need for face-to-face relations in daily and community life is not in itself sufficient as an explanation. In reality these relations could remain anonymous, indifferent and dormant in respect to cultural transmission (this is what happens in the cities, where relations with neighbours or work colleagues often occurs without any "human" communication or communicative and cultural exchange).

The relationship "education-work," per se, can be evoked only up to a certain point to illuminate the process of the socialisation and the acquisition of competence. It should be remembered: a) that a uniform educational system has rather different results in socially different contexts; b) that productive systems with specific organisational and professional characteristics require specific training institutions to form an adequately trained and socialised work-force.

The term socialisation of competencies (which was coined more than 20 years ago) underlines the double meaning of socialisation. In the normal sense of the term, it is a process that describes the interaction of many actors who share and exchange *redundant* pieces of knowledge and information, by doing things together. At the same time, this relationship among many actors has a technical meaning: the objective of this communication, interaction, familiarisation, learning, gathering experience through interaction with others, creates channels for the propagation of knowledge/innovation. Within each community that forms a local production system or a district, this means a privileged communication system among producers (workers and entrepreneurs) is created, and knowledge is propagated in the daily interactions of work and community life.

From research done on some local production systems in the region of the Marches, the specific skills of the work force were related to "knowledge of production methods" or to the "ability to produce": it was found that they did not necessarily derive from direct work experience, acquired over time, but this was the result of the indirect accumulation of knowledge about the process that permeated the area. When this indirect knowledge of how to perform a given manufacturing process, permeates a local social system, enhancement of the (active or potential) labour force occurs which we can define as the "socialisation for the manufacturing activity" of the population.

This industrial qualification of the labour force in a given area is greater the more the industrial activity in the area considered is developed.

The process of socialisation can act on two different components of the local social system: 1) the potential labour force; 2) potential local entrepreneurship (small artisans, "rising" entrepreneurs, and workers who set up their own businesses). Manufacturing socialisation has several effects on the territory. New enterprises are generated when this process is accompanied by knowledge of the production cycle, the existence of channels for distribution, the availability of economic-financial resources and technical, economic and commercial assistance.

In short, the socialisation of manufacturing competencies by the work force is based more on workers' prior knowledge of the tasks and a tendency to "know what to do", rather than direct experience of a specific task. It is also different from general "socialisation or basic cultural competence"[4] in as far as it is not the acquisition of a general, multifaceted cultural abilities.

Furthermore, general socialisation can be distinguished from specific socialisation. General socialisation means the predisposition and potential of a population in a specific area to carry out manufacturing activities generally. Specific socialisation means the predisposition of labour force in a given area to carry out particular activities. Specific and general socialisation of competencies are interrelated. A vast range of industrial products may require specific skills from the work force that form a preparation for other types of production.

Human resources and the socialisation of competencies: a case study[5]

In this section, an analysis of the "socialisation of competencies" of a ceramics production centre involving 7 towns geographically isolated from large urban industrial areas which has a large European and world market share,[6] is presented (Calza Bini, Bosco, Oteri, and Pieri, 1996).

Historically, the local production system of Civita Castellana, which developed industrially after the Second World War,[7] highlights a particular and unusual socio-productive phenomenon: a large number of co-operatives. The local economic system, based on a few craft shops, was in crisis during the war years, forcing the local owners to close down. In order to protect their only source of revenue, the workers decided to combine their forces and take over ownership of the shops, giving rise to the so-called "co-operative" firms,[8] which has characterised the local economic production infrastructure for many years.

The vitality of local entrepreneurs and the economic boom in the building industry, due to post-war reconstruction, made the initiatives of the entrepreneurs/workers successful. Thereafter, there was continual growth in the area with the creation of new enterprises through widespread start-ups of new firms that lasted until the 1980s. This was a process that we could define as a "proliferation" process where groups of workers decided to leave a factory in order to set up their own. Old worker-associates say that: "firms were created over dinner, different specialised workers that worked in a factory got together and said: we only need a little investment, we have the know-how, all we need is a shed."

From the interviews with older worker-associates, it emerges that there is widespread awareness of the value of human resources and professional competencies needed for manufacturing.

In the wake of the intense and rapid economic expansion, strong bonds between the local community and the ceramic sector developed in Civita Castellana. There was also a general consensus on this productive activity, so much so that the disease (silicosis) was accepted as a fact of life associated with a potter's work. The ceramic district of Civita Castellana followed the same path as that of other Italian districts where new factories and new products continued to be created - even though in this case it involved mainly the "craft" sector. Because the raw material is all imported, the real basis of the district's wealth is clear: it is the workers, the entrepreneurs and their relations with international markets, intensified through their participation in fairs or through contacts with relatives living abroad. Manual labourers still make up the backbone of the district. "I was a builder, I had always worked in construction, then in 1970, some friends, a couple of engineers, and I decided to set up a plate-manufacturing firm. We had some American friends who were looking for these articles. What we learned, we learned from the market." (our interview with an entrepreneur).

In the 1980s, the morphology of local manufacturing, small homogeneous independent enterprises, changed because of financial and credit problems. Almost all the co-operative firms disappeared and a few groups were created controlling several factories. A new order is taking shape that is still evolving: it is being polarised between small independent enterprises and *group enterprises*. But, between the two poles, there is a range of different situations.

Our research in the field leads us to underline some of the diverse features that form the complex skills and competencies of the local pottery workers:
- manual skill: rapidity and precision of action (in the touch up phase), a trained eye (to pinpoint imperfections), perceptive hearing (to recognise from its sound if a dish has a flaw), etc.;
- knowledge of ceramic mixtures (its visual characteristics and consistency, their variation with respect to the external (dampness of the air) and internal (extent of dampness of the moulds) environment; knowledge of the entire production cycle; etc.;
- autonomy: on the basis of knowledge of the mixture and humidity gradient, that can vary from one day to the next, he evaluates and decides on when to "withdraw" (solidify) the mix; etc.

But where does this professional heritage come from? The "know-how of ceramics is in the air" say the inhabitants of Civita, unconsciously quoting Marshall and his "industrial atmosphere." In our research, we tried to identify empirically this "industrial atmosphere".

Interviews with the workers and entrepreneurs underlined that there is only one model of learning based on on-the-job training - the eldest workers teach the youngest, who also try to learn the skill (and the speed with which each task is performed) of the best workers (in factories, payment is partially based on piece-work). We found no connections with the local professional school. Both entrepreneurs and workers were convinced that each inhabitant of Civita Castellana could become a good potter in time (the length of time depends on the task). The best workers enjoy celebrity among the local factories that try to hire them away.

But the process of knowledge transmission goes on outside the factory. At the café or in the square, where the workers gather in the afternoon, they talk about problems encountered at work, about how a piece did not come out right because of a certain error. This probably happens by making fun of the worker who made the mistake; or they talk about the automatic gluing machine that has just arrived and the difficulties or innovations that have come about at work.

The exchange of information and "education" does not only happen in the factory, but also outside, in the community, in the places where the workers spend their "free time."

And also in the family, where the presence of one or more people linked to the world of ceramic production, brings home the latest news concerning the factories that are shutting down or opening up and the reasons for their successes or failures.

This accumulation of competencies in local human resources (be they workers or managers) is a decisive source of competitiveness for the enterprises, even though they do not enjoy exemplary modern technology for production, new organisational models, or advanced advertising and marketing techniques. The firms of the district of Civita Castellana however are able to offer good quality products, to penetrate and hold their own in new markets and to compete or coexist with the biggest multinationals of the sector.

Many interviews with privileged witnesses have uncovered the processes creating specific competencies through the reconstruction of life stories of manual workers, through which the importance of what workers have learned on "the job", and how skills and competencies were acquired, developed and accumulated, making many workers into almost irreplaceable experts, who are crucial for the (qualitative and/or quantitative) competitiveness of the firms, just as important as the introduction of the most recent technological innovations.

The accumulation, evolution, innovation, re-organisation of know-how were induced by the continual socialisation processes in everyday life, even those not strictly connected to work. The development and/or obsolescence of knowledge, were defined and re-defined by knowing what to do, how to resolve a specific new problem, how to adapt new machinery. A part of this knowledge is still tacit and difficult to be codified and it is owned by manual workers of the areas or by technicians.

This world is quite different from typical Taylorist or Fordist organisations, where the knowledge of the productive process is organised by scientific work management operations, through which the know-how of the pool of knowledge and information possessed by the worker is reduced to a specific position in the work place. In our case, the social model spreads knowledge and information more widely among social actors, so a richer division of labour is obtained.

In the past, in the world of craftsmen, there was a long apprenticeship through which the creative talents of the master and solidarity among the workers produced skilled workers whereas, in the

Fordist-Taylorist world, engineers and personnel managers set levels, limits and forms of promotion for professional skills. This attitude has often destroyed competence, but there has been a rediscovery of the need for training, as an exogenous educational factor. Entrepreneurs did not want to invest in the cognitive development of human resources, as this was perceived as a pure cost. Thus, often these organisations were very weak in their ability to produce, develop and accumulate competence. Our field work has demonstrated that in the specific industrial district studied, competencies were developed in many work and social places and not only in "traditional" forms of training. This means that "the environment," intended as a system of social relations that characterises a specific territory, is involved in the process of socialising competencies through numerous social actors (schools, families, friends, etc.).

Notes

1 This text is the result of a joint effort: sections 1, 3 and 5 were written by P. Calza Bini, section 2 is attributed to both authors while section 4 was written by M. C. Bosco.

2 NEC is North East Central (Italy).

3 This knowledge, referred to the small Italian *microcosm of small firms model*, developed in research in the 1970s, did not manage to avoid being snubbed by the most accredited experts on the enterprise and industrial relations. The delay, by one or two decades, of the acknowledgement of these findings has produced some negative effects in the comprehension of the macro differences that discriminate the social economic situation of the country (i.e. the Mezzogiorno) (Mingione and Pugliese, 1995); this has also given space to autonomous tendencies in privileged areas (The Northern League).

4 This is a typical interactive process among several elements, therefore it would be difficult and misleading to define it according to a simplistic classical model of relations between one independent or mono influential variable and the others.

5 The empirical analysis was conducted during the period 1994-5. Fourteen representative firms were selected, where the life stories of these firms and of many manual workers were collected.

6 Italy is the first producer of sanitary pottery. The district studied represents nearly 21% of the total Italian production. In Civita Castellana the production is manufactured by about 100 firms, with 4,000 employees and with 354 billion lira.

7 The production of artistic ceramics at Civita Castellana has very old origins. It began in pre-Roman times (about the tenth century B. C.) characterising the local production activity up until the nineteenth century because of the presence of raw materials, and its closeness to Rome. At the beginning of the twentieth century it turned to producing crockery and sanitary articles. Therefore the historical memory of the local labour force is in the "raw material" processed.

8 The workers who had lost their jobs decided to take over what was left of the firms that they worked in, thereby becoming the owners. They set up companies of capital divided up in equal shares. The number of associates of a firm could be

as many as 20 or 30. In this way a collegial entrepreneurial figure was created — the characteristic figure of the co-operative-worker that carried out the dual role of worker/owner in the firm.

References

Amin A. and Robins K. (1990), 'The Re-Emergence of Regional Economies? The Mythical Geography of Flexible Accumulation, Environment and planning', *Society and Space*, 8, 1 March, pp. 7-34.

Bagnasco A. (1988), *La costruzione sociale del mercato,* Bologna, il Mulino.

Balloni V. (1976), Il sistema imprenditoriale di Fermo: un esempio di modello Centro-Nord-Orientale, *Economia Marche*, n.1.

Becattini G. and Rullani E. (1993), 'Sistema locale e mercato globale', *Economia e Politica*, n. 80.

Becattini G. (1987), (ed.) *Mercato e forze locali: il distretto industriale,* Bologna, il Mulino.

Becattini G. (1979), 'Dal settore industriale al distretto industriale', *Rivista di Politica ed Economia industriale*, n. 1.

Brusco S. (1975), 'Organizzazione del lavoro e decentramento produttivo nel settore metalmeccanico', *Inchiesta*, n. 17.

Brusco S. (1974), Ruolo delle piccole imprese nell'economia capitalistica in AA.VV., *Occupazione, lavoro precario, piccola impresa,* Rome, Ed. Coines.

Brusco S. and Fiorani G. (1995), Competitività, partecipazione e condizione operaia in Bartolozzi P. and Garibaldo F. (eds.), *Lavoro creativo e impresa efficiente,* Rome, Ediesse.

Calza Bini P. (1976), *Economia periferica e classi sociali,* Naples, Liguori Editore.

Calza Bini P. (1981), 'Per un'ulteriore riflessione su: doppio lavoro e politiche dell'occupazione', *Economia e Lavoro* n. 1.

Calza Bini P. (1989), 'Classes sociales et flexibilitè' M. Maruini, L. Reynaud, and C. Romani Mire (eds.), in *La flexibilitè en Italie: debats sur l'emploi,* Paris, Syros.

Calza Bini P. (1994), Il mercato del lavoro negli approcci socio-economici: processi di qualificazione e dequalificazione delle risorse umane e del territorio, paper presented at the meeting 'Colloque Education-travail: etat d'un champ de recherches dans trois pays europeens', Paris, 17th-18th March.

Calza Bini P., Bosco M.C., Oteri C., and Pieri D. (1996), *Sistema locale e distretto industriale: il caso di Civita Castellana,* Civita Castellana, Edizioni Biblioteca Comunale.

Dei Ottati G. (1995), *Tra mercato e comunità,* Milan, F. Angeli.

Favaretto G. (1988), 'Minore impresa partecipe delle trasformazioni produttive' *Progetto e Economia,* n.1.

Frey L., (1974), 'La problematica del decentramento produttivo', *Economia e Politica industriale* n. 6.

Garofoli G. and Mazzoni R. (1994), (ed.), *Sistemi produttivi locali: struttura e trasformazione,* Milan, Franco Angeli.

Irpet (1969), *Lo sviluppo economico della Toscana: un'ipotesi di lavoro,* mimeo, Florence.

Mingione E. and Pugliese E. (1995), 'Modelli occupazionali e disoccupazione giovanile di massa nel Mezzogiorno' in *Disoccupazione perché,* Giullari B. and La Rosa M., (eds.), Milan, Franco Angeli.

Mingione E. (1991), *Fragmented societies,* Oxford, Basil Blackwell.

Mollenkopf J. H., and Castells M. (1992), *Dual City,* New York, Russell Sage Foundation.

Paci M. (1982), *La struttura sociale italiana,* Bologna, Il Mulino.

Piore M. and Sabel C. (1984), *The second industrial divide,* New York, Basic Books.

Rainbrid H. (1996), La costruction sociale de la qualification, in Jobert A. and Marry C., Tanguy, (eds.), *Education et Travail,* Paris, Armand Collin.

Sassen S. (1991), *The global city: New York, London, Tokyo,* Princeton, Princeton University Press.

Sassen S. (1994), *Cities in World Economy,* California/Pine Forge, Sage.

9 The evolution of the chair-manufacturing industry in Friuli-Venezia Giulia

MONICA TAMISARI

Introduction

Italian industrial districts have been the subject, in the last decade, of a large number of studies, because of their performance and original model of organisation based on a division of labour, both horizontal and vertical, among local firms. This model of development characterises the economy of Northeast and Central of Italy, forming the "Adriatic development belt". In the extreme Northeast of this area, there is the chair-manufacturing district of Manzano. This local production system is the subject of this analysis and focuses on the most recent structural changes that have occurred as a consequence of the radical change in its competitive context.

This interest in the chair-manufacturing industry is justified by its importance in both the local and the regional economy. In fact, the chair industry is a large contributor to the total sales revenue of industry in the Region of Friuli-Venezia Giulia, and it is even more important for the economy of the Province of Udine, where most of the chair-manufacturing firms are located.

More than 1,000 firms specialised in the production of wooden chairs (or in processing components of the final product) are concentrated within this small area. Together these firms produce more than 30 million chairs a year, with total sales of over $ 1,300 million, and employ nearly 9,000 people (15,000 if those employed in the whole *filière* of activities are considered). The area accounts for over 80% of the national production of chairs, 50% of the EU's and 30% of the world's. 90% of this production is exported to foreign markets. Most of the firms in the chair manufacturing system (64%) are craft firms, accounting for 30% of total employment.

The area formed by the villages of Manzano, S. Giovanni al Natisone and Corno di Rosazzo (the "Chair Triangle"), is the heart of the chair manufacturing area, accounting for 63% of employment and 67% of the productive capacity of the entire chair-manufacturing system. The surrounding area—to which manufacturing has spread over the years—contains related intermediate activities and supplies the manpower required by the industry.

Table 9.1 Productive structure of chair-manufacturing system

COMMUNES	Shops	Craft	%	Industrial	%	Employees
Buttrio	29	23	79	6	21	163
Chiopris-Viscone	15	7	47	8	53	101
Cividale del Friuli	35	35	26	74	9	98
Cormons	16	1	6	15	94	299
Corno di Rosazzo	107	81	76	26	24	700
Manzano	323	194	60	129	40	2805
Mariano del Friuli	8	2	25	6	75	126
Medea-Romans-Dolegna	5	1	20	4	80	43
Moimacco	28	16	57	12	43	343
Pavia di Udine	90	46	51	44	49	1119
Premariacco	101	66	65	35	35	900
Prepotto	5	5	100	0	0	5
Remanzacco	32	24	75	8	25	111
San Giovanni al Natisone	356	245	69	111	31	2698
San Vito al Torre	28	16	57	12	43	261
TOTAL	1178	762	64	490	36	9772

Source: Chamber of Commerce of Udine (1995)

This analysis of the chair-manufacturing district is based on interviews with chair producers and other relevant actors, such as representatives of business associations, service centre managers and sector experts. The interviews with these informed participants during the data-gathering phase has yielded valuable information, particularly in outlining the dynamics of the most recent changes within the industry. The other source of information comes from the recent publications about the district.

The paper is structured as follows: first the history of the area is briefly outlined; then the results of our research on the recent evolution of the system are presented; finally, a few conclusions based upon this research are drawn.

The phases of the structural evolution of the chair-manufacturing industry

The history of the chair-manufacturing district began about 1880, with the arrival in the district of the first chair-makers from the nearby village of Mariano, when the new national border left the village under Austrian rule.[1]

Near Manzano the chair-makers from Mariano found

circumstances favourable to continuing their activity: most importantly easy access to the Italian market, good transport (because of the recent construction of bridges, roads, railways), an abundance of hydroelectric power (from the numerous mills along the river Natisone) and raw materials, and an abundance of low-priced manpower willing to move from agriculture to industry.[2]

Ten years later, there were eleven firms engaged in chair-manufacturing in the area. They were industrial firms performing the whole production process, run by craftsmen from Mariano and employing local manpower. They spread throughout the entire province.

However, these firms were destroyed during World War I.

Later, during the post-war reconstruction, development was characterised by important changes in the industry's dimensions. Small craft firms (performing the whole production process), run by ex-farmers who were attracted by the expectation of high profits, proliferated.

In fact, demand was growing steadily, both public—for rebuilt public offices—and private—to replace old furniture, particularly among the lower classes.

In this period the largest firms suffered, due to competition from both local craft firms, which enjoyed lower capital, labour and tax costs, and foreign firms, whose industrial organisation ensured greater economies of scale.[3]

During the fifties and the sixties there was a boom in demand, both internationally—due to international specialisation, which assigned furniture manufacturing exclusively to less industrialised areas—and nationally—due to the general increase in income and the development of a consumption pattern typical of developed countries.

The dynamics of demand, together with low technological entry barriers—due to the minimal requirement in terms of initial fixed capital and availability of technical and managerial skills—sparked a process of widespread industrialisation.

In the following decade demand re-structuring began, connected to the evolution of consumer tastes and towards more "fashionable" items. Production shifted from standardised products to small batch production. In particular, the demand for turned and folding chairs increased the technological content and consequently the level of technical skill required.

The local chair-manufacturing system reacted to the structural change in the demand by beginning a process of vertical disintegration. This was possible because of the technical divisibility of the production process.

The functional aggregation of several small firms created economies outside the single firm, but within the territory, that normally characterise industrial district development (Bagnasco, 1988; Becattini, 1987, 1989; Garofoli, 1991). The dense web of informal relationships was regulated by a particular mixture of "competition and co-operation" (Becattini, 1992), "market and community" (Dei Ottati, 1986). The management of the manufacturing process, according to the district model, allowed for a greater reduction of transaction costs because of the low degree of opportunism, and the frequency of interaction reduced the co-ordination costs (in comparison with a much more integrated model) as well. A high level of production flexibility was created. In comparison to the model of standardised mass production, the district model was better equipped to adjust rapidly to the new demand conditions. This ability was due to limited restructuring costs and a flexible distribution of roles among firms (prime contractors and subcontractors), and from a high level of adaptability and flexibility in the labour force.

Then, chair-manufacturing firms could count on a series of competitive factors:

- the presence of economies of specialisation allowing for a reduction in fixed costs and for greater exploitation of production facilities;
- the development of economies of learning (allowing for the acquisition of specific knowledge);
- the introduction of technological innovation through specialised assembly firms and machinery production (the imitation mechanism was sustained by envy, emulation, and fast-copying). This process involved the continuous production of incremental innovation—normally embodied in machinery—and a predisposition to renew equipment (supported by the relatively low costs for new machinery as well as by the existence of an efficient market for the second-hand equipment);
  the creation of a skilled labour market: the existence of a widespread "industrial atmosphere" encouraged the accumulation of skills inside the area;
- the supply of collective services: in the chair-manufacturing district several co-ordinating institutions were created as a result of the initiative of local policy makers and firms; for example, a centre for technological research called CATAS (centre for technical assistance to chair-manufacturing firms), a professional training school called IPSIA (State professional institute for industry and handicrafts), a credit system serving the needs of chair-manufacturing firms,[4] and various export associations.[5] PROMOSEDIA was also important, an institution formed by the Chamber of Commerce and some leading firms to promote sales in Italy and abroad and to identify new markets.

Pulled by an ever increasing demand, the chair-production district grew steadily.[6]

The number of craft firms set up by ex-workers increased. Many firms expanded their productive capacity (investing in fixed capital without investing in "soft" activities, such as research, marketing, data processing, or training), moving from a craft to an industrial scale. This led to growth in the number of medium-sized firms.[7]

The chair manufacturing district and change

The early eighties represented a period of profound crisis for the chair-manufacturing industry.[8]

The most significant factors which contributed to the crisis of the traditional model were:

- reduced European consumption and declining international demand;
- high domestic inflation and increased cost of raw materials and labour; this became particularly serious because of Italy's participation in the EMS which made a policy of competitive devaluation unsustainable;
- globalisation of the market, and increasing Eastern European competition (which enjoyed lower labour and lower raw material costs)[9] as well as that of large integrated American and European (German, Belgium, Dutch) groups (which were able to control final markets to a significant degree).

The *product-oriented* strategy, traditionally pursued by the firms in the district—largely based on three factors: price, production flexibility and the technical quality of the product—was no longer adequate to cope with the increasing complexity of the competitive context.

In this situation some of the largest firms began restructuring processes based mainly on building new distribution channels.[10]

In recent years many firms have developed independent commercial and distributive functions which has allowed them to avoid having their earnings controlled by intermediaries. In addition, they have initiated manufacturing strategies based upon diversifying product and improving the quality of product.

Through diversified, high-quality products sold under their own brands, these firms have partially succeeded in repositioning themselves in the new competitive context.

A largely unstructured system

However, the fall in demand of the early eighties brought several small and medium firms to their knees. In particular, firms which had gone from craft to industrial size firms during the prior expansion suffered. This significant negative trend has been offset by positive trends within the category of smallest firms. Some of the firms that had expanded in the previous period are craft size firms again. Thus, the micro and craft firms proved to be resistant, thanks to their flexible organisation; but this involved the decentralisation of several intermediate manufacturing phases. The largest firms have been able to survive the crisis.[11] While the survival of many smaller firms can be explained by the large increase in subcontracting.

The recession, for different reasons, strengthened both the largest firms—which could exploit economies of scale—and the craft firms—which have flourished as a result of the marked trend towards the decentralisation of the intermediate manufacturing phases of the largest firms. Many old factories have been "converted" into craft shops in search for greater production flexibility.[12]

In such a context, the high level of internal competition caused by the huge increase in small firms has further reduced the profit margins of the firms (already eroded by a general increase in costs), and by the increasing bargaining power of large retailers. This has led to a higher incidence of self-exploitation and increased the risk of bankruptcy.

For all these firms the strategy of cutting costs by sub-contracting out parts of the manufacturing processes has been prevalent. Only recently have some firms developed more structured forms of inter-firm relationships to allow more rigorous business planning.

These leader firms have retained for only the most critical phases of the production cycle (assembly and quality control, design, research, financing and marketing) themselves and are now able to fill even the more demanding niches of the market. These firms also have begun to build information links with suppliers and subcontractors in order to improve co-ordination and thereby minimise the time and cost of filling orders.

However, they have been very slow in implementing "just in time" strategies, as the high average value of product inventory indicates. The examples of stable co-operation in the chair-manufacturing area are still limited to policies of production rationalisation. Mergers and acquisitions (or simply *de facto* control) very often do not represent a real evolution towards more structured groups of firms.

In general, however, chair-manufacturing firms, even the largest ones, are tightly anchored to the local context, particularly with respect to the organisation of production. They prefer to rely on local subcontractors, because of their high level of professional competence, not only for sophisticated but also for standardised operations. The difficulty of managing distant relationships is explained by the lack of both experienced technicians and an entrepreneurial mentality. In addition, social and political instability have created problems in co-operative relationships with foreign partners.[13] Furthermore, the transfer of know-how and technology is strongly resisted by local entrepreneurs, who are afraid of encouraging competition in a sector already characterised by very low barriers to entry.[14]

The most successful cases of sub-contracting for foreign customers have occurred in seats, upholstery, finishing and padding.[15]

Some attempts to internationalise production in accordance with the principle of a more global division of labour have also been made (although most of them are still in the planning stages). Specifically, these attempts have included:

- The outsourcing of the simple and low value-added phases of manufacturing directly to the countries providing the raw materials: for example, chair stuffing, which, until a few years ago, was performed by local female workers who performed the work at home, has disappeared from the area. This phase is now performed in Eastern European countries or in Asia. Sometimes the early manufacturing phases are performed directly in Eastern European wood exporting countries;
- The outsourcing of the assembly process directly to the outlet markets[16]: for instance, to Mexico and Costa Rica for products destined for the American and Canadian markets, in order to reduce transport costs and exploit the provisions of NAFTA.[17]

Long-term sub-contracting agreements have been stipulated with local firms, saving on labour—even if in the past few years these costs have increased—and transport costs.[18]

However, wider forms of internationalisation have yet to be implemented. On the whole, a traditional entrepreneurial mentality prevails. Therefore, the process of opening towards the outside carried out by district firms can be mentioned as a process of "incomplete internationalisation" (Grandinetti, 1990; Rullani, 1990).

The end of a model of spontaneous development: some concluding remarks

To develop successfully, a local production system must be able to dynamically balance the robustness of its internal tissue and its openness to the outside world (Bramanti and Miglierina, 1995).

At the same time the process of the structural evolution of the chair manufacturing district appears to be tied ever more to the drive of individual firms which led its transformation.

These firms emerged from among district firms by successfully responding to the competitive challenges which derives from a market with a new behavioural logic different from that of the district's. They are firms which no longer base their competitiveness merely on exploitation of spontaneous positive externalities embedded in the district's environment (normally of a technical-productive nature), but on individual strategies designed to acquire new skills and resources. The implementation of these strategies generally did not occur through a process of internal growth, i.e. by expanding the size of the firm, but rather through external growth, by organising a rather unstabilise form of inter-firm co-operation (Varaldo 1993; Rullani 1993; Lorenzoni, 1990; Mistri 1993). From this interpretative framework, the chair-manufacturing district seems to have been a system which had difficulty digesting organisational changes because of the lack of leadership within the district. The impact of business strategies on the structural evolution of the chair-manufacturing district is still limited and restricted to the reorganisation of the production process. The advantages of globalisation, mainly the possibility to co-operate with several international agents that are centres of the production of knowledge, skills and information remain unexploited and unexplored (Vaccà and Zanfei, 1989).

A policy that creates real services for firms should be adopted. This would provide:

- assistance to the entrepreneurial function (by showing not only which strategic resources should be created, but also how to create new "non-material" strategic resources);
- introduction of tools to facilitate co-operative interaction among firms in a global context, easing the flow of information among firms and therefore promoting advanced systems for co-ordinating the global network of firms (service centres, promotion of contacts and co-operation with foreign enterprises).

Notes

1   In the village of Mariano the chair-manufacturing activity has been practised since the eighteenth century. There was a pronounced craft and commercial tradition in wood-working deriving from some Carnic families who emigrated to the area after Turkish raids and epidemics. In these two towns, in the province of Gorizia, the chair industry developed quickly, by taking advantage of a series of favourable conditions: its geographic position on the Udine-Trieste and Cividale-Cormons roads (the latter being a major marketplace for raw materials), the availability of low-priced manpower (chair-mending work performed by women and children at home), state-sponsored facilities for the exploitation of wood (in Ternova), lack of competition and steady growth in demand coming from Lombardy and Venetia (Exner, 1879). When, in 1866, Friuli was annexed by the Kingdom of Italy, the new boundary left the village of Mariano in Austrian territory, thus irreparably compromising the principle market for the chair-manufacturing industry. Later on, the situation became worse, when, following the Italo-Austrian agreements of 1878 high customs duties were imposed. Some Mariano chair-making families decided to leave and emigrated to the nearest Italian villages (Bosco and Deganutti, 1980). So the long history of the district began.

2   For centuries agriculture constituted the only livelihood and offered an uncertain and meager income.

3   See, for example, the Austrian Thonet.

4   Nearly 90% of investments by *Cassa Rurale di Manzano* are in the chair-sector.

5   The first export associations were the Consortium for chair-manufacturing development and the Gessef (Group of Friulian chair exporters), then the Conseg (Consortium of chair makers).

6   The chair industry continued to expand with the reconstruction that began after the 1976 earthquake. This event—which effected much of the Province of Udine—acted as a powerful amplifier of the area's industrial growth. The availability of easy loans and subsidies, created to encourage the area's economic recovery, stimulated investment in fixed capital (facilities, equipment, plants and so on), thus accelerating the renewal of the industrial structure.

7   The dynamism in the chair industrial structure is linked to the high level of labour mobility.

8   The period between 1982 and 1984 was the worst for local industry.

9   Between 60% and 75% of the total cost of a chair comes from raw material and labour (Bednatz and Mattioni, 1985) and competition from countries, endowed with these resources, becomes more and more threatening as these countries adopt more modern technologies.

10   For instance Calligaris (240 employees and an annual production of 1.5 millions chairs, 45% for export) has developed a new sales organisation covering the entire national territory (through 7000 furniture shops). The development of such a structure has allowed the firm to consolidate its market share and to strengthen its bargaining power with customers. Today the firm produces 100 models of chairs and tables, in more than 600 different versions by varying the colour and material. The firm distinguishes itself by the high quality standards which characterise its products, both in design and in reliability, durability (certified by CATAS), and by a very good quality to price ratio.

The precision in design and the large distribution network are the basis for the success of another firm in the area, Tonon (135 employees); it serves numerous markets (exports account for 85% of total production) with its line of chairs. Its production (about 160 models with 40 standardised versions and 100 different fabrics) is destined for the medium-high end of the market and with high degree of flexibility to meet their customers desires.

Another interesting firm is Lisa (110 employees), operating in three sectors: subcontracting for 50% of its total output, contracting (furniture for restaurants, hotels) and home furniture. Like the other firms mentioned, Lisa takes part in all the most important international fairs of the sector (Milan, Cologne, Paris, Munich, Genoa and, obviously, Udine) and counts on a large distributive structure. More then 90% of the total production is exported.

Distinguishing itself from the other firms in the area, Moroso (85 employees) operates solely in the high quality upholstery sector. Its production is mainly by hand and requires great skill and specialisation (for the most valuable operations the firm makes use of decentralised work). The distributive structure consists in direct agencies in various countries (exports being about 50% of the total).

While Top Sedia (75 employees) operates in the medium-low segment of the market, and produces a standardised product for foreign markets (since the national market is more demanding in product differentiation). The firm is part of a group of firms including Crabo (specialised in the production of benches), Ms (tables), Pan and Daron (sub-contractors) which together employ 260 people, and produce 1 million pieces a year.

The strategy undertaken by Potocco (115 employees and 120 thousands pieces a year, 75% for export) has been to increase its value added by launching specially designed products. The other strong point of the firm is in contracting, which represents 50% of its total sales revenue.

Montina International (35 employees) is a leader in the production of sophisticated chairs, with a long tradition of collaboration with famous designers (Gio Ponti, Magistretti, and Coppola) The peculiarity of this firm is that the entire production cycle is performed inside the firm itself, in order to control each phase with great care. This firm operates at the top end of the Italian market while exporting around 40% of its output. Moreover, Montina is one of the few firms in the area to attach importance to advertising through specialised magazines, as well as taking part in international fairs and expositions.

11   With the exception of Sabot, the only firm with more than 100 employees that was forced to close.

12   For example, Moroso makes use of former employees who have formed craft firms to perform some phases of the manufacturing process that require a certain level of quality. Decentralised work is also used to give the firm the flexibility required to meet seasonal peaks. Calligaris makes use of external workers for specialised manufacturing processing.

13   Manzano entrepreneurs think that the district "industrial atmosphere" is not exportable, and therefore production elsewhere cannot achieve the level of refinement (for instance, in optimal level of wood drying process) that originates from the high degree of specialisation characteristic of the production organisation within the chair-manufacturing district. As far as the more standardised phases of manufacturing, "buying intermediate-goods from abroad—says Angelo Speranza, director of CATAS— is difficult because transport often damages materials and consequently the final product may be defective".

14   Calligaris started, some years ago, to decentralise some upholstering requiring a high level of professional competence and extended manufacturing times to Romania, because these phases were costly in Italy. However, lower quality made it necessary to transfer technical knowledge and know-how. Today, due to the rise in manpower costs, this firm is pulling out of these markets. The attitude is to internationalise the distribution function, not production
Similarly, Lisa's attempts to internationalise production in Eastern Europe did not have brilliant results because the low labour costs and proximity to supplies were offset by imperfections in manufacturing and rigidity in delivery.

15   Adler, a paint producer, recently created a joint-venture in Costa Rica, after expanding in Syria, Korea and Malaysia.

16   An example is Top Sedia: this firm is developing an internationalisation plan that foresees a first phase in the cycle of production directly at the source of raw materials, quick shipment to Italy for the most complicated manufacturing, and final assembly in the destination country. The firm has already taken the first steps in this direction: a new plant has opened in France, close to a market that absorbs more than 25% of firm's total production, as well as a joint-venture with a firm in Slovenia for upholstering.

17   NAFTA is a mutual trade agreement among North American countries.

18   Importing semi-finished goods rather than unfinished wood permits savings up to 60% in weight and bulk and the same applies to the handling of components rather than assembled chairs (a transport truck can carry 600 assembled chairs or the components of 3,500 chairs).

References

Bagnasco, A. (1988), *La costruzione sociale del mercato* [The Social Construction of The Market], Bologna, Il Mulino.

Becattini, G. (1987), (ed.) *Mercato e forze locali: il distretto industriale* [Market and Local Forces: The Industrial Districts], Bologna, Il Mulino.

Becattini, G. (1989), (ed.) *Modelli locali di sviluppo* [Models of Local Development], Bologna, Il Mulino.

Becattini, G. (1992), Concorrenza e cooperazione: la formula italiana [Competition and co-operation: the Italian formula], *Il Ponte*, n.4.

Bednatz, F. and Mattioni, F. (1995), *Seggiolai e mercati* [Chair-manufacturing firms and markets], Udine, Cooperativa Editoriale Il Campo.

Bianchi, P. (1989), Concorrenza dinamica, distretti industriali e interventi locali, in F. Gobbo (ed.), [Dynamic Competition, Industrial Districts and Local Intervention], *Distretti e sistemi produttivi alla soglia degli anni '90* [Districts and production systems on the edge of the 1990s], Milan, Angeli.

Bosco, F. and Deganutti, A. (1980), *Manzano, S. Giovanni al Natisone, Corno di Rosazzo. Aspetti sociali ed economici tra Sette e Novecento* [Manzano, S.Giovanni al Natisone, Corno di Rosazzo. Social and Economical Aspects between the seventeenth and the twentieth centuries], Tergeste, University of Tergeste.

Bramanti, A. and Miglierina, C. (1995), Alle radici della crescita regionale: fattori, fenomeni, agenti [At the root of regional growth: factors, phenomena, agents], *L'industria*, n.1.

Chamber of Commerce Udine (1995), *Situazione economica del sistema manifatturiero della sedia in Friuli- Venezia Giulia* [Economic Situation of The Chair-manufacturing System in Friuli- Venzia Giulia], Udine, Chamber of Commerce.

Dei Ottati, G. (1986), Distretto industriale, problemi della transazione e mercato comunitario: prime considerazioni [Industrial District, transactions problems and communitary market: first considerations], *Economia e Politica Industriale*, n.51.

E.S.A.- Friuli Venezia Giulia (1982), *Indagine sulle aziende produttrici di sedie e affini nel Friuli orientale* [Survey on the firms producing chairs and similar products in Eastern Friuli], Udine, Ente Sviluppo Artigianato.

Exner, G. B. (1879), *Il villaggio di Mariano* [The Village of Mariano], Gradisca.

Garofoli, G. (1991), *Modelli locali di sviluppo* [Models of Local Development], Milan, Angeli.

Grandinetti, R. (1990), Apprendimento ed evoluzione nei percorsi di internazionalizzazione delle piccole e medie imprese [Learning and evolution in small and medium firms undergoing processes of internationalisation], *Piccola impresa*.

Lorenzoni, G. (1990), *L'architettura di sviluppo delle imprese minori* [The development architecture of small firms], Bologna, Il Mulino.

Mistri, M. (1993), *Distretti industriali e mercato unico europeo. Dal paradigma della localizzazione al paradigma dell'informazione* [Industrial Districts and European Common Market]. From The Paradigm of Localisation to The Paradigm of Information], Milan, Angeli.

PROMOSEDIA (1988), *L'universo Promosedia. Indagine di marketing delle aziende produttrici di sedie friulane* [The Universe Promosedia. Marketing Survey on The Firms Producing Chairs in Friuli Region], Udine, Promosedia.

PROMOSEDIA (1992), *Il distretto della sedia in Friuli nella competizione internazionale: affrontare le sfide del futuro* [The Chair-manufacturing district in Friuli Region in The Face of the International Competition: facing the future challenges], Udine, Promosedia.

Rullani, E. (1990), L'internazionalizzazione incompiuta: apprendimento ed evoluzione nell'esperienza internazionale di un campione di piccole e medie imprese, [Incomplete internationalisation: Learning and Evolution the International Experience of a Sample of Small and Medium Firms], working paper of finalized project CNR Servizi e strutture per l'internazionalizzazione delle imprese italiane e sviluppo delle esportazioni, [Services and Structure for the Internationalisation of Italian Firms and the Development of Exports], sub-project 2.

Rullani, E. (1993), L'internazionalizzazione delle imprese nei distretti industriali, [The Internationalisation of the industrial district firm], paper presented at the workshop *I distretti industriali verso gli anni 2000* [Industrial districts in the XXI century], Prato.

Vaccà, S. and Zanfei A. (1989), L'impresa globale come sistema aperto a rapporti di collaborazione [The Global Firm As a System Open to Co-operative Relationship], *Economia e Politica Industriale*, n.64.

Varaldo, R. (1993), *La natura e la dinamica dell'impresa distrettuale*, [The Nature and Dynamics of the District Firm], Pisa, Edizioni tecnico-scientifiche.